Other Books by Isaac Bashevis Singer

Books by Isaac Bashevis Singer

Novels

THE MANOR

I. THE MANOR · II. THE ESTATE

THE FAMILY MOSKAT · THE MAGICIAN OF LUBLIN

SATAN IN GORAY · THE SLAVE

ENEMIES, A LOVE STORY

SHOSHA · THE PENITENT

Stories

A FRIEND OF KAFKA · GIMPEL THE FOOL · SHORT FRIDAY

THE SÉANCE · THE SPINOZA OF MARKET STREET · PASSIONS

A CROWN OF FEATHERS · OLD LOVE · THE IMAGE

Memoirs

IN MY FATHER'S COURT

For Children

A DAY OF PLEASURE · THE FOOLS OF CHELM

MAZEL AND SHLIMAZEL OR THE MILK OF A LIONESS

WHEN SHLEMIEL WENT TO WARSAW

A TALE OF THREE WISHES · ELIJAH THE SLAVE

JOSEPH AND KOZA OR THE SACRIFICE TO THE VISTULA

ALONE IN THE WILD FOREST · THE WICKED CITY

NAFTALI THE STORYTELLER AND HIS HORSE, SUS

WHY NOAH CHOSE THE DOVE

THE POWER OF LIGHT

THE GOLEM

Collections

AN ISAAC BASHEVIS SINGER READER

THE COLLECTED STORIES

STORIES FOR CHILDREN

Isaac Bashevis Singer

LOVE and EXILE

Including A LITTLE BOY IN SEARCH OF GOD

A YOUNG MAN IN SEARCH OF LOVE

LOST IN AMERICA

and a new Introduction ''THE BEGINNING''

FARRAR, STRAUS AND GIROUX   NEW YORK

This paperback edition first published 1986 by arrangement
with Doubleday and Company, Inc.

Library of Congress Cataloging-in-Publication Data
Singer, Isaac Bashevis
Love and exile.
Memoirs, including A little boy in search of God,
A young man in search of love, and Lost in America.
1. Singer, Isaac Bashevis   —Biography.
2. Authors, Yiddish—Biography.   I. Title.
PJ5129.S49Z466   1984   839'.0933   79-7211

CONTENTS

AUTHOR'S NOTE

While *Love and Exile* is basically autobiographical in style and content, it is certainly not the complete story of my life from childhood to my middle thirties, where the book ends. Since many people I describe are still alive, and for a number of personal reasons, I had to change names, dates, and, in some exceptional cases, the course of events. Actually, the true story of a person's life can never be written. It is beyond the power of literature. The full tale of any life would be both utterly boring and utterly unbelievable.

In the author's notes to parts of this work, I call the writing spiritual autobiography, fiction set against a background of truth, or contributions to an autobiography I never intend to write. However, if I am given more time, I may try to continue this work in the same manner for the sake of some interested readers and perhaps for a potential biographer who may need help in devising my life story.

As a believer in God and His Providence, I am sure that there is a full record of every person's life, its good and bad deeds, its mistakes and follies. In God's archive, in His divine computer, nothing is ever lost.

I. B. S.

THE BEGINNING

Long before I began to write—
actually in my early childhood—I became interested in the question: "What differentiates one human being from another?" The
problem of human individuality became my problem. I toyed
with this riddle too often for a child of my age. I was barely
over five years old when my parents, my father, Pinchos Menachem Singer, and my mother, Bathsheba, moved to Krochmalna
Street in Warsaw. But unbelievable as this may sound, I already
carried the memories of two former homes with me: the village
of Leoncin, where I was born and where my father served as
a rabbi, and the little town of Radzymin, where my father had
become the head of a yeshivah. Both of these places were near
the Vistula, the largest river in Poland. I was about three years
and five months old when we moved to Radzymin. But I remember Leoncin, and episodes I lived through there, until today. When I told this to my mother in later years she refused to
believe me. She questioned me about details, and I convinced
her that I was telling the truth. I described each house, each
store, and many of the Jewish families who lived there. I also
remembered a number of Gentiles, both Poles and Germans:
the so-called "Volksdeutschen" who had their own community
in the suburbs. I could recall a long walk to the Vistula taken
with my sister Hindele and two other girls, as well as the circumcision party of my younger brother Moishe who was three
years younger than I. My mother kept saying, "What a memory!
Let no evil eye befall you." Even the summer day we said goodbye to the Leoncin families and rode away in a wagon to Rad-

zymin was still vivid in my memory. In Radzymin I began to
attend cheder. My teacher, Reb Fishel, an old man with a long
white beard, had his school not far from where we lived. He
was the teacher of the Radzymin wonder rabbi when this famous man was a cheder boy. This rabbi had founded the yeshivah in which my father taught. As far as I can remember, Reb
Fishel's house had two rooms: a bedroom and a large room that
was both the kitchen and the cheder. Reb Fishel's old wife always stood at the oven cooking soups or stews in large pots,
since the pupils were also fed there. They sat at a long table on
two benches. I had never yet heard of a cheder where boys and
girls studied together, but there is always an exception to the
rule. For some reason Reb Fishel was also teaching a few little
girls. None of us had yet learned how to read. All we knew was
the alphabet. Reb Fishel had a cat-o'-nine-tails to whip us for
misbehaving, but I don't remember his ever using it. Every
weekday he ate cabbage soup for lunch with black bread and
washed it down with water from a copper pitcher. On the table
he kept a wooden pointer and an alphabet pasted on cardboard.
Reb Fishel's wife had a face with deep wrinkles. Her bonnet had
many beads and colored ribbons. She put mushrooms, potatoes, and fried onions into her soups. Each pupil got a bowl,
and we had to recite a blessing beforehand at the table. Reb
Fishel's wife took us out to urinate and helped us keep our
pants or little skirts dry. Everyone in that cheder was older
than I. The boys were also taller and stronger, and they made
fun of me and played tricks on me. The girls protected me.
The boys considered it beneath their masculine dignity to play
with the girls, but I was too young to be a male chauvinist. In
the courtyard, the girls and I played with shards, a broken
spoon, an old shoe, and other such toys that Reb Fishel's wife
had thrown into the garbage. We sat on logs and told stories.
We played husband-and-wife games. I was the father, one of the
girls was my wife, and the other two or three were our children. I went to the synagogue—some shed—to pray while my
wife cooked a meal for me. I pretended to pray, saying, "Munia,
munia, munia," nonsense syllables. This was my prayer. Soon

my wife gave me a little sand in the broken spoon. This was my lunch or my supper. The boys laughed at us and called me "donkey monkey." Sometimes the boys threw a chip of wood at us, a pebble, or spat. The oldest girl, Esther, cursed them with the words: "You should spit with blood and pus," something she must have heard from the grown-ups.

The most important memory of Radzymin was a fire in the wonder rabbi's court. It happened on a Friday. Two thick pillars of smoke went up from the rabbi's study house. Bearded neighborhood Jews were saving scrolls of the Torah, volumes of the Talmud, and other holy books from the fire. Housewives packed garments and linens into sheets, bound them together, and brought them into an orchard near the house in which we lived. Young men carried buckets of water from the well. Both men and women were screaming—warning one another not to desecrate the approaching Sabbath, God forbid.

Already in Radzymin I began to realize how different our family was from the others. Our family was made up of unique characters. My father did not wear a cap like the other Jews, but a round velvet hat. He wore no boots with high uppers, but half shoes. He was not a merchant, the owner of a store, but stood all day at a lectern studying large volumes and writing small letters in a composition notebook. Once when I asked him what he was writing he said, "Commentaries." And when I asked him what commentaries were he said, "The Torah is bottomless. No matter how much one studies it, one can never grasp all of it. The deeper you dig into the Torah, the more treasures you uncover. Without the Torah the world would not exist. With the letters of the Torah, God has created Heaven and Earth."

I thought a lot about those words. Was my father trying to create a new heaven and a new earth? Sometimes he wrote a line and then erased it. He dipped his pen in the inkwell and then wiped it on his skullcap. While studying he drank many glasses of watery tea and smoked a long pipe. Not far from our house lived the father of a girl who studied at Reb Fishel's. Her name was Dvorele. Her father was a coachman and owned a wagon and a horse. Sometimes he took Dvorele with him, and they traveled far to where the sky and the earth merged. Why didn't my father have a cart and a horse? I wondered. Why didn't he own a store where one could buy candy, halvah, cookies, chocolate bits? I asked my mother the reason, but she never gave me a clear answer. All she could say was, "We are different." One boy in the cheder named Benjamin always had toys in his pockets: a whistle, a colored pencil, tin foil, or gilded buttons. The house where his parents lived was decorated with pictures, flowerpots, copper pans, a brass pestle and mortar, trays that looked like silver. In our house there was nothing but books. I used to play with the books, turning the pages back and forth. Sometimes I found among the pages a red hair from my father's beard or a thread from the fringes of his prayer shawl. These were considered sacred objects one was not permitted to throw away. Since there was always talk in our house about God, I asked my father, "Papa, does God have a beard?" My father smiled, thought it over and said, "You are not allowed to say such things."

"Why not?"

"God has no body. However, everything that exists on Earth has its counterpart in Heaven. Here everything is matter; there everything is spirit."

"What is spirit?" I asked.

"Soul."

"What is soul?"

"No one can see the soul or touch it," my father said. "But without the soul, one cannot live."

I wanted to ask more questions, but my father said, "Please, let me study."

In the kitchen it was somewhat cozier than in my father's study. True, my mother also read a book, but it was not as large and heavy as my father's volumes. A fire was burning in the oven and a soup was boiling. Once in a while my mother put some kindling wood into the oven. I watched it catch fire, making crackling sounds as it burned. My mother did not wear a bonnet like Reb Fishel's wife, but a wig. When she took it off for a second I saw red hairs sprouting from her skull. She immediately put the wig back on and secured it with hair pins. Her skirt was so long it covered her ankles. One could only see the points of her shoes. "Mama, what are you reading?" I would ask, and she would answer, "You see, it's a book."

"What is written there?"

"It is written that people should be good to one another."

"Benjamin isn't good to Dvorele," I said. "He pulled her hair. Is this being good?"

"No, my child. This isn't right."

"Will God punish him?"

"Not immediately. But one is not allowed to pull another child's hair. If you do something wrong to someone, you have to apologize."

"He stuck his tongue out at her."

"This is not nice."

"Mama, I love Dvorele," I said.

My mother raised her eyes from the book. "Is that so? Why do you love her?"

"Because her papa has a horse."

My mother smiled. "Is this a reason for loving her? Oh, you talk like a little fool. You love a girl because she's clever, gentle, friendly. Anyone can buy a horse for twenty rubles."

"Mama, does a horse have a soul?"

My mother knit her brows and said, "Don't ask me so many questions, one after the other. Let me read my book."

"I also want to read a book."

"You will read when you grow up. You will study all the books. For the time being, go out and play with the children."

2

Krochmalna Street in Warsaw was always full of people, and they all seemed to be screaming. One day there was a fire and the firemen came with their wild horses. The firemen wore brass helmets and dragged along fire hoses. Another day someone got run over by a cart and an ambulance came blaring its sirens. Once an automobile passed by—a horseless vehicle—and crowds gathered to gape at the wonder. People in our courtyard, and even some of the visitors in our house, constantly told harrowing stories about the revolution in 1905, the strikes, and how Jewish boys and girls had undertaken to dethrone the Tsar. They shot at Russian officials and threw bombs. On Bloody Wednesday hundreds of those rebels marched to city hall demanding a constitution, and most of them were killed. Blood streamed through the gutter. Those who remained were chained and exiled to Siberia. Many of these tales I did not understand, but in 1908 I felt the turmoil behind them.

We lived in a walk-up in Warsaw, and we had to learn to climb stairs. Our apartment had a balcony, and high buildings, slanted roofs, broad gates, and stores could be seen from there. The windows were open in the summer, and grown-up girls sang songs with trilling voices. In some of the windows there were cages with parrots that spoke like people, whistled, screeched, even uttered profanities. I had never seen it before, but some of the Jews kept dogs. My mother complained that Warsaw was a Gehenna, but my sister Hindele and my brother Joshua, both already adults, were delighted with the big city. Hindele stood for hours at the window observing the passersby. Girls in short-sleeved blouses with gauze necklines wore hats with flowers and feathers and carried pocketbooks. My father warned Joshua not to look at those salacious females who uncovered their flesh to arouse men to evil thoughts. But my brother never heeded his warning.

In his debates with my father, Joshua questioned God's intentions and my father kept defending Him. Joshua mentioned that in the war with Japan tens of thousands of innocent soldiers were killed. Ships were sunk with their entire crews. In the city of Kishinev and in many other Russian cities there were pogroms against the Jews. How could God see all this and keep silent? Can a God like this be called merciful? My father choked on the answers. God has given man free choice and he could choose between good and evil, between life and death. Besides, we cannot grasp God with our little brains. Those innocent people who perished were martyrs and their sacred souls will live on in Paradise.

My father was not the only one on God's side. Chassidim came to our house and told of the miracles worked by their wonder rabbis and of their great piety. One of those hangers-on was my father's former pupil in Leoncin, a young man by the name of Mattes. Mattes was a follower of the Bratslav rabbi—one of a sect nicknamed "dead Chassidim." They were disciples of a rabbi who had died some hundred years ago, Rabbi Nachman who preached religion through joy. Mattes would speak about this dead rabbi and dance. He cried out Rabbi Nachman's slogans: "As long as your candle burns, everything can be corrected." Mattes would sing out the verse in the book *Ethics of the Fathers*: "If I'm not for myself, who will be for me? And if I'm only for myself, what am I? And if not now, when?"

I was listening to everything: to the stories of the Chassidim, to my brother's debates with my parents, to the arguments of the litigants who came for a "Din Torah," mostly a peaceful settlement of a business argument. I was especially interested in the conflict between couples who sought divorce. There were also struggles in our own household. My sister Hindele accused my mother of not loving her. I have heard her weep and cry out, "You don't love me, this is why you are pushing to marry me off to anybody who comes along. If you could, you would send me far away behind the Mountains of Blackness." Young as I was, I grasped that Hindele was telling the truth. My mother could not stand her constant complaints. Hindele suffered from nerves. This is what the doctor told us. He applied electric treatments to her head and prescribed massages and pills twice a day, but they did not help. Several times Hindele attempted to jump out the window. Still, people liked her. Our neighbors praised her looks, her light skin, brown hair, and blue eyes. She, too, waged war against my father's extreme piety. She wanted to dress according to fashion, to attend the

Yiddish theater and marry a modern young man, not some yeshivah boy who lived on charity. However, because my father could not afford to give her a dowry the matchmakers tried to marry her off to some widower, divorced man, or someone twice as old as she was. Hindele cried, laughed, tore the hair from her head, and threatened to drown herself in the Vistula. Joshua said that Hindele was suffering from hysteria.

The summer was over and then the winter, but I was still not enrolled in a new cheder. I learned everything at home: to recite the prayers and also to read storybooks in Yiddish—tales about kings, princesses, frightening events about devils, imps, dybbuks, vampires. My brother Joshua bought the Yiddish newspaper every morning and I tried to read this too. My father maintained that all the secular writers were unbelievers, liars, mockers. Their writings were an abomination. About the Yiddish theater my father said that charlatans sit there all day long, eat pork, play around with loose women, and speak profanities. But my brother said that the theater was a part of culture. He praised the Yiddish writers Mendele Mocher Sforim, Shalom Aleichem, Peretz, as well as the mother of the Yiddish theater, Esther Rachael Kaminsky and her play, *Mirele Efrat*. Joshua brought home translations into Yiddish of Tolstoi, Dostoevski, Turgenev, Knut Hamsun, Mark Twain. He called their writings literature, and he said that to write the way they do, one must have talent and great knowledge of the human soul. My mother upbraided Joshua and Hindele for reading these worldly books, but she herself used to glance into them. In the newspaper *Der Haint* they published a novel in a serial with the title *The Bloody Lady*—a story of a woman who drove men crazy with her caprices and demands. Some of her admirers fought duels over her and killed one another. Some sent spies to follow her. They showered her with gold and precious gifts. She possessed a devilish beauty. Behind her veiled face looked out two fiery black eyes that drove men to madness.

Not only were men driven to madness and to death in Petersburg and Paris but also on Krochmalna Street where we lived.

A tailor's assistant in Number 11 had fallen in love with the daughter of a Chassid, and when her parents refused to consent to their marriage the young man threw himself to the ground from the fourth floor. A maid whose groom-to-be stole her dowry and ran off to America with another woman poisoned herself with iodine. A striker, who was sentenced to life in the Citadel prison, poured kerosene on his clothes and burned himself to cinders. He had left a letter written in blood to his bride-to-be: "I'm dying so that you should live in a world of freedom."

Every day I learned the most astonishing things from these newspapers. In Italy a Jew was Prime Minister, only one step away from being a king. In London a Jew was given the high title of Lord. The Tsar wanted to borrow money from Baron Rothschild, but the Baron refused him credit. There were also articles about science: the earth is fifty times as large as the moon. Some of the stars are as large as the sun or even larger, and many times as bright. In Italy, in Portugal, in the United States of America, and in other countries earthquakes took place where hundreds and thousands of people were killed. There were stories in this newspaper about giants, midgets, about a baby born with two heads, and Siamese twin brothers who were doomed never to be separated. Meteors fell from the sky and formed deep holes in the earth. Volcanoes spat out fiery lava. Rivers overflowed their banks and covered whole villages. In China thousands of people starved to death. In India a man walked barefoot on burning coals. In America a millionaire gave a birthday party for his sixteen-year-old daughter, and the flowers alone cost five thousand dollars or ten thousand rubles.

I craved learning how to read these newspapers and especially the books whose writers had all the knowledge about the human soul. Joshua said that novels didn't have to be completely true. Some of these stories were invented, but in such a clever way that they were more interesting than real facts. Sometimes Joshua spoke about philosophers who attempted to reveal all the secrets of Heaven and Earth. A lot was written in

the newspapers about an inventor from America by the name
of Edison. He had invented a machine that could talk, sing,
make jokes, laugh, cry. He had devised the electric light bulb.
He slept only four hours a day and the rest of the time he spent
thinking profound thoughts about science. Joshua had mentioned the philosopher Baruch Spinoza who believed that God
is nature and nature is God. All men, all animals, even snakes
and worms were part of the Godhead. The laws of nature are
also God's laws. God does not reward the just and punish the
evildoers. Many saints died young and in bitter poverty. Some
of the wicked became rich and lived a hundred years. According to this philosopher there was no Paradise, no Gehenna. The
Messiah would never come, the dead would never rise from
their graves. No cloud would ever carry away all the virtuous
Jews to the Land of Israel.

"So what will happen to us Jews?" my mother asked. "Will we
always remain in exile?"

"Doctor Herzl wanted to create a Jewish state," my brother
said. "He believed that we should become a nation like all the
other nations and have our own country."

"Doctor Herzl is not alive anymore," my mother said, "and
his whole plan was nothing but an idle dream."

"There are already Jewish colonists in Palestine," my brother
argued. "They have just opened a Gymnasium where the children speak Hebrew."

I absorbed all this information and strange words with a decision to always retain them. I fantasized about becoming a second Edison or a writer of books or like the Count who resisted
the "Bloody Lady" and made her expire from yearning for him.
In our house there lived a woman by the name of Bashele and
her daughter Shosha who was about my age. I told Shosha all
the astounding things my brother told us from the newspapers
and books. I also contrived facts of my own. I had saved up two
kopeks from my daily allowances (one groschen every morning) and bought two colored pencils; one blue and one red in
order to draw for Shosha the fire I had seen in the court of the
Radzymin rabbi.

3

For a time I attended a number of cheders but didn't stay in any one for long. My father taught me the Gemara and my mother was my Bible teacher. There was little left for my teachers to instruct me, and my fellow students were envious. They called me nicknames and teased me. I had become an expert on human character. I looked at a boy and knew if he was honest or a cheat, clever or foolish. Faces generally, and eyes especially, revealed a lot to me. Voices and words did the same. I spoke to a boy for a few minutes and was sure I knew who he was and what I could expect from him. I had once heard my father quote Maimonides: "Just as the faces of humans are different, so are their thoughts and opinions." Noses, ears, and lips revealed secrets to me. I read somewhere that the soul looks out from the eyes, and I was baffled to realize how much truth there was in these words. There were silly eyes, clever eyes, sly eyes, eyes full of goodness, eyes full of wickedness, eyes that expressed sheer joy, and eyes full of sadness. They all told stories that I could not put into words. I had heard from my brother that the fingerprints of each human being were different. Also I knew that every person had a different handwriting so that bank officers and policemen could identify forged signatures. How could God have created so many eyes with so many different expressions.

My brother had said to my mother that literature deals mostly with the characters of people—their feelings, their way of talking, and behavior in various circumstances, and I decided to become a writer. I began to look inside myself and my own soul. There was constant turmoil there. I suffered, but what my suffering consisted of was not clear to me. There was a time when I used to catch flies, tear off their wings and put them into boxes of matches with a drop of water and a grain of sugar for nourishment. Suddenly it occurred to me that I was committing terrible crimes against those creatures just because I was bigger than they, stronger, and defter. While I was always

angry with the wicked, I was wicked myself toward those who
were weaker than I. This thought tormented me to such a degree that for a long time I could think about nothing else. I
began to repent and to pray to God to forgive my vicious deeds.
I took a holy oath never again to catch flies. But what about the
flies I had already caught? True, I still could be punished as I
deserved to be. But can those creatures still get retribution for
their pain? Has a fly a soul? Can its soul go up to Paradise and
be compensated for its suffering?

The ponderings about the suffering of flies expanded and
soon included all people, all animals, all lands, all times. I had
passed Yanash's bazaar a number of times and had seen the
slaughterers killing chickens, ducks, geese. The butchers began
to pluck their feathers even while those creatures were still
alive and wallowing in their own blood. I once saw my own
mother kill a trembling fish for the Sabbath. My mother told me
that when a fish is eaten for the honor of the Sabbath and a
pious Jew makes a blessing over it, its spirit is elevated. Sometimes sinful souls of humans enter fish and the fish's death is
an atonement for sins of those souls. But how about the fish
that are not killed for the Sabbath? How about the fish that are
eaten by Gentiles or by sinners? And how about the pigs that
are killed, scorched in hot water while still alive? What spirit
was atoned in them? Where is their compensation for the tortures they went through? Neither my father nor my mother nor
the morality books that I began to read in Yiddish translation or
even in Hebrew, could give me a satisfying answer. I had studied in the Book of Leviticus about the sacrifices the priests used
to burn on the altar: the sheep, the rams, the goats, and the
doves whose heads they wrung off and whose blood they
sprung as a sweet savor unto the Lord. And again and again I
asked myself why should God, the Creator of all men and all
creatures, enjoy these horrors?

My brother Joshua, who had become a non-believer, had one
answer to all these questions: "There is no God. He never
spoke to Moses and bade him to offer these sacrifices. All existence is nature, and nature knows of no pity. According to na-

ture, might makes right. All living species are a result of a fight wherein the weak perished and the strong survived." However, this explanation did not satisfy me. If nature is so clever that it watches over each star in the sky, each animal in the forest, each mouse, each worm, how can it be without compassion? How can great wisdom care so little about the torments of innocent creatures? This question, which began to agonize me when I was six or seven years old, still haunts me today. I still cannot accept the ruthlessness of nature, God, the Absolute, or whatever name these high powers are given.

I heard that there were vegetarians who ate no meat and no fish, but even they seemed to care little about such despised creatures as mice, rats, spiders, bedbugs. With each step a person takes, he crushes some living being. I heard from my brother that in some faraway country rabbits had multiplied in such numbers that people had to erect fences to keep them out. And thousands upon thousands of hunters did nothing but shoot them or kill them with axes and knives. I heard of locusts that were poisoned, burned by the myriads. Wolves attacked sheep; lions and tigers ravaged whole villages. Nature had given to its creatures horns, nails, claws, venom to assail other creatures. In the oceans big fish swallowed little fish. People waged wars or made bloody revolutions. I was reading the Bible and the whole history of the Israelites was full of wars and assassinations. One day the Philistines killed twenty thousand Israelites. Another day these Israelites slaughtered thirty thousand Philistines. Every second or third king was assassinated, and the assassin took over his throne, put on his crown, and became a king. They all served idols. They were constantly invaded by Egypt, Aram, Babylonia, and other enemies. One year there was a pestilence and the next a famine. One misfortune followed another until the Babylonians, the Greeks, and the Romans destroyed the Temple and drove the Jews into Exile, where for almost two thousand years they paid for the sins they themselves did not commit. How can a merciful God allow all this to happen and keep silent?

I began early to realize that there is no answer to these questions either in the holy books or in the explanations of my parents. They kept contradicting themselves. They spoke of a hereafter from which no one ever returned. Only my brother Joshua seemed to tell the whole truth, but there was no comfort in his words, no solution to the great riddle called life.

Sometimes I thought, "Who knows? Maybe I would find some answer. Perhaps I will go on searching until the truth will be revealed to me." In the process of listening to myself I came to the conclusion that my soul or my heart was always yearning for something new. I was constantly hoping for some new event, some new information, renewed courage. I began to study a new treatise of the Gemara, and I soon got tired of it. I read a storybook, and after some ten or twenty pages it became tedious. I was always waiting for some good tidings, a miracle, a joyful revelation. Repeating the same prayer every day had become a burden to me, and I began to deceive my parents saying that I had already prayed, said grace, recited this or that supplication. Once I saw in the newspaper the expression, "a novel of suspense," and I asked my brother what it meant. He told me it is a book that keeps you curious as to what would happen later. You can barely wait to turn the page. My brother seemed to disapprove of this kind of novel. He made fun of the serialized novels in the Yiddish newspapers. But I felt that expectation adds zest to life. I went to sleep every night with the hope that next morning I would get two groschen instead of one for allowance, that I would be able to buy a new storybook or a composition book, or that I would hear some new facts about the war between the Turks and the three little countries whose names I could never repeat. There was in the *Haynt* a column called "News from the Four Corners of the World," and there was always something astounding there. Once a month one could read about those who won big sums of money in the Warsaw lottery. The Chassidim in the Radzymin study house were all buying lottery tickets. The highest prize was seventy-five thousand rubles. Even my father used to buy these tickets. The owner of the lottery was the rabbi of Gora Calvaria. His adversaries criticized him for presiding over this kind of gambling, but the rabbi assured his Chassidim that the profits all went for religious purposes. There was also a small lottery on the square of Krochmalna Street where you paid a penny to draw a number, and you could win chocolate or halvah worth as much as ten groschen. The gambling went on from early in the morning until late in the evening. There was a lot of card gambling on Krochmalna Street. Women often came to my father and complained that their husbands gambled away their salaries. Once a woman told my father that her husband lost their stove in a card game after gambling away his last penny. Not only did she not get household money for that week, but four men came in and although it was freezing outside they removed the stove. I remember my father saying, "Once a man surrenders to the powers of evil, there is no limit to how deep he can fall." Across the street lived a man who worked all day making paper bags that were used in grocery stores. At night he sat down with some other men and they often played cards until the morning. My mother used to say, "These people don't seem to sleep at all. They are ruining their health and their families." In our house there was often talk about evil passions and what damage they could cause when not curbed. I myself had quite a number of them. I could not get enough of observing the acrobats who performed in the courtyards. There were days when I accompanied them from courtyard to courtyard neglecting my studies. There were always three men and one girl. The men ate fire, swallowed knives, juggled balls. One of them put a heavy log on his teeth and balanced it that way for minutes. They never wore jackets or shirts because one of their tricks was to lie down with their naked backs on a board of nails. The girl had flaxen-white hair cut short like a boy's, and she wore a velvet blouse with tinsel and short pants over her narrow hips. She rolled a barrel on the soles of her feet and turned a wheel with a glass of water on it that never spilled. While the men performed, she played a little drum with bells and caught the groschens or kopeks which tenants threw from their windows. Once in a while she also walked on her hands. I was always amazed when watching these shows.

In the Book of Kings in the Bible I was fascinated with the story of the Queen of Sheba who had visited King Solomon. She came with a great train of camels bearing spices and gold and precious stones as gifts to the wise king. She spoke to King Solomon all that was in her heart, and Solomon answered all her questions and showed her all his treasures. I don't remember where I read it, in Rashi or in some other commentary, that when she returned to the Land of Sheba she carried Solomon's child in her womb. I could not connect acquiring wisdom and showing treasures with giving birth to a child, but I also remembered the stories of Abraham with his two wives, Sarah and Hagar, as well as those about Jacob marrying Leah, Rachel, and the concubines Bilhah and Zilpah. King Solomon had loved many foreign women—Moabites, Ammonites, Edomites, Zidonians, and Hittites and married the daughter of Pharaoh. More than that, he had seven hundred wives and three hundred concubines, who in later years turned his heart away from God and made him serve idols. It seemed that adults in history were as confused and greedy for excitement in their own way as I was in my fashion.

4

Things happened every day. It was worthwhile to hear and read about them and to tell it all to Shosha with additions of my own imagination. A ship called *Titanic,* which was almost as large as a town, with stores, restaurants, and a theater, had hit an iceberg and sunk in the ocean with hundreds of millionaires on board. The enemies of the Jews in Russia had falsely accused a Jew by the name of Mendl Bailys of killing a Christian child to use his blood for matzoh—a wild and malicious accusation. In Russia there were new strikes and demonstrations by those who tried to dethrone the Tsar. They had killed a great dignitary and some of the assassins were hung. A peasant from distant Siberia

by the name of Rasputin became an important figure in the
Tsar's palace in Petersburg. The newspapers hinted that he had
a romance with the Tsarina and some of her court ladies. Many
new things happened in our own family. My sister Hindele had
become engaged to a young man who lived in the town of Antwerp in Belgium, and the wedding took place in Berlin, Germany. My father and mother went there leaving me alone for a
week with Joshua. Who took care of younger brother, Moishe, I
don't remember. A few months after my sister's wedding a letter
came that she was pregnant and my parents sent her a gift. A
boy had divulged to me the secret of how children are born.
The thought that even such pious people as my parents, who
always talked about the Torah, good deeds, should indulge in
such abominations shocked me terribly. When I told this to
Shosha, she told me that she herself had seen her father and
mother in one bed. If the adults committed sins like these, why
should I try to be better? I fantasized about lying with Shosha
in bed. I actually kissed her forehead. Like King Solomon, I told
Shosha all my secrets. I myself did not possess treasures of gold
and precious stones, but I told her that my father was a king
and he had a palace not far from Warsaw full of gold, silver,
diamonds, pearls, and other precious stones, the kind that the
High Priest used to wear on his breastplate. I also revealed to
her that I was studying the cabala in the middle of the night
and that the Prophet Elijah came to instruct me. I had learned
holy names of God that when uttered could allow one to fly
like a bird and become invisible. I could with the power of one
of those names kill all those who made pogroms against the
Jews and take those who remained alive to the Land of Israel. I
could, if I chose to, become the King of Jerusalem with golden
lions, leopards, eagles, and other animals decorating my throne
and with sixty mighty men around my bed guarding me from
the dread of the night.

I had not yet become the King of Jerusalem, but my nights
too were full of dread and wonders. The moment I closed my
eyes I saw lights of many colors: yellow, red, blue, green, violet.
The colors changed turning into flowers, swans, doves, parrots.

I saw giants with spears and golden helmets, their points reaching to the sky. Were these the same mighty men who watched over the bed of King Solomon? Or were they demons? I wasn't asleep, but I dreamed while awake. I flew together with all those colors and monsters over fields, forests, rivers, seas. I landed on the islands I read about in the storybooks. Outlandish people spoke to me in languages similar to Yiddish and Hebrew as well as in the Aramaic translations of the Pentateuch I had learned to recite in the cheder. I flew over the desert where the Jews ate manna for forty years, as well as over Egypt, the store-cities of Pithom and Ramses. I saw the Land of Israel—Rachel's grave, the Wailing Wall, the cave of Machpelah, and places perhaps not of this world.

There was one dream that repeated itself almost every night. I came to a cemetery with mounds over graves. I knew that children were buried there. Suddenly the children would emerge from under the earth. They wore little white blouses and skirts. They played together and danced in a circle. They also swung on swings. But they never said a word. Were they mute? Was this the resurrection of the dead? I recognized one little girl, Jochebed, who had died not long after we came to Warsaw. Her parents lived in the same building as we did and on the same floor. I had gone out on the balcony and saw Jochebed's funeral—a black, rectangular hearse with compartments not unlike the philacteries adults put on their heads and arms. The horses were wrapped in black with holes cut out for their huge eyes. The driver came out from our gate carrying a black narrow box and I knew that Jochebed was in it. He took her to a darkness of no return. Even now, so many years later, I still see all these visions in my dreams.

Looking back on my life I see that all my qualities, good and bad, were with me then. Even my ideas about literature. I had often heard my mother and Joshua say that many misfortunes in the world resulted from human boredom. So painful is boredom that people would risk their lives to escape it. Nations tire from long epochs of peacefulness and try to create a crisis, a conflict, in order to start a war. Some men get tired of their family life and indulge in quarrels that lead to divorce. Youngsters from wealthy homes leave their parents and seek out adventures that do them harm. In my father's courtroom I constantly heard tales of human ferocity and madness. Some men ran off to America with other women, leaving their families without bread. I heard of girls who began to live a life of shame (I didn't know exactly what that was) because their days and nights seemed so dreary to them. When I began to read I saw that the good writers always had some surprises and twists which the reader could not have foreseen. My brother had said that Talmudic casuistry was developed among Polish Jews as a means to make the Torah more playful, to sharpen the students' minds, to bring the joy into learning, and to increase the scholar's competition. The cabala from Isaac Luria, the belief in false messiahs like Sabbatai Zevi and Jacob Frank as well as Chassidism were all created to enliven Jewishness, which became stagnant under the rigid rules of the rabbis and the rigor of the law. I heard my brother say that the Baal Shem, who was born at the beginning of the eighteenth century, was afraid that the Enlightenment might seduce the Polish Jews. Chassidism preached that the way to serve God was through joy. Melancholy and boredom separated men from God.

At the time I began to fantasize about becoming a writer I had already realized that the masters always entertained the reader. Also, I could see that nothing engages the reader as much as a love story. I had read in the Gemara that for men and women to find their right mates is as much a miracle as the splitting of the Red Sea. A good marriage does not always happen and is different with each union. The various encounters of love could never be exhausted. Every human character appears only once in the history of human beings. And so does every event of love. My father's courtroom was like a school to me where I could study the human soul, its caprices, its yearnings, its barriers. I was amazed to hear the strong complaints of the couples who asked for a divorce or to end an engagement or who just came to open their hearts to my father and my mother. Men and women craved happiness together, but instead they indulged in silly quarrels, spiteful accusations, various lies, and acts of treachery. Each wanted to be stronger than the other and often to belittle and denigrate the weaker. Sometimes I got a desire to give them advice myself, especially when the couples were young and good looking. I often fell in love with the young woman and her way of speaking about her troubles. Once an unusually elegant couple came to my father to end an engagement. The young man accused the young woman of becoming too familiar with his friends, and she said that he behaved the same way with her girl friends. Suddenly the young man slapped the girl. She tried to slap him back and they wrangled for a while like two youngsters. Later, after my parents made peace between them and they left, he took her arm and they both kissed. I remember thinking to myself, "This is what literature must be about." I heard my mother say, "So beautiful and so crazy. It would be a sin for them to part."

I remember one case where an elderly man accused his wife—she was his second—of oversalting his dishes. Doctors had forbidden him to eat too much salt, pepper, and other sharp spices. But no matter how much he pleaded with her to use less salt and pepper, she always put in a lot. My father asked the woman why she didn't do what her husband asked of her. He quoted the Gemara that "a kosher wife fulfills the demands of her husband." The woman said that she could not cook without salt and spices because then the food had no taste. My mother said, "You can always put salt in later. Salt has the same flavor whether you put it into the pot or into the plate." But the woman said that was not so. I could see in that woman's eyes the stubbornness of a peasant who has taken something into her head and can never free herself of it. She told my mother that, God willing, she would find a man who would not look into the pots. Her smile had evil intentions. Perhaps she wanted her husband to get sick and die.

My father was never in a rush to let people get divorced—he always told them to come back next month or even half a year later. He talked it over with my mother after they left, and I heard my mother say, "Human stupidity has no limit." To which my father answered, "It is all the Evil One. His mission is to tempt people."

I could see that every human being acted and spoke differently and found different excuses for his or her follies. For example: The Jews in the Radzymin study house all worshipped the same wonder rabbi, told of his miracles, quoted his sermons. But everyone did it in his own fashion. Some faces expressed blind faith and God-fearing fervor. In other faces I could see not more than the desire to belong to this particular group of Chassidim, to be one of the crowd. Some of these Chassidim were always berating their rabbi's adversaries, trying to prove how ignorant and vicious they were. Some of the Chassidim were known to be men of their word, honest merchants, or artisans. Others were known to break their word or to swindle whenever they got a chance. My father and mother were both honest and charitable, but still what a difference between the two of them! My mother's eyes were sharp and I could see in them impatience with the ways of the world, with men and women—a resentment toward life and all its tribulations. She always had to search for comfort in her morality books. I once heard her say, "I hate the human species." I knew that no one could fool her. She saw through a person, behind all his or her masks. She could be sarcastic and biting. My father was the opposite; good-natured, full of faith in almost all people. He never seemed to have any doubts. His only desire was to have time and strength to serve God and to study His Torah. I had inherited some traits from my father and many from my mother. I can say that she suffered not only her own afflictions but also those of all mankind. I could see in her eyes great compassion when she read in the Yiddish newspaper about those who were run over, robbed, raped, beaten. Every news item made her wince in resentment against the Creator who could see all this misery and remain silent. Once I heard her say, "Newspapers are pure poison."

Just the same she read the newspapers daily and even stealthily leafed through my brother's books. I heard her express opinions. She would say, "People don't speak that way." Or,

"This is wooden talk. This writer really does not know how people behave." Once I heard her say about the Yiddish writer David Berglson that he tried to imitate Knut Hamsun. I had not read either of them, but I saw my brother's eyes light up and he exclaimed, "Mother, you understand literature better than all our critics!"

My mother was, even at that time, an ardent feminist, or a suffragist as they called them then. Whenever she read about the cruelties in war, she would say that only women could end these murderous events. Her recipe was that all women should unite and decide not to live with their husbands until they had resolved to make peace once and forever. My mother elaborated on this idea many times, and my brother answered her, "Neither men nor women will ever unite. Nature always accomplishes what it had intended, that all life must fight for its existence." My mother's narrow face became pale, and she said, "In that case, there will never be peace in this world."

I dedicate this book to her and my father's sacred memory.

A LITTLE BOY IN SEARCH OF GOD

One

THOSE WHO HAVE READ MY WORKS, particularly my autobiographical volume, *In My Father's Court,* know that I was born and reared in a house where religion, Jewishness, was virtually the air that we breathed. I stem from generations of rabbis, Chassidim, and cabalists. I can frankly say that in our house Jewishness wasn't some diluted formal religion but one that contained all the flavors, all the vitamins, the entire mysticism of faith. Because the Jews had lived for two thousand years in exile, been driven from land to land and from ghetto to ghetto, their religion hadn't evaporated. The Jews underwent a selection which has no parallel in any of the other faiths. Those Jews lacking strong enough religious convictions or feelings fell to the wayside and assimilated with the Gentiles. The only ones left were those who took their religion seriously and gave their children a full religious upbringing. The Diaspora Jew clung to only one hope—that the Messiah would come. Messiah's coming was not some worldly redemption, a recovery of lost territory, but a spiritual deliverance that would change the whole world, root out all evil, and bring the Kingdom of Heaven to earth.

In our house the coming of the Messiah was taken most literally. My younger brother, Moishe, and I often spoke about it. First, the sound of the ram's horn would be heard. It would be blown by the Prophet Elijah, and its sound would be heard round the world proclaiming the news: "Redemption came to the World! Salvation came to the World!" All the malefactors and enemies of Israel would perish leaving only the good Gentiles whose privilege it would now become to serve the Jews. According to the Talmud, the Land of Israel would extend over all the nations. A fiery Temple would descend unto Jerusalem from heaven. The Kohanim, or priestly class (we were Kohanim), would offer sacrifices—possibly fiery sacrifices—because already then the slaughter of oxen, sheep, and turtledoves seemed to me not conducive to redemption. Abraham, Isaac, Jacob, and their tribes; Moses, King David, all the prophets, sages, geonim, and saints, would be resurrected along with the rest of the Jewish dead. My father had published a book in which there was a family tree tracing our descent from Shabatai Cohen, from Rabbi Moshe Isserlis, from Rashi, until King David. My brother Moishe and I would enter the palace where King David sat with crown on head on a golden throne and call him "Grandpa! . . ."

How poor seemed the Gentiles with their kings, princes, soldiers, and wars in comparison with what awaited us! But in order to achieve all this, we had to be pious Jews, study the Torah, do good deeds, pray with fervor, and obey our parents. . . .

All this would have been good and fine except that at an early age I already started asking myself: "Is it true?"

The only proof my parents could offer me was the holy books, which said that it would be so. But books were only paper and ink and written by people. I knew already that the Gentiles had books, too, in which it was written that the Jews were a sinful race and that on Judgement Day they would be condemned to eternal damnation for having failed to accept Jesus. I also knew of heretical books which denied both Moses and Jesus. My brother Joshua, who was eleven years older than I (two girls in between had died of scarlet fever), often discussed this with my mother. These modern books claimed that the world was millions of years old, hundreds of millions. The people stemmed not from Adam, but from apes. God hadn't created the world in six days; the earth had torn away from the sun, and after taking millions of years to cool, it developed liv-

ing creatures. Traces of ancient creatures were found in stones
and in amber. Bones and horns were found of animals that had
lived forty and fifty million years ago. Moses hadn't parted the
Red Sea, Joshua hadn't stopped the sun in Gibeon, and the Messiah would never come. My brother spoke not of God's wonders, but of the wonders of nature. How mighty and magnificent
nature was! There were stars whose light reached our eyes after
millions of years. Everything that existed—people, dogs, pigs,
bedbugs, the sea, the rivers, the mountains, the moon—was part
of this nature. But for all its greatness, nature was blind. It
couldn't differentiate between good and evil. During an earthquake, saints perished along with sinners. The floods inundated
synagogues and churches, the mansions of the rich and the
shacks of the poor. The pious and the heretics both died during
the epidemics. This nature had never begun and could never
end. It followed its own laws. It was sand, rocks, electricity,
light, fire, water. Our brains were part of this nature, too. Our
heads thought, but nature did not. Our eyes saw and our ears
heard, but nature was blind and deaf. It was no smarter than
the cobblestone in the street or the refuse in the large garbage
bin in our courtyard.

I recall a Sabbath in summer following the holiday meal.
Mother and Father took a nap as was the custom on Sabbath
day; my younger brother, Moishe, had gone down to play in the
courtyard; my older brother, Joshua, had gone off somewhere
to "those streets" where there were libraries with heretical
books, museums, and theaters, and where students carried on
affairs with rich, pretty, and educated girls. Who knows what
sins my brother committed there? Maybe he rode the streetcar
despite the Sabbath, handled money, or kissed a girl. According
to the holy books I had studied, he would roast in hell or be
reincarnated as an animal, a beetle, or maybe even as the sails
of a windmill. Joshua was already writing stories that he called
literature and painting portraits.

I went out onto our balcony—a boy with a pale face, blue
eyes, and red earlocks—and I tried to think about the world. I
pondered and at the same time observed what went on in the

street below. The passers-by were as divided in their beliefs and attitudes as were the children in our house. Here, a bearded Jew with earlocks walked by in a fur-lined hat and satin gabardine—probably one of the Chassidim late after services—and soon a dandy came by in modern clothes, yellow shoes, a straw hat, clean-shaven and with a cigarette between his lips. He smoked openly on the Sabbath demonstrating his lack of faith in the Torah. Now came a pious young matron with a bonnet on her shaven head, to be closely followed by a girl with rouged cheeks, a kind of blue eye shadow, and a short-sleeved blouse that revealed her bare arms. She stopped to talk to the street loafers and even exchanged kisses with them. She carried a purse, even though this was forbidden on the Sabbath. A few years before, such boys and girls had tried to launch a revolution and overthrow the Tsar. They threw bombs and shot a grocer on Krochmalna Street for allegedly being a bourgeois. Some of the rebels had been hanged; others were in prison or exiled to Siberia. This crowd laughed at my father and his piety. They predicted that after the revolution there would be no more synagogues or study houses, and they called the Chassidim fanatics. Other young men and women on our street felt that the Jews shouldn't wait for the Messiah but should themselves build up the Land of Israel, which they called Palestine. They argued that all peoples had their countries and that Jews being a people, too, needed a land of their own. The Messiah would never come on his donkey. Their leader, Dr. Herzl, had died the year I was born. There were also thieves on our street, gangsters, pimps, whores, fences who bought stolen goods. The fact was that not all Chassidim were such honest people themselves. Some of them were known to be swindlers. They went bankrupt every few months and settled for a half or for a third with the manufacturers.

"What does all this mean?" I asked myself. "Wherein lies the truth? It must be somewhere, after all!"

At first glance, my brother Joshua seemed to be right. Nature demonstrated no religion. It didn't speak or preach. It apparently didn't concern nature that the slaughterers in Yanash's

Market daily killed hundreds or thousands of fowl. Nor did it bother nature that the Russians made pogroms on Jews or that the Turks and Bulgarians massacred each other and carried little children on the tips of their bayonets. Well, but how had nature become that which it was? Where did it get the power to watch over the farthest stars and over the worms in the gutter? What were those eternal laws by which it acted? What was light? What was electricity? What went on deep inside the earth? Why was the sun so hot and so bright? And what was that inside my head that had to be constantly thinking? At times Mother brought brains home from the market—brains were cheaper than beef. Mother cooked these brains and I ate them. Could my brains be cooked and eaten, too? Yes, of course, but so long as they weren't cooked, they kept on thinking and wanting to know the truth.

Two

THERE WERE A NUMBER OF HOLY
books in my father's bookcase in which I sought the answers to
my questions. One was the *Book of the Covenant,* which I believe was already at that time a hundred years old and full of
scientific facts. It described the theories of Copernicus and Newton and, it seems, the experiments of Benjamin Franklin as well.
There were accounts of savage tribes, strange animals, and explanations of what made a train run and a balloon fly. In the
special section dealing with religion were mentioned a number
of philosophers. I recall that Kant already figured in there, too.
The author, Reb Elijah of Vilna, a pious Jew, proved how inadequate the philosophers were at explaining the mystery of the
world. No research or inquiry, wrote he, could reveal the truth.
The author of the *Book of the Covenant* spoke of nature, too,
but with the constant reminder that nature was something that
God had created, not a thing that existed of its own power. I
never tired of reading this book. Things had already evolved in
my time of which the author of the *Book of the Covenant* could
not know. In the delicatessen near our house there was a telephone. From time to time, a car drove down our street. My
brother said that rays had been discovered that could photograph the heart and the lungs and that an instrument existed
that revealed the stuff of which stars were made. The Yiddish
newspaper read in our house often printed articles about Edison, the inventor of the phonograph. Each such account was for

me like a treasure find. Because of my deep curiosity about
science, I should have grown up a scientist, but I wasn't satisfied
with mere facts—I wanted to solve the mystery of being. I
sought answers to questions which tormented me then and still
do to the present day.

The street was crowded with people, and our balcony
swarmed with living creatures. Here came a butterfly and there
a big fly with a green-gold belly; here landed a sparrow and
suddenly a pigeon came swooping in from somewhere. An in-
sect lighted on the lapel of my gabardine. In cheder we called it
Moses' little cow. Actually it was a ladybug. It was odd to consider that all these creatures had had fathers, mothers, grandfathers, and grandmothers just like me. Each of them lived out
his or her time and died. I had read somewhere that a fly had
thousands of eyes. Well, but despite all these eyes boys caught
flies, tore off their wings, and tortured them in every manner
only man could conceive while the Almighty sat on His Throne
of Glory in seventh heaven and the angels sang His praises.

There were cabala books in my father's bookcase which in-
trigued me immensely. I was forbidden to study them. Father
constantly reminded me that you couldn't take to the cabala
before you reached thirty. He said that for those younger, the
cabala posed a danger. One could drift into heresy and even
lose one's mind, God forbid. When Father wasn't at home or
was taking his Sabbath nap, I browsed through these books.
They listed names of angels, seraphim. God's name was printed
in large letters and in many variations. There were descriptions
of heavenly mansions, transmigrated souls, spiritual copulations.
The writers of these books were apparently well versed in the
ways of heaven. They knew of combinations of letters through
which you could tap wine from a wall, create pigeons, even
destroy the world. Besides God Himself (there were no words
or satisfactory terms to describe what He is), the one who had
the main say above was Metatron, who ranked just a notch below God. A second mighty and awesome angel was Sandalphon.
All the angels, seraphim, cherubim, had one desire—to praise
God, to revere Him, to extol Him, to enhance His name. Their

wings spread over many worlds. They spoke Hebrew. I had
learned in the Gemara that God understands all languages and
that you could pray to Him in your own tongue, but the angels
resorted only to Hebrew. Well, but this wasn't the same ordinary Hebrew that I knew. Holy names spurted from their fiery
mouths, secrets of the Torah, mysteries upon mysteries. So vast
were these heavens that three hundred and ten worlds were
reserved for every saint. Every soul, big or small, the moment it
passed the process of being cleansed in fires of hell, found a
place in Paradise—each according to its origin and its deeds. All
the heavens, all the upper worlds, all the spheres, all the angels
and souls, were concerned with one thing—to learn the secrets
of the Torah, since God and the Torah and those who believed
in the Torah, the Jews, were one and the same. . . . Every
word, every letter, every curlicue, contained hints of Divine wisdom which no matter how often it was studied could never be
learned, since, like God, the Torah was infinite. God Himself
studied the Torah; that is to say, He studied His own depths. All
the heavens, the entire eternity, were one great yeshivah. God
even found time to study with the souls of little children who
had left the world early. In my imagination I pictured the Almighty sitting at a heavenly table surrounded by little souls in
skullcaps and earlocks, all of them anxious to hear the word of
Him who was beyond words of praise and beyond human
knowledge, and of Whom the best thing that could be said was
silence.

Leafing through the cabala books, I discovered that even as
they studied the Torah in the heavens, so did they indulge in
fiery loves. In fact, in heaven Torah and love were two sides of
the same entity. God copulated with the Divine Presence, which
was actually God's wife, and the people of Israel were their
children. When the Jews transgressed and God grew angry at
them and wanted to punish them, the Divine Presence in-
terceded for them like any Jewish mother when the father is
angry. The authors of the cabala books constantly warned
against taking their writings literally. They were always afraid of
anthropomorphism. Still, they did present a human concept.

Not only God and the Divine Presence but all the male and female saints in the heavens loved one another and coupled both face to face and front to back.

Jacob again mated with Rachel, Leah, Bilhah, and Zilpah. The Patriarchs, King David, King Solomon, all the great people of the Scriptures and the Gemara, had wives and concubines in heaven. These couplings were unions performed for the glory of God. I already knew from reading the *Book of the Covenant* and maybe from glancing into my older brother's books that there were male trees and female trees. Winds and bees carried the pollen from one tree to another and fructified them. But I realized now that even in heaven the principle of male and female prevailed. I myself began to long for the mysteries of the girls in our street and courtyard. They seemed to eat, drink, and sleep just like men, but they looked different, spoke differently, smiled differently, dressed differently. Their lips, breasts, hips, throats, expressed something I didn't understand but was drawn to. The girls laughed at things that evoked no laughter in me. They thrilled over doodads that left me cold. They said words that struck me as silly and childish, yet their voices appealed to me. Not only God but also objects down here on earth had a language that defied interpretation. Hands, feet, eyes, noses— all had their own speech. They said something, but what? I had read somewhere that King Solomon understood the language of animals and birds. I had heard of people who could read faces and palms, and I yearned to know all this.

Three

SOME OF THE CABALA BOOKS WERE chiefly concerned with sacred matters, but others, such as the *Book of Raziel* and the *Book of the Devout,* devoted much space to the powers of evil—demons, devils, imps, hobgoblins—as well as to magic. God had His kingdom, and Satan, or Asmodeus, had his own. The devil had secrets, too—dark secrets. The powers of goodness nourished themselves on the Torah and good deeds. They sought only to attain the truth, whereas the powers of darkness fed on lie, blasphemy, hate, envy, madness, cruelty. There were synagogues, houses of prayer, and Chassidic study houses on our street where Jews prayed, studied the Torah, and served God, but the street also contained taverns, brothels, and a den for thieves, pimps, and whores. There was a woman on the street of whom it was said that if she even glanced at a child she promptly gave it the evil eye. I knew her. A raging fire burned in her black eyes. It was said that three of her husbands had died and two had divorced her. She was capable of hitting a child she didn't know, tearing off his cap, or spitting at him. Every third word she uttered was a curse. She wore her own hair instead of a wig, but this wasn't hair but a kind of tangle of tufts, elflocks, and thorns. The crooked eyes and wide nostrils brought to mind a bulldog. Her lips were thick, her teeth long, black, and as pointed as nails. My mother said that Satan gazed out of her eyes. She was allegedly a supplier of domestic help, but it was said that she in-

duced country girls into prostitution and sold some of them
into white slavery in a city far across the sea—Buenos Aires.

Because my brother Joshua had left the path of righteousness
and denied both God and the devil, my parents often spoke of
both these forces in order to overcome his arguments. If there
were demons, there had to be a God. I heard countless stories
of dybbuks, corpses that left their graves at night and wandered
off to visit miracle workers or to attend distant fairs. Some of
them forgot that they were dead and launched all kinds of business ventures or even got married. In Bilgorai, my mother's
home town, there was a ritual slaughterer, Avromele, on whose
window an evil spirit had been beating for weeks on end. Every
evening the whole population of the town gathered in the
house to listen to the invisible force knock on the pane. One
could discourse with it. One asked it questions and it tapped
out the answers—mostly "yes" or "no" but occasionally entire
words according to an agreed-upon code. The town *nachalnik*,
a Russian, was apparently an enlightened man who didn't believe in evil spirits. He sent the police and soldiers to search
the house—the attic, the cellar, every nook and cranny—to discover the source of the noises, but they found nothing. Well,
and what about the girl in Krasnik who was possessed by the
soul of a sinful man which in a male voice recounted the sins
and abominations he had committed during his lifetime? The
girl was of common stock and didn't even know the alphabet,
yet the dybbuk spouted passages and quotations from the Gemara, the Midrash, and other holy books. Often, wag that he
was, he transposed the sacred words so that they emerged ob-
scene but in a way apparent only to those who were learned. I
read about such demons in storybooks. They were even mentioned in the Gemara, which spoke of Jewish demons and of
Gentile demons.

I lived in dread fear of these invisible beings. Our stairs were
dark at night, and going up and down them became for me a
terrible burden. I often counted the fringes on my ritual garment to see that none were missing. I mumbled incantations
from the Gemara and from other sacred books. My brother

Joshua laughed at me. He argued that there was no such thing
as evil spirits. It was all fantasy, fanaticism. Well, but had a whole
world conspired to make up the same lie? An anthology of German poetry had somehow found its way into our house. Since
German is similar to Yiddish and because my eagerness to read
was so great, I had learned to read German and I read Goethe's
"Der Erlkönig," Heine's poem about the Lorelei, and many
other mystical poems. The whole world believed in ghosts. If it
could be shown that a piece of mud in the gutter housed millions of unseen microbes, why couldn't hordes of invisible
ghosts be flying around in the air? Even my astute brother
couldn't come up with an answer to this question.

There was a book in our house called *The Pillar of Service,*
which explained the cabala in simpler terms. It claimed that
God had existed forever. The author, Reb Baruch Kossover,
"proved" the existence of God using the same arguments I
found years later in Spinoza's *Ethics* and in other philosophical
works. God's essence and His existence are identical. When we
say that one and one makes two or that the sum of the angles
in a triangle equals two right angles, we don't need a wooden
triangle or two groschen to prove us right. One and one would
equal two even if there were no objects in the world.

Once Reb Baruch Kossover had reassured the reader that
there is a God, he went on to describe Him without any further
proofs. Before God had created the world, all His traits or qualities had been completely merged within Him. Wisdom blended
with mercy, beauty with strength, perpetuity with understanding
and love. But it seemed that the urge to create was one of God's
attributes, too. How could there be a king without a people?
How could one be merciful when there wasn't anyone to receive the mercy? How could God love when there was no one
to be loved? So long as God didn't create the world, all His
traits were latent, not realized—potential, not factual. God
needed a world, many worlds, to become what He was. Creativeness was God's most obvious attribute.

But how could He create the world when He Himself and His
radiance flooded everything? The answer given by the cabala,

especially by Rabbi Isaac Luria, is that in order to be able to create and to make room for Creation, God had to shrink or reduce Himself. It lay within His power—if He so desired—to dim or even extinguish part of His light. In the midst of the infinity He created a vacuum, where the Creation would come into being. Rabbi Baruch Kossover constantly warned the reader not to take him literally. God wasn't matter, and the emptiness He created wasn't one of space but one of quality. When a teacher taught a child just entering cheder, he wouldn't try to make him grasp the intricacies of the Talmud or the commentaries. The teacher had, in a sense, to compress his thinking in order to adjust it to the capacities of his young pupil. According to the cabala, Creation was a process of diminution and emanation. First God created the World of Emanation. This world was still close to God, as spiritually elevated as can be conceived, but even *it* already revealed God's traits or *sephiroth:* the Crown, Wisdom, Understanding, Mercy, Power, Splendor, Infinity, Magnificence, Fundamentality, Kingdom. This spiritually exalted world then emanated a world that was lower, the World of Creation, which possessed the same ten *sephiroth.* Later came the World of Form, and only then the World of Deed or the World of Matter, with all the stars, galaxies, comets, planets; and, it seems, at the very end was created our world. Actually, we were all part of God's light, but through the process of emanation and diminution God's light grew ever darker, ever more specific and accessible, until it turned into matter—earth, rocks, sea, animals, people. According to the cabala, Creation was a kind of gradual revelation and popularization of divinity. The cabala is pantheistic. My later interest in Spinoza stemmed from trying to study the cabala.

Four

ALTHOUGH I WAS STILL YOUNG WHEN
I began to browse through the cabala books, I realized that
their particulars weren't as important as was their concept that
everything is God and God is everything; that the stone in the
street, the mouse in its hole, the fly on the wall, and the shoes
on my feet were all fashioned from the Divinity. The stone, I
told myself, might appear dead, mute, cold, indifferent to good
and evil, but somewhere deep within it, it was alive, knowledge-
able, on the side of justice, united with God from Whose substance it was kneaded. Matter was a mask over the face of spirit.
Behind smallness hid bigness, stupidity was crippled wisdom,
evil was perverted mercy. Years later when I read that a stone
consisted of trillions of molecules constantly in motion and that
these molecules consisted of atoms and that these atoms were
in themselves complicated systems, whirls of energy, I said to
myself: "That's the cabala, after all!" Even as a boy I had heard
that atoms were not merely dead balls of matter. Certain atoms
such as radium emitted rays of light and energy for hundreds
of years. I had heard the words "proton" and "electron." Slivers
of scientific knowledge found their way into our pious household through the newspapers and the Yiddish and Hebrew
books my brother brought home. Science, just like the cabala,
spoke of light that could be seen with human eyes and of invisible light. I had read somewhere about the ether that filled the
endless space and whose vibrations allowed eyes to see, trees

to grow, creatures to live and love. Later, I read that certain
scholars denied the existence of this all-encompassing ether.
There were heretics in science, too. There, too, they served an
idol one day, and the next they dragged him through the
slime. . . .

I existed on several levels. I was a cheder boy, yet I probed
the eternal questions. I asked a question about the Gemara and
tried to explain the mysteries of Zeno. I studied the cabala and
I went down to play tag and hide-and-seek with the boys in the
courtyard. I was aware of being quite different from all the
other boys, and I was deeply ashamed of this fact. Simultaneously I read Dostoevski in Yiddish translation and penny
dreadfuls that I bought on Twarda Street for a kopek. I suffered deep crises, was subject to hallucinations. My dreams
were filled with demons, ghosts, devils, corpses. Sometimes before falling asleep I saw shapes. They danced around my bed,
hovered in the air. In my fantasies or daydreams I brought the
Messiah or was myself the Messiah. By uttering magic words, I
built a palace on a mountaintop in the Land of Israel or in the
desert region, and I lived there with Shosha. Angels and demons served me. I flew to the farthest stars. I discovered a po-
tion which when drunk revealed all the world's wisdom and
made one immortal. I spoke with God and He disclosed His
secrets to me.

My moods varied swiftly. Now I was in ecstasy and soon deep
in despair. The cause of my gloom was often the same—unbearable pity for those who were suffering and who had suffered in all the generations. I had heard about the cruelties perpetrated by Chmielnicki's Cossacks. I had read about the
Inquisition. I knew about the pogroms against Jews in Russia
and Rumania. I lived in a world of cruelty. I was tormented not
only by the sufferings of men but by the sufferings of beasts,
birds, and insects as well. Hungry wolves attacked lambs. Lions,
tigers, and leopards had to devour other creatures or die from
hunger. Hunters wandered through forests and shot deer,
hares, and pheasants for pleasure. I bore resentment not only
against man but against God, too. It was He who had provided

the savage beasts with claws and fangs. It was He who had made
man a bloodthirsty creature ready to do violence at every step.
I was a child, but I had the same view of the world that I have
today—one huge slaughterhouse, one enormous hell. My
brother had brought home a brochure about Darwin which
contained a chapter about Malthus. Making sure my father
shouldn't see me, I read the book in a single day. Malthus
proved in a way that couldn't be clearer that countless creatures
were born to die, for otherwise the world would fill with so
many creatures that everyone would starve to death or simply
become crushed. Wars, plagues, and famines sustained life on
this earth. Darwin went even further and maintained that the
continuous struggle for food or sex is the origin of all species.
The Cossacks who massacred the Jews, the Russians, the Tartars,
all the tribes that kept on killing each other, actually imple-
mented the plans of Creation. Kill or be killed was the rule of
life and of God. Malthus' contentions denied all the claims of
the Scriptures that God despised bloodshed. Actually He had so
constructed the world that blood should spill, that children
should starve to death, that beasts should devour each other. I
read these truths that I knew no one could deny, yet at the same
time I felt as if I were swallowing poison. I closed this terrible
book and began to browse through the Scriptures. I had long
been aware of the amazing contradictions contained in this holy
volume. The same Moses who said, "Thou shalt not kill" also
said, "Thou shalt save alive nothing that breatheth." The wars
waged by Joshua bore an uncanny resemblance to the outrages
perpetrated by Chmielnicki's Cossacks. King David, the alleged
author of the Psalms, hardly conducted himself like a psalmist
should. Before my eyes the vision had long lingered of how he
measured prisoners with a rope to indicate which would live
and which would die. Since a murderer was a malefactor, how
could King David be called a saint? And why must the Messiah
descend from King David? And when the Messiah came, how
would I be able to call King David, a murderer, "Grandpa"? In
the Psalms it said that people of violence and falseness are an

abomination to God. Well, but how could God abominate them if they carried out His bidding?

No, I could find no answer in the Scriptures. The Scriptures indirectly confirmed the theories of Malthus. When the Jews were stronger, they killed the Philistines, and when the Philistines were stronger, they killed the Jews. According to the Scriptures, the Jews fell before their foe because they had sinned, but was every soldier in the war a sinner? And what about the children who were frequent victims of these wars? It seemed that God didn't punish individual sinners directly—He punished the entire group. But this same God had also said that fathers mustn't die for the sins of their children nor children for the sins of the fathers, but that everyone must die for his own sins.

I did find a trace of comfort in the cabala books. These books described the earth as the meanest of all the worlds. The evil spirits, the dissenters, Satan, Lilith, Naamah, Machlat, Shibta—all had dominion in this den of evil. Our world was the lowest of all the worlds, far removed from God and His mercy. But just because we were so far from God and His benevolence, He had given us the greatest gift in His treasury—free will. The angels have no choice, but man could choose between good and evil. This world is, you might say, the weakest link in God's chain, and a chain is only as strong as its weakest link. When man chooses virtue, he strengthens all the spheres. Angels and seraphim look forward to a man doing a good deed, since this brings joy and strength to all the worlds. A good deed helps God and the Divine Presence to unite. A sin, on the other hand, evokes gloom in all the worlds.

Assume it was so. But does a cat have a choice? Does a mouse? I once heard the scream of a mouse that a cat had caught, and this cry haunts me still. Do the chickens slaughtered in Yanash's Market have a choice? Do they have to suffer because of *our* choice? Well, and those children that died of scarlet fever, diphtheria, whooping cough, and other diseases—how were they guilty? I had read and heard that the souls of the dead were reincarnated in cattle and fowl and that when the slaugh-

terer killed them with a kosher knife and said the blessing with
fervor, this served to purify these souls. What about those cows
and hens that fell into the hands of Gentile butchers? . . .

"I'm becoming a heretic!" I said to myself, or thought it.

My urge to know what the unbelievers or the scientists had
to say grew ever stronger. Who knows—perhaps the truth lies
with them? A Jewish publisher in Warsaw had begun to issue a
series of popular books on science, and I asked my brother to
bring them to me. My brother and I now shared a secret. I read
a popular book on physics. I read about astronomy. To the scientists, the universe was larger than the World of Deed as described in the cabala. In infinite space floated countless bodies,
some already cooled, others of a temperature of thousands and
millions of degrees, others still composed of gases or mists. All
these bodies were ruled by one law—gravity. The book provided the cosmological theory of Kant and Laplace. Earlier, the
universe had consisted of one immense fog. This fog existed in
a state of equilibrium. But something occurred so that in one
place in this fog the molecules grew denser and began to attract
the surrounding molecules. A body formed which grew from
moment to moment—a cosmic ball. In time, this ball grew so
immense that it tore apart and formed the sun, the other stars,
the planets, and the comets. The sun itself grew too big and
unwieldy so that a part of it tore away and later became our
Earth and the moon. . . . I discussed this theory with my
brother. "Where did the first fog come from?" I asked him, and
my brother replied: "Where did God come from? You must accept the fact that something has existed forever and you can just
as well say that nature existed forever as you can say that God
did. It's the same with gravity and all the other laws. They were
a part of nature forever, but so long as the cosmic fog was in a
state of equilibrium these laws remained passive (more or
less)."

Even a child could detect the similarity between the cabala
and the cosmology of Kant and Laplace. The only difference lay
in the fact that the infinity as described by the cabala possessed
consciousness, wisdom, beauty, and mercy, whereas the fog of

Kant and Laplace was dead. The question of how this dead golem could have produced trees, blossoms, birds, lions, Maimonides, Copernicus, Newton, and the Baal Shem, the scientists had
one answer: development, evolution. My father called it by another name—an inkwell that had spilled on a scroll and written
a book full of wisdom. . . .

In the midst of all this, World War I erupted. Some assassin
had killed the Austrian archduke and his wife, and millions of
soldiers and civilians had to pay with their lives for this crime.
The scholars of all the nations harnessed the eternal laws to
decimate the enemy peoples. The Jews in the Radzymin study
house where my father worshiped (we had moved from number 10 to number 12 Krochmalna Street) said that there were
such cannons now that could kill a thousand soldiers with one
shot. The airplane had been invented, a kind of heavier-than-air
balloon. Until the war we had to be careful with the Yiddish
newspaper in our house. Father said that the newspapers were
full of blasphemy and heresy. He said that to start the day by
reading the paper was like eating poison for breakfast. But as
the armies fought around the towns and villages where we
came from and the Tsar's uncle, Nikolai Nikolaevich, ordered
the Jews driven out of those towns and even took Jews as hos-
tages and sent them to Siberia, Father started to glance into the
papers, too—not the first thing in the morning but later in the
day, after praying and studying. New words had emerged which
Father had never before heard. The Jew who had been in exile
for two thousand years and never mixed into the Gentile wars
had almost no names for arms and ammunition. Nor did he
have words for strategy and tactics. The Yiddish journalists had
to adapt all these words from the German and occasionally
from Russian and Polish. Father read the reports. The enemy
(the Germans) was constantly being repulsed—still he kept ad-
vancing steadily despite the heavy losses. The numbers of dead
and wounded were listed. At times the writer added: "We suffered heavy casualties, too." Father gripped his red beard while
his blue eyes gazed out the window and up to heaven. They
fought and shed blood over some poverty-stricken village, some

muddy stream. They burned the wooden shacks and the meager possessions of paupers who often had to flee into the cold nights with their children. I heard Father mumble: "Woe, woe is us, God in heaven!"

I wanted to say: "Papa, this isn't the fault of God but of evolution. Had the fog remained in a state of equilibrium, we would all be in peace."

Five

WE STARVED AT HOME. BITTER FROSTS raged outside, but our stove wasn't lit. Mother lay in bed all day and read her books of morals—*Duty of the Heart, The Rod of Punishment, The Good Heart,* and occasionally the aforementioned *Book of the Covenant.* Her face was white and bloodless. She, too, sought the answers to the eternal questions, but her faith remained firm. She didn't cast a speck of doubt upon the Almighty. Mother argued with my older brother: "It isn't the Creator's fault. He wanted to give the Torah to Esau and Ishmael but they rejected it." My brother asked: "Were you there?" He denied the concept of free choice. There was no such thing as free will. If you were born into a Jewish house, you believed in Jewishness; if you were born into a Christian home, you believed in Jesus; if you were born a Turk, you believed in Mohammed. He said to Mother: "If someone abducted you as a child out of your father's house and raised you among Gentiles, you'd keep on crossing yourself, and instead of the Jewish books you'd be reading the history of the Christian martyrs now."

Mother grimaced at this blasphemy and said: "May the Almighty forgive your words."

"There is no Almighty. Man is an animal like all animals. This whole war is on account of oil."

This was the first time I had ever heard such words. Oil, of all things? All the time we had lived in number 10 we had used oil or kerosene in our lamps. Now that we lived in number 12 we used gas. It seemed incredible that Germany, Russia, England, and France should fight over such a filthy thing as oil, but my brother soon explained it.

Mother heard him out and said: "They only need an excuse to fight. Today they fight over oil; tomorrow it'll be over soap or cream of tartar. The fact is that they are evildoers and the evildoer wants to commit evil. All he needs is an excuse."

"When the Jews had a country, they fought, too. The whole notion of the 'chosen people' isn't worth a row of beans. We're the same animals as all the others. We have our share of swindlers, fakers, and charlatans."

"It's all because of the accursed Exile."

I didn't know myself with whom to agree—I loved them both deeply—but it appeared that my brother was right. Whatever home one was raised in, that was the faith one accepted. The home hypnotized people like that hypnotist Feldman described in the newspapers. That which Feldman did in a minute the home did gradually. If you heard day in and day out that there is a God, you believed in God. If you raised children to believe that everything resulted from evolution, they would believe in evolution. But which was the truth? I, Isaac, or Itchele, from Krochmalna Street, wouldn't let myself be hypnotized by anybody. I had to consider everything on my own and come to my own conclusions! I realized by now that reading popular books on science wouldn't reveal the secret of the world to me. Kant and Laplace were men, too, not angels. How could they possibly know what had happened millions and myriads of years ago? Since one cannot dig a pit seven miles deep and see what goes on beneath the earth, how could they know how the universe had formed? It was all supposition or plain guesswork. Both the cabala and the astronomy book spoke of presences that existed forever, but I couldn't for the life of me conceive of such a thing. If God or the fog had existed forever, this would mean you could take a wagonful of pencils and write the number of years these presences had existed and it still wouldn't be enough. The fact was that you couldn't write this total with all the pencils in the world on all the paper in the world. In the book on astronomy it stated that space was without limit as was the number of heavenly bodies. But how could something stretch on without an end? On the other hand, how could time have a beginning? What was *before* the beginning? And how could space have a limit? I spoke of this to my brother, and he said: "Your questions have to do with philosophy, not with science, but you can't find the truth there either."

"Where can you find it?"

"The real truth was never known, it isn't known, and it will never be known. Just like a fly can't pull a wagon of coal or iron, our brain can't fathom the truth of the world."

"In that case, what's to be done?"

"Eat, drink, sleep, and if it's possible, try to create a better order."

"What kind of order?"

"One in which the nations stop slaughtering each other and people have work, food, and a decent place to live."

"How can this be done?"

"Oh, there are all kinds of theories."

My brother waved his hand. He himself was in deep trouble. He was hiding from the Russian military authorities. He lived under a false passport listing a different name and different place of birth. He was living in some unheated studio of a sculptor and starving along with the rest of us. He risked his life every moment, since deserters were shot. Mother cried her eyes out as she prayed to God that no harm befall him. Although I doubted the existence of God, I, too, prayed to Him (whenever I forgot that I was a heretic). After all, you couldn't be sure about such things.

My brother left after a short visit, but before leaving, he glanced out the window to see that no military patrols were roaming about. I began to pace to and fro like a caged beast. How could you live in such a world? How could you breathe when you were condemned to never, never know where you

came from, who you were, where you were going? I looked out
the window and saw a freight wagon of sacks drawn by a skinny
nag. I compared myself to this creature that pulled a load without knowing what it was or where it was going or why it had to
strain so. My brother had just now advised me, like Ecclesiastes,
to eat, drink, and sleep, but I had nothing to eat and it wasn't
even easy to drink a glass of water, since our water pipes had
frozen. No matter how I covered myself at night I still felt cold.
The mice in our apartment were apparently starving, too, since
they grew ever bolder in their desperation—they even leaped
over our beds. Well, and how would I go about creating a better
order? Should I write a letter to Nicholas II or to Wilhelm II or
to the English King that it didn't pay to go to war over oil?
Hadn't Malthus said that wars and epidemics were useful—actually vital to man's existence?

My brother had mentioned the philosophers, and although
he said that I could learn nothing from them, they had to
know something, after all. Otherwise, why were they called
philosophers? But where did one get such a book? I could
have asked my brother, but first of all, he seldom came home
now, and secondly, he often forgot what I asked him for and it
took him weeks to remember. But I had to learn the answer
right now! I began to rummage among my brother's papers,
and I found what I wanted—a book from Bresler's Library listing its address somewhere on Nowolipki Street. Now I was
ready to launch the biggest adventure of my life—namely, I resolved to go to this library and try to get a book out on philosophy. It was my feeling that my brother had probably already
read this book and that it was high time he brought it back. A
few times cards had come from the library demanding from my
brother that he bring back books that were overdue. I would
therefore take this book back and ask for another in its stead,
one on philosophy. It was true that if my brother found out
what I had done, he might grow terribly angry and might even
slap me for going where I didn't belong. But what was a slap
compared to the joy that a book on philosophy would grant me?
I burned with the urge to read what the philosophers had to

say about God, the world, time, space, and, most of all, why people and animals must suffer so. This to me was the question of questions.

I took the book and started off toward Nowolipki Street. It was freezing outside. The Germans had pushed so close to Warsaw that I could hear their cannonfire in the streets. I pictured to myself how a thousand soldiers died from every shot. Freezing blasts blew, making my nose feel like a piece of wood. I had no gloves, and the fingers of the hand holding the book had become stiff. I was terribly afraid they would yell at me at the library or make fun of me. Who knows? My brother might even be there. I raced against the wind, and a voice within me shouted, "I must learn the truth! Once and for all!"

I went inside the library and, for a moment, saw nothing. My eyes grew bedazzled and my head spun. "If only I don't faint!" I prayed to the forces that guided the world. Gradually the dizziness subsided, and I saw a huge room, actually a hall stacked with books from floor to the astoundingly high ceiling. The sun shone in through the windows casting a bright wintery light. Behind a wide counter stood a corpulent man—bareheaded, beardless, with longish hair and a mustache—who placed paper patches on the margins of a book. For a long time he didn't look up, then he noticed me, and his big black eyes expressed a kind of amiable surprise.

He said: "What do you say, young fellow?"

I savored the title "young fellow." It was a sign that I was already half grown.

I replied: "I brought back my brother's book."

The librarian stuck out his hand and took the book. He stared for a long time at the inside of the cover and knitted his brow. Then he asked: "Israel Joshua Singer is your brother?"

"Yes, my older brother," I replied.

"What's happened to him? It's a year since he took out this book. You're not allowed to keep a book longer than a month. A pretty big fine has accumulated. More than the deposit."

"My brother is in the Army," I said, astounded over my own lie. It was obviously either my way of justifying my brother's failure to return the book or a means of drawing sympathy to myself. The librarian shook his head.

"Where is he—in the war?"

"Yes, the war."

"You don't hear from him?"

"Not a word."

The librarian grimaced.

"What do they want—those savages? Why do they drag innocent victims into their murderous wars?" He spoke half to me, half to himself. He paused a moment, then said: "Your brother is a talented young man. He writes well. He paints well, too. A talent. A born talent. Well, and you obviously study at the study house, eh?"

"Yes, I study, but I want to know what goes on in the world, too," I said. I had the feeling that my mouth was speaking of its own volition.

"Oh? What do you want to know?"

"Oh—physics, geography, philosophy—everything."

"Everything, eh? No one knows everything."

"I want to know the secret of life," I said, ashamed of my own words. "I want to read a book on philosophy."

The librarian arched his brows.

"What book? In what language?"

"In Yiddish. I understand Hebrew, too."

"You mean, the sacred language?"

"My brother read the *Ha-tzephirah,* and I read it, too."

"And your father let you read such a heretical paper?"

"He didn't see."

The librarian mulled this over.

"I have something about philosophy in Yiddish, but a boy your age should study useful things, not philosophy. It'll be difficult for you and it'll serve no practical purpose."

"I want to know what the philosophers say about why people must suffer and how the world came about."

"The philosophers don't know this themselves. Wait here."

He went to search among the books and even climbed a ladder. He came down with two books and showed them to me. One was in Yiddish, the other in Hebrew.

He said: "I have something for you, but if your father should see them, he'd tear them to pieces."

"My father won't see them. I'll hide them well."

"When you take out books from a library, you have to leave a deposit and pay for a month in advance, but you probably haven't a groschen. All right, I'll take the chance, but bring them back when you're finished. And keep them clean. If you bring them back in time, I'll find something else for you. If a boy wants to learn the secret of life, you have to accommodate him."

The librarian smiled and marked something down on cards. He handed me the books, and I barely restrained myself from kissing his hand. A great surge of affection swept over me toward this good person along with the desperate urge to read what was written in these books.

Six

I FINISHED THE YIDDISH BOOK THAT same day. I became so engrossed in it I even forgot my hunger. There were only a few pages devoted to most philosophers in this book. Some of them—Plato, Aristotle, and Democritus—were familiar to me from browsing through *Guide to the Perplexed, The Khuzari,* and *Faiths and Opinions* and other volumes in our house as well as the *Book of the Covenant.* I understood only a little of what I read, but I plowed right through lest my father catch me, tear these heretical books to pieces, and slap me besides. I was anxious to discover as quickly as possible why men and animals had to suffer. The philosophers offered various opinions regarding the creation of the world, but I clung to the question "How do they know?" Since they weren't in heaven, and neither God nor the First Cause nor the Entelechy spoke to them, how could I reply to them? I encountered such words as idea, form, categories, substance, monads, idealism, materialism, empiricism, solipsism, but the questions of how things could exist forever, how the world could be without limit, and why cats caught mice remained unanswered. Only one philosopher, Schopenhauer, mentioned the sufferings of men and animals, but according to this book, he offered no explanations for it. The world, he said, consisted of a blind will, of passions that had no reason and that the intellect served them like a slave. . . .

After a while, I turned to the Hebrew book. Reading about

philosophy in Hebrew was even harder for me than in Yiddish. Actually I didn't read but scanned through the pages for parts that would answer my questions in clear fashion, but there was less clarity here than in the books on the cabala, particularly *The Pillar of Service*. The pleasure that I got from these two books gradually turned into despair and rage. If the philosophers didn't know and couldn't know—as Locke, Hume, and Kant themselves indicated—what need was there for all those high-flown words? Why all the research? I had the suspicion that the philosophers pretended, masked their ignorance behind Latin and Greek phrases. Besides, it seemed to me that they skirted the main issues, the essence of things. The question of questions was the suffering of creatures, man's cruelty to man and to animals. Even if it provided answers to all the other questions but this one, philosophy would still be worthless.

Those were my feelings then, and those are my feelings still. But in reading about these philosophers I got the impression that the question of suffering was of little consequence to them.

My brother had left a dictionary of foreign words and phrases in the house, and I looked up the more difficult words. On one page of one of the philosophy books it discussed whether the sentence "Seven and five equals twelve" is *a priori* or synthetically *a priori*. I looked up the meaning of *a priori* and "synthetic" as well as of "analytic," which was mentioned there, too, and at the same time I thought: "How can it help the chewed-up mouse or the devoured lamb whether the sentence 'Seven and five equals twelve,' is analytic or synthetic?" I know today that the whole Kantian philosophy hangs on this question, but the problem of problems is still to me the suffering of people and animals. I have the same feeling today when I try to read the convoluted commentaries of Wittgenstein and his disciples who try to convince themselves and others that all that we lack is a clear definition of words. Give us a dictionary with crystal-clear definitions (if such a thing is even possible) and the pains of all the martyrs of all times and of all the tortured creatures would become justified forever. . . .

In the course of the month that I kept the two books (I don't know to this day who their authors were) I read them virtually day and night. I constantly referred to the dictionary, but the more I read and probed in these books, the more obvious it became to me that I would find no answers to my questions in them. Actually, the philosophers all said the same thing I had heard from my mother—that the ways of God (or of nature or of Substance or of the Absolute) were hidden. We didn't know them and we couldn't know. Even then I detected the similarity between the cabala and Baruch Spinoza. Both felt that everything in the world is a part of God, but while the cabala rendered to God such attributes as will, wisdom, grandeur, mercy, Spinoza attributed to God merely the capacity to extend and to think. The anguish of people and animals did not concern Spinoza's God even in the slightest. He had no feelings at all concerning justice or freedom. He Himself wasn't free but had to act according to eternal laws. The Baal Shem and the murderer were of equal importance to Him. Everything was preordained, and no change whatsoever could affect Spinoza's God or the things that were part of Him. Billions of years ago He knew that someone would assassinate the Austrian archduke and that Nikolai Nikolaevich would have an old rabbi in a small Polish town hanged for being an alleged German spy.

The book said that Spinoza proposed that God be loved with a rational love *(amor Dei intellectualis),* but how could you love such a mighty and wise God who didn't possess even a spark of compassion toward the tortured and beaten? This philosophy exuded a chill, though still I felt that it might contain more truth (bitter truth) than the cabala. If God were indeed full of mercy and benevolence, He wouldn't have allowed starvation, plagues, and pogroms. Spinoza's God merely fortified the contentions of Malthus.

When the Germans entered Warsaw, the hunger became even worse. An epidemic of typhus broke out. My younger brother, Moishe, caught the spotted typhus and was taken to the municipal hospital. His life was in danger, and Mother cried her eyes out begging God (or whoever was in charge) in his behalf. Spinoza taught me that prayers couldn't help in any way, but the cabala books said that prayers recited with fervor went straight to the Throne of Glory and could avert the worst decree. How could Spinoza be so sure that God had no will or compassion? He, Spinoza, was no more than blood and flesh himself, after all. Thank God, Moishe recovered.

Between 1915 and 1917, hundreds of people died on Krochmalna Street. Now a funeral procession passed our windows and now the ambulance taking the sick to the hospital. I saw women shake their fists at the sky and in their rage call God a murderer and a villain. I saw Chassidim at the Radzymin study house and in the other study houses grow swollen from malnutrition. At home we ate frozen potatoes that had a sweetish, nauseating taste. The Germans kept scoring victories, but those who foretold that the war wouldn't last longer than six weeks had to admit their error. Millions of people had already perished, but Malthus' God still hadn't had enough.

In the midst of all this, the Revolution broke out in Russia. The Tsar was overthrown, and the Jews in the Radzymin study house promptly began to say that this was an omen presaging the coming of the Messiah. The dead rotted, but new hopes were aroused in those still living. It was possible that this Revolution was an act of Providence, but the hunger and sicknesses in Warsaw grew steadily worse. Father became so dejected by the situation that he just about stopped paying attention to me, and I was free to read all the books I could get my hands on. Nor did I neglect to study the Gemara and the commentaries. I studied, read, and let my imagination soar. Since both the cabalists and the philosophers made everything up out of their heads, why couldn't I ferret the truth out with my own brain? Maybe it was destined that *I* should uncover the truth of Creation? But all my ruminations came smack up against the exasperating enigma of eternity and infinity and against the even deeper mystery of suffering and cruelty.

Seven

IN THE SUMMER OF 1917 MY MOTHER took me and my younger brother, Moishe, to Bilgorai where her father had been the town rabbi for forty years. He had fled from the Russians to Lublin and had died there of the cholera. My grandmother Hannah was no longer living either. My uncle Joseph, Mother's brother, had become the Bilgorai rabbi. I have described this trip in detail in my book *In My Father's Court*. The library in Bilgorai was a small one, but I had already started reading Polish then, and I also had the opportunity to read the history of philosophy as well as Spinoza's *Ethics* in German. I even read Karl Marx's *Das Kapital* in Yiddish. Materialism—historical materialism particularly—never attracted me. In my worst moments of doubt I knew that this world hadn't evolved on its own but that behind it lay some plan, a consciousness, a metaphysical force. Blind forces couldn't create even one fly. But in Spinoza's *Ethics* I found a kind of cheerless greatness. Since according to Spinoza substance possessed an endless number of attributes, this left some room for fantasy. I even toyed with the notion of changing some of Spinoza's axioms and definitions and bringing out a new *Ethics*. You could easily say that time was one of God's attributes, too, as well as purpose, creativeness, and growth. I had read somewhere about Lobachevski's non-Euclidian geometry, and I wanted to create a non-Spinozian pantheism, or whatever it might be called. I was ready to make will a divine attribute, too.

This kind of revisionist Spinozism would come very close to the cabala.

There was an enlightened Jew in Bilgorai, Todros the watchmaker, who took an interest in science and philosophy. I tutored his daughter—a beautiful girl—in Hebrew, and her father and I discussed the loftier matters. He subscribed to several scientific periodicals from Warsaw, and I learned from him about Einstein, Planck, and the fact that the atom was a kind of solar system with electrically positive protons and electrically negative electrons. The indivisibility of the atom had always puzzled me. No matter how small a thing was, you could always imagine a half of it, a quarter of it, and so on ad infinitum. I said to Todros in a Gemara chant: "Since the atom is not the final measure of smallness, why should it be the electron? A few years hence scholars will probably discover that the electron can be split, too, that it also consists of a system, and so on without an end. If bigness has no limit, then neither has smallness. It's altogether possible that each atom is a universe and that the electron is actually a planet inhabited by tiny people and animals. It's not inconceivable that on one of these planets sit an Isaac and Todros carrying on more or less the same discussion as we are."

A half-burned match lay on the table, and I said: "Nor is it inconceivable that this match contains countless worlds where people study, learn, marry, and breed—that there are universities there and philosophers writing books."

I wanted to add that there were loves there, too, since I was in love with his daughter, my pupil. Todros smiled and gazed at the match stub.

I went on: "Maybe our world is also part of some cosmic match. Maybe there exist such persons in the infinite universe who could stick our solar system in their pocket, and maybe they actually do this without our knowledge. . . ."

"Well, well, the things that all *could* be. . . . Science speaks only of things known to exist, not of the possibilities."

"I read that there are such rays that vibrate a million times a second. Maybe there are creatures, too, that can experience in one second what we experience in a hundred years."

"Yes, maybe. But meanwhile the situation on our planet grows ever worse. In the Ukraine they're slaughtering Jewish children like in Chmielnicki's times. I got a bunch of newspapers from Warsaw yesterday. It's hard to believe that such savageries are being committed in the twentieth century."

"The same savageries will be committed in the thirtieth century, in the fiftieth century, and in the hundredth century."

"Why do you say this, eh? Don't you believe in progress?"

"God wants murder—He must have it," I said. "Did you ever hear of Malthus?"

"Yes, I've heard of him and I've read him. But you can control human birth. French women have only two children. If people would stop breeding like rabbits, you wouldn't need all the wars and epidemics. In the civilized countries they've just about eliminated cholera. Typhus is rare there. Even here, smallpox is becoming extinct. You can regulate everything with knowledge and patience."

"If they will eliminate one sickness, others will crop up. God is evil," I said, astounded at my own words. "A good God wouldn't arrange it that wolves should devour lambs and cats should catch innocent mice."

"He is neither evil nor good," Todros said. "He doesn't exist and that's all there is to it. And nature doesn't care about morality."

"Where did nature come from?"

"Where did God come from? Nature is here and we must come to terms with it and use its laws for the good of humanity."

"What about the animals?"

"We can't worry about the animals."

The wick in the kerosene lamp cast a bright glow; the stove gave off warmth. My pupil brought two glasses of tea from the kitchen. Her face was pale, but her eyes were coal-black. She listened to our conversation and smiled. Girls never discussed such matters. They talked about shoes, dresses, engagements, weddings, and bargains you could pick up in the market. . . .

My new friend, Notte Schwerdscharf, made speeches and proposed that the Jews go to Palestine, but the girls didn't take him seriously. What difference did it make what Notte said anyway? Each Monday and Thursday he got a new crazy notion. There were already communists in Bilgorai, too. There was even one Jewish youth who was a Polish patriot and had enlisted in Pilsudski's Legion. The pious Jews had organized an Orthodox party.

When my mother took me and my brother Moishe to Bilgorai, my brother Joshua remained in Warsaw. He hadn't the slightest desire to bury himself away in such a Godforsaken hole as Bilgorai. My father went back to Radzymin to help the Chassidic rabbi there compose his books. The Radzymin rabbi had a poor handwriting, and his spelling in Hebrew was atrocious. His commentaries were fatuous, and the scholars scoffed at him. The rabbi needed a "wet nurse," and my father fulfilled this capacity. Eventually, my brother went to Kiev, which the Germans had occupied, and he worked there in the local Yiddish press.

Later came the Bolshevik Revolution and with it, the bands that committed pogroms. Long months went by that we didn't hear from my brother. My sister Hindele had been living in Antwerp with her husband, and when the Germans invaded Belgium, the couple fled to England. He being a Russian citizen, the English authorities sent him back to Russia to report for military duty. However, the Revolution had broken out in the meantime and he was stuck in Russia. My sister lived with a child in London without any means of support. The mails didn't function between England and Poland. For all these problems Mother had but one solution—praying. Compared to us, Todros lived in luxury and it was peaceful there. Todros' wife had a candy store which stayed open until late. I drank the tea, nibbled along on a cookie, and discussed the higher matters with Todros.

I argued: "If there is no God and if nature knows of no morality, why should man behave in a moral way? Why actually *shouldn't* he make pogroms?"

"And if—as you say—God is evil, why should man be good?" Todros countered my question with a question in Jewish fashion.

"To spite God," I replied. "Just because God wants men to kill each other and to slaughter innocent animals is why man must help man and animals, thus demonstrating that he doesn't approve of the way God runs the world."

"If God exists, don't you think He would have His way anyway? You think man is stronger than God?"

"No, I don't mean that at all. But man still has the right to protest if he considers God's deeds unjust."

"And how will this protest help?"

"It doesn't have to help. This is a form of statement that one opposes God's ways. If God kills and man kills, too, it means that we approve of the killing, and we can no longer blame God for the evils of the world."

I don't guarantee that these were my exact words, but this more or less was my contention. Todros shrugged. He was a humanist, a liberal, and an atheist, and he could conceive of no reason for reckoning with a God that didn't exist anyway. His approach was pragmatic. If you didn't kill others, others wouldn't kill you. Todros, incidentally, had been a pupil of my grandfather's. When Todros began to utter heretical remarks, Grandfather ordered him out of his house. My mother often spoke of Todros, and I had the feeling that as a young girl she had figured on becoming his wife. Mother was sixteen and a half when she married my father.

Another time, we got to talking about evil spirits. Todros, enlightened man that he was, naturally didn't believe in such things. I asked him if he recalled the incident of the spirit knocking on Avromele the slaughterer's window. The question apparently embarrassed Todros, for he began to stutter and shook his head.

After a while, he said: "I don't only remember it, I was there. We, the boys from the study house, went there every evening after the services."

"Did it really knock?"

"Yes, it did."

"A demon, eh?"

"I didn't say that."

"Who then did the knocking—a person?"

"I really don't know."

"Is it true that the *nachalnik* sent police and soldiers to see if someone was playing tricks?"

"I didn't see it, but it seems it was so. The whole town talked about it. Not only soldiers, other people searched around, too."

"Who was it that did the knocking?"

"I really don't know. There must have been some cause for it. One thing is sure—it wasn't a spirit because there are no such things."

I told Todros about my mother's dream, three days before the numbers were drawn, that a Bilgorai woman would win the lottery, and Todros said: "Yes, I remember that they spoke of this in your grandfather's house. It was nothing but a coincidence."

And Todros explained it to me this way—millions of dreams that made no sense or that predicted things that didn't happen were ignored. Among all those dreams it happened sometimes that one became true, and that was the one that was noticed. Many miracles could be explained this way.

Several years went by. Poland had become independent again. My brother Joshua had come back from Russia with a wife and a child. I was straining to go back to Warsaw. I was writing then, too, but neither my brother nor I was pleased with the results. My father had accepted a rabbinate in a small town in Galicia. I had gone to Warsaw a few times with the hope of getting some job there, but I came back each time after a few weeks to Bilgorai. My brother had already written some of his best short stories by then, but he had no job either, and he lived in an alcove at his in-laws. Neither of us was good at any other kind of work, but to draw a living from Yiddish literature at that time was impossible. Literary Warsaw was dominated by the communists. A great number of the young writers and readers believed that communism would once and for all put an end to the Jewish problem. In a communist order there would be no Jews or Gentiles, only a single united humanity. Religion and superstition would become a thing of the past. Neither my brother nor even less I fitted into this kind of ideology. I often spoke with great rage against God, but I had never ceased to believe in His existence. I wrote about spirits, demons, cabalists, dybbuks. Many Yiddish writers and readers had cut loose from their Jewish roots and from the juices upon which they had been nourished. They yearned once and for all to tear away from the ghetto and its culture—some as Zionists, others as radicals. Both factions preached worldliness. But I remained spiritually rooted deep in the Middle Ages (or so I was told). I evoked in my work memories and emotions that the worldly reader sought to forget and factually had forgotten. To the pious Jews, on the other hand, I was a heretic and blasphemer. I saw to my astonishment that I belonged neither to my own people nor to any other peoples. Instead of fighting in my writings the political leaders of a decadent Europe and helping to build a new world, I waged a private war against the Almighty. From my viewpoint, the literature produced at that time in Soviet Russia, in Warsaw, and wherever the radicals held sway was fashioned to suit party resolutions rather than to express artistic truths. In the name of alleged progress, writers turned into liars and destroyed the little bit of talent God had bestowed upon them.

I lived on what I made by giving private lessons in Bilgorai. Actually, I suffered extreme privation during those years, but I didn't take this to heart. I stopped reading the new literature and to the best of my ability read all the popular science books I could obtain as well as the magazines that described in everyday language what went on in the world of science. I speak here of the so-called exact sciences. I was less interested in works of psychology. Neither Freud, Adler, nor Jung seemed to touch on any truths that were previously unknown. The astronomers had rejected the cosmology of Kant and Laplace, but as far as I could determine, they hadn't come up with a better theory. Each time I read an article about the origin of the universe, I found that the author sooner or later came to the concept of a cosmic explosion that had erupted billions of years ago and made the universe flee from us with great rapidity. With each article I read, the universe grew larger, older, loaded with rays or particles that vibrated with fantastic frequency. Matter and energy had become one and the same. Those who studied the atom soon began to realize that the protons and electrons were insufficient to maintain the atom in balance. Long before neutrons were discovered, conjectures were made that the atom was more complicated than it had been assumed. Discoveries were made in chemistry and biology, too, but the mystery of the world and my own puzzlement grew no smaller. I myself was a collection of innumerable miracles—my skeleton, my flesh, my brain, my nerves. When I light a match, its light rays radiate at a speed of three hundred thousand kilometers a second. When I unwittingly step on a worm, I destroy a divine masterpiece. I myself was such a worm that could be squashed at any moment. I wanted to hope, but I had nothing to hope for. I wanted to resign, but I couldn't do that either. I read Tolstoi's sermons about Christian love and the nobility of the Russian peasant, but I knew that Tolstoi had never managed to acquire this Christian love himself and that the Russian muzhik wasn't so noble and honest as Tolstoi pictured him. His proposals that the land be divided among the peasants had come to naught. Millions of Russians starved to death; others had been sent to Siberia, rotted in prisons, or been stood against the wall by the GPU. I read the literary idols of the day—Romain Rolland, G. K. Chesterton, Thomas Mann. What I was searching for I could not find in their work.

Eight

IN 1923 MY BROTHER JOSHUA BE-
came coeditor of the literary journal *Literary Pages,* and the
mail brought me the news that I was given the post of proofreader. I had spent nine months in the half-bog, half-village
where my father was rabbi. I had gone there because I had
gotten sick in Bilgorai. In this village there were no worldly
books, and all I had with me were some old algebra textbooks
and a copy of Spinoza's *Ethics.* I came to this village so broken
in spirit that I was ready to give in to my parents, let them
arrange a match for me (my love for Todros' daughter involved
so many complications that I had to abandon all hopes), and
become a storekeeper, a teacher, or whatever fate held in store
for me. I stopped shaving my beard and let my earlocks grow.
The inhabitants of the village were semi- or total peasants. Many
Jews owned land in Galicia. I had no other company but my
parents and my brother Moishe, who had become exceedingly
pious during the time I had been away from home. The Jews
there were all Chassidic, followers of the rabbi of Belz, but my
brother had discovered that great Jewish mystic Rabbi Nachman
Braclawer, and he became what was then called a Dead Chassid,
which is to say, the disciple of a rabbi who no longer lived. I
had heard of Rabbi Nachman Braclawer while we were still living in Warsaw. I had read his wondrous tales years before I had
glanced into his other works. My brother Moishe had obtained
all of Rabbi Nachman's works, and since I had so much time on

my hands, I began to read them. Rabbi Nachman was one of those blessed thinkers and poets whom—no matter how often you read or reread them—you always come away from with something new. As I've already mentioned, Rabbi Nachman didn't write these stories himself. He offered words of wisdom and told stories, and his pupil, Nathan the Nemirover, wrote them down. No one will ever know how much was lost in this process of transcription, but that which has remained is both great and deep. The famous Martin Buber discovered Rabbi Nachman Braclawer in his own fashion and translated his tales into German. Spirits such as Rabbi Nachman Braclawer cannot be forgotten. In each generation they are discovered anew.

Outside of his stories and maybe his prayers, Rabbi Nachman cannot be translated. His wisdom is closely bound up with passages in the Torah, in the Talmud. He ascribed to the Torah and the Gemara things that their writers never dreamed of. He often warped the meaning of their words, but what he had to say was always grand, fantastic, and full of psychological insight. I can firmly state that although Rabbi Nachman was a true saint, his spirit shouted a protest against the cruelties of life. To the best of his ability, he tried to justify the Almighty and to show that only good and mercy issued from Him, and that we ourselves were in great measure responsible for the sufferings that were visited upon us. At the same time he constantly wrestled with the dilemma of the good who suffered and the malefactor who enjoyed the best of everything. Like all great men, Rabbi Nachman was full of compassion. Each of his followers came to him with his own bag of troubles, and he had to comfort each one in turn while he himself was terribly ill and suffering unbearable pain. Rabbi Nachman died young, a victim of consumption.

I had lots of time in my father's town. I went through Spinoza's *Ethics* again and again. Out of Rabbi Nachman Braclawer's works screamed a kind of saintly hysteria, an exultation that often goes hand in hand with a deep melancholy, whereas Spinoza's *Ethics* was allegedly cold, pure logic. Spinoza didn't believe in feelings, in emotions, or, as he called them, affects. But it is obvious that beneath this cold logic lurks a person with a strong feeling for justice and truth. Just like Rabbi Nachman, Spinoza was a victim of consumption and died young. Both Rabbi Nachman and Spinoza suffered persecution. Other rabbis and their followers agitated against Rabbi Nachman for years. They even sought to excommunicate him. His worst enemy was a rabbi called the Spola Grandfather. In one of his better moments Rabbi Nachman said: "They've invented a person and they wrangle with him." The Jews of Holland actually excommunicated Spinoza. He was also in constant danger from the Inquisition, which was very powerful at that time. Rabbi Nachman found solace in a God who was full of benevolence and love, even though we humans could not comprehend His goodness. Spinoza found solace in a God who lacked will and feelings and possessed only great power and eternal laws. According to Spinoza, feelings, suffering, and justice were human concepts, passing modes.

I could find solace neither in Rabbi Nachman's God nor in Spinoza's. I had concluded that man had every right to protest against the violent acts of life. Man wasn't obliged to thank God for all the plagues and catastrophes that assailed him virtually from the cradle to the grave. The fact that God possessed immeasurably more knowledge and power than we did not give Him the right to torment us even if His motives were of the purest and wisest. The argument that the Lord presented to Job that He was wise and mighty while Job was a mere ignorant human was no answer to Job's anguish. Even the fact that toward the end of his life Job had more donkeys and camels and prettier daughters was little reward for his prior sufferings. I said to myself: I believe in God, I fear Him, yet I cannot love Him—not with my whole heart and soul as the Torah commands nor with the *amor Dei intellectualis* that Spinoza demands. Nor can I deny God as the materialists do. All I can do is to the best of my limits treat people and animals in a way I consider proper. I had, one might say, created my own basis for an ethic—not a social ethic nor a religious one, but an ethic of protest. This ethic of protest, I told myself, existed in all people, in all animals, and in everything that lived and suffered. Even the evildoers protested when things started going badly for them and other malefactors did to them what they had done to others. As his diaries indicate, Napoleon, who sent millions of people to their deaths, protested bitterly on the island of St. Helena because he wasn't fed decently or tendered the proper respect. The moral person protests not only when he is personally wronged but also when he witnesses or thinks about the suffering of others. If God wants or feels compelled to torture His creatures, that is His affair. The true protester expresses his protest by avoiding doing evil to the best of his ability.

With this view of life and in this mood I went to Warsaw to become the proofreader of the *Literary Pages.*

Already on the train I had opportunity to witness the depths of human degradation, of Jewish anguish. A bunch of hooligans had boarded the third-class wagon that was filled with Jewish passengers—paupers traveling with sacks, bundles, and crates. The hooligans promptly turned their attention to these Jews. First they abused them with every kind of foul name. Every Jew, they insisted, was a Bolshevik, a Trotskyite, a Soviet spy, a Christ-killer, an exploiter. By the light of the tiny lamp hanging there I could see these "exploiters"—ragged, broken people, most of whom were standing or squatting atop their belongings. The hooligans had earlier pushed the Jewish passengers off their seats and had sprawled themselves across the benches. One of them boasted that he had been an officer in the war. Several young Jewish men tried to defend the Jews and to point out that Jewish soldiers had fought at the front and suffered heavy casualties, but the hooligans hooted them down and heaped them with abuse. Soon, words turned into deeds. They grabbed the Jews' beards and yanked them. They tore the wig off an elderly Jewish woman. They began to stomp the Jews' belongings. The Jews could have easily beaten the hooligans to a pulp, but they knew how this would end. There were soldiers riding in the other cars, and it could have easily led to bloodshed.

After a while the hooligans demanded that the Jews sing "Come, My Beloved," the hymn celebrating the coming of the

Sabbath. It was a form of stigma and humiliation that many Polish hooligans had learned from the time when General Haller's soldiers had had their way with the Jews, had shaved off their beards often along with a piece of the cheek. I stood there frightened in a corner of the carriage near the toilet, gripping my bundle that consisted almost entirely of manuscripts and the few books that I possessed. Something inside me laughed at my own illusions. I knew full well that what I was seeing now was the essence of human history. Today the Poles tormented the Jews; yesterday the Russians and Germans had tormented the Poles. Every history book was a tale of murder, torture, and injustice; every newspaper was drenched in blood and shame. The two most pessimistic philosophers I had read, Schopenhauer and Von Hartmann, both condemned suicide, but at that moment I knew that there was only one true protest against the horror of life and that was to hurl back to God His gift. It was entirely possible that had I had a pistol or poison with me at that time, I would have killed myself.

After much talk and pleading, the Jews began to sing "Come, My Beloved." It was a half-song, half-lament. Until that night I had often fantasized about redeeming the human species, but it became obvious to me then that the human species didn't deserve redemption. To do so would actually be a crime. Man was a beast that killed, ravaged, and tortured not only other species but its own as well. The other's pain was his joy, the other's humiliation his glory. The Torah tells us that God regretted having created man. Adam's son murdered his brother. Ten generations later, God caused the Flood because the world had grown corrupt. There isn't a book that so candidly and clearly tells the truth about man and his nature than the Scriptures. Even the allegedly good people are evil. Yesterday's martyrs often become today's bullies. Man, as a species, deserves all the whippings he gets. It is not mere chance that most of the monuments man is erecting are to murderers—be it patriotic murderers or revolutionary murderers. In Russia there is even a monument to Bogdan Chmielnicki. The real innocent martyrs on this earth are the animals, particularly the herbivorous.

After a while the hooligans grew tired, leaned their heads against the backs of the seats, and began to snore. The little storekeepers in this car were obviously innocent, but I knew for a fact that Jewish youths in Russia also tortured and killed innocent people in the name of the Revolution, often their own Jewish brothers. The Jewish communists in Bilgorai predicted that when the Revolution came, they would hang my uncle Joseph and my uncle Itche for being clergymen, Todros the watchmaker for being a bourgeois, my friend Notte Schwerdscharf for being a Zionist, and me for daring to doubt Karl Marx. They also promised to root out the Bundists, the Poale Zionists, and, naturally, the pious Jews, the Orthodox. For these smalltown youths it had been enough to read a few brochures to turn them into potential butchers. Some of them even said that they would execute their own parents. A number of these youths perished years later in Stalin's slave camps.

Nine

THE NEW POLISH REPUBLIC WAS
barely four years old, but in that brief time it had already gone
through a war with the Bolsheviks, party struggles that led to an
assassination of a President, attacks upon Jews in a number of
towns, bitter disputes with the Ruthenians who had become
part of the new Poland, and a rising inflation. Lenin still lived,
but he was already paralyzed, and Comrade Stalin was beginning to make a name for himself. In Germany a former paper
hanger named Hitler had launched an abortive *Putsch*. In Italy
Mussolini forced castor oil down his opponents' throats. The
typhus epidemics and hungers had decimated who knows how
many people, but the streets of Warsaw still swarmed with pedestrians and you couldn't get an apartment. All cellars, all gar-
rets, were jammed with tenants and subtenants. From all the
provinces people tore to come to Warsaw, but there was no
work to be had there. Even as the Polish Socialist party trum-
peted that the proletariat of all nations must unite, its professional unions barred Jewish workers. Actually there wasn't even
enough work for the Gentile workers. The Bundists, the Jewish
socialists, sharply criticized their Christian comrades for their
nationalistic and capitalistic deviations from Karl Marx's teach-
ings. The Warsaw communists, Jews nearly all, heaped brimstone and fire upon all the parties and insisted that only in Soviet Russia did true social justice prevail. The Zionists argued
that there was no longer any hope for Jews in the lands of the

Diaspora. Only in Palestine would the Jew be able to live freely and develop. But England held the mandate and wouldn't allow any Jewish immigration. The Arabs had already begun to threaten the Jews with pogroms.

From my very first day in Warsaw I had no place to stay, since my brother lived with his wife and child in a tiny room at his in-laws and in the direst poverty. Melech Ravich, one of the editors of the *Literary Pages,* took me into his apartment for free, an apartment which consisted of several attic rooms on the fifth floor. Just as I was a skeptic, so was Ravich a believer. He believed in the redeeming power of literature, in socialism, in humanism, in the philosophy of Spinoza. At that time I wasn't yet a vegetarian. How could someone who had nothing to eat be a vegetarian? But Melech Ravich was already a vegetarian. He was tall, stout, eleven years older than I, and handsome. I actually could speak nothing but Yiddish, even though I could read several languages. But Melech Ravich spoke good Polish and German. He had spent years in Vienna working in a bank. His wife had a good voice and aspired to a singing career. Outside of my brother, Melech Ravich was my first contact with the literary world and with the so-called big world. We began our discussions immediately. Ravich believed with absolute faith that the world of justice could come today or tomorrow. All men would become brothers and sooner or later, vegetarians, too. There would be no Jews, no Gentiles, only a single united mankind whose goal would be equality and progress. Literature, Ravich felt, could help hasten this joyous epoch. I respected his talent and his worldly knowledge, yet at the same time I wondered at his naïveté. All the omens pointed to the fact that the human species had learned nothing from the war that had cost twenty million lives, if not more. In all the cities of Europe people did the latest dances—the Charleston, the fox trot, or whatever they were called—dances over graves. Sociologists propounded theories that were allegedly new, but they exuded the evils of generations. Poets babbled their empty verses. The *Literary Pages,* of which I was proofreader, was radical, socialistic, half communistic, full of bad articles, poor poems, and false criticism. My brother soon turned away from the editorship. The one who had top say there were Nachman Maisel, who had for years flitted between socialism and communism before becoming a full-fledged communist, and Peretz Markish, who sang odes to Stalin until Stalin had him liquidated. Peretz Markish and Melech Ravich were also the editors of an anthology called *The Gang*, which flattered the rabble and catered to its basest instincts. It cast aspersions upon Jewishness and Jewish history; it denigrated the classicists of world literature, and as an example of the new literature, it featured the hollow phrases of Mayakovsky. Although I was young and far from being a mature writer, I wasn't fooled by all these lies and flatteries. Behind this gabble lurked the urge to destroy, the will for a new mass violence. Malthus' God wasn't yet sated. The emissaries of Moscow called for a world pogrom upon all the bourgeois and middle classes as well as upon all socialists who dared deviate from Lenin by even a hair. Provincial youths—yesterday's yeshivah students who never in their lives had done a lick of work nor had been able to do so—spoke in the name of the workers and peasants and condemned to death all those who wouldn't stand on their side of the barricade. I looked on with alarm and astonishment at how a few pamphlets could transform into potential murderers the sons and daughters of a race that hadn't held a sword in hand for two thousand years. It had become the fashion among the girls to wear the leather jackets worn in Russia by the female members of the Cheka. The mothers and fathers of these murderers were scheduled to become their first victims. . . .

Spinoza had warned me against the emotions, affects that darkened reason and actually constituted a form of madness. In the books of morals I had scanned during the nine months I had spent in my parents' town, these same emotions were called evil thoughts, the persuasions of Satan. Rabbi Nachman Braclawer, a man in whom the emotions seethed and stewed, offered all kinds of advice on how to outwit and master them. Man was a pauper when it came to reason, but a millionaire when it came to emotions. I myself was a ferment of passions

and doubts. Dreams assailed me like locust. My nights were
filled with nightmares. I hadn't yet been with a woman, but in
my imagination I had already committed all the excesses that
could only be fancied. I wanted to write and to study, but 90
per cent of my spiritual energy was squandered on yearning for
the forbidden, that which would be harmful to me and to others. Like all tyrants of all times, I wanted to force my ideas upon
others. I flew to the farthest galaxies with a speed a hundred or
a thousand times faster than light. I discovered such potions that
granted me Divine wisdom. Like the legendary Joseph de la Ri-
nah, about whom I had read as a boy, I lured all the beauties
of the world to my bed through magic. The summer had passed
and it started to turn cold. I couldn't stay on forever in Melech
Ravich's congested apartment, and I started to look for a room
of my own. I suffered hunger, cold, sickness. The financial situation of the *Literary Pages* was such that they couldn't even pay
me the few groschen I had been promised. In my despair I
allowed many errors to go by and stood to lose even this miserable job. My brother's lot was no better than mine. In the
midst of all my grandiose daydreams, a voice within me cried:
"Put an end to it! You have nothing to wait for. With a rope or
a razor you can free yourself of all this misery. There is but one
redemption and that is death."

That winter in Warsaw there were two institutions that kept
me alive. One was the Writers' Club, where I was allowed to
come as a guest. It was warm there, one could read the Yiddish
and Hebrew newspapers from all over the world or play chess,
and the food at the buffet counter was reasonable. Occasionally,
the waitresses even extended credit. Every few evenings a lecture was held, and I met many young writers—beginners like
myself in the same dire straits as I. They all strove to have something published in the *Literary Pages,* and they may have assumed that I had some influence there. They heaped scorn on
the established writers whose poems, stories, and articles I corrected. I realized something then that I had actually already
known for a long time—that poor writers are often astute critics
of other writers. Their criticism was sharp and accurate. Some

even correctly pinpointed the errors of the great writers. But this didn't stop them from writing with a clumsiness that astounded me. The same held true in the way they appraised the character of others. Egotists spoke with contempt of egotists, fools derided the stupidity of fools, boors demonstrated refinement in pointing out other men's boorishness, exploitative traits, vanity. A mysterious chasm loomed between their estimation of others and of themselves. It seemed that somewhere within, each person was able to see the truth if only he was determined not to overlook it. Self-love was apparently the strongest hypnotic force, just as it is written in the Pentateuch: "For the bribe blindeth the wise, and perverteth the words of the righteous." The sage becomes blind and the saint will compromise with the evildoer when it suits his purpose, or when he *thinks* that it suits his purpose.

The other institution that sustained me was the libraries. For years I had suffered a hunger for books. In Warsaw I could get all the books I wanted. I went to the same Bresler's Library and spent hours browsing there. There was a table where you could sit and read. I read and scanned through books on philosophy, psychology, biology, astronomy, physics. I went to the municipal library on Koszykowa Street and read scientific journals.

I didn't understand everything I read, but I didn't have to. Science offered me scant comfort. The stars were composed of the same matter as earth—hydrogen, oxygen, iron, copper, sulfur. They radiated vast amounts of energy that were lost in space or maybe transformed into matter again. From time to time a star exploded and became a nova. Enormous clouds of dust floated in space in the process of becoming stars billions of years hence. As far as the astronomers could tell, there was no life on the other planets of our solar system. As for probing the possibilities of life beyond the solar system, there was no hope for that. Neither Einstein's theory nor any other theories held out any promise for the species of man. We already had radio sets in Poland, and when you put on the earphones you might hear jokes from vaudeville, a report on the political situation, or possibly even an anti-Semitic speech. Writers predicted tele-

vision and airplanes that would cross the Atlantic, but these pre-
dictions did nothing to elevate my spirit. . . .

Once as I browsed in Bresler's Library, I came across a complete translation or an abridgment of Edmund Gurney, Freder-
ick W. H. Myers, and Frank Podmore's *Phantasms of the Living*.
I took to this work with an eagerness that astounded even me.
If even a hundredth part of the cases described there was true,
all values would have to be reassessed. The writers were men
who hadn't the slightest reason to lie or falsify. Almost all the
incidents had been thoroughly investigated. I learned of the English Society for Psychical Research. Even here in Poland such
investigations were being conducted. Each day brought me
some fresh news. The French astronomer Camille Flammarion
had investigated hundreds of cases of mind reading, clairvoy-
ance, true dreams and had written works about this that had
been translated into Polish or German. Poland had a Professor
Ochorowicz and a world-famous medium, Kluski. The Italian
scholar Cesare Lombroso, who had been a materialist all his
life, in his old age had become a spiritualist and participated in
séances. I got the opportunity to read the works, or fragments
of works, of Sir Oliver Lodge, Sir William Crookes, Sir Arthur
Conan Doyle—the creator of Sherlock Holmes, which I had
read as a boy in Yiddish translation and which had so enthralled
me. In the science taught at the universities, man was ashes and
dust. He lived out his few years and became lost forever. But
the psychical researchers stated directly or indirectly that the
body contained a soul. The twenty million people who had perished in the war were somewhere about. I read cases of dogs,
cats, and parrots coming back to their owners after death and
giving signs of their love and devotion.

I was inclined to believe that which I read without further
guarantees, but I recalled what I had told myself only two weeks
earlier—that self-love and self-interest were a colossal hypnotic
force. I had read a translation of William James's *The Will to
Believe*. Every kind of fantasy nourished itself upon this will.
The fact that official science offered me no comfort was no
proof that it lied. As much as I yearned to believe the psychical

researchers, I realized full well that all their contentions were
based on what this or the other person had related to them. I
also got hold of books by writers who denied all the assertions
of spiritualists and psychical researchers. Even at that time they
had already unearthed many swindlers among the mediums. I
didn't dare let myself be bribed by my own desires! I had to
investigate personally and reassure myself that I wasn't paying
myself off to close my eyes to the truth.

I became so deeply engrossed in these matters that I forgot
all my troubles. I read books about psychical research well into
the night until my eyes closed. In the morning I rose with renewed curiosity. I had rented a room that was unheated and
had bedbugs to boot. My clothes had grown tattered, nor did I
get enough to eat, but I didn't let these petty annoyances get
me down. I no longer played chess at the Writers' Club nor
waged debates about literature. I took along books and read
them at the club. The writers made fun of me. To this day elderly writers from Warsaw remind me of how I sat at the club
reading books. The writers used to glance at the titles of these
books and shrug. In the Yiddishist circles they virtually didn't
know that such reading matter even existed.

The winter passed—I rightly didn't know how—and spring
came. My room was no longer so cold. At this time I met a man
and a woman who came to influence my life.

Ten

EVEN BEFORE COMING TO WARSAW I had heard of Hillel and Aaron Zeitlin. Two giants—father and son—had evolved in Yiddish literature in the radical, atheistic atmosphere of a Jewish culture that was ignorant and provincial besides. The father, Hillel Zeitlin, who was learned in philosophy and a cabalist, had come to the early conclusion that a modern Jewishness (whether in nationalistic or socialistic form) that lacked religion was a paradox and an absurdity. Hillel Zeitlin lived in a milieu that dictated worldly Jewishness. Bialik the Hebraist and Peretz the Yiddishist both maintained that the Jews could be a people even without religion. Bialik contended that this could be possible only in a Jewish land, whereas Peretz advocated that Jews should fight for national autonomy in the lands where they lived. But Hillel Zeitlin postulated powerful arguments that Jewishness without religion—a Jewishness based on a language or even upon a nation—lacked the force to keep the Jews united. What's more, such Jews wouldn't be Jews but Gentiles who happened to speak Yiddish or Hebrew. Even prior to Zeitlin, Ahad Ha-am had offered similar opinions, but Ahad Ha-am had himself been an agnostic, a doubter of the religious truths, one for whom religion had been merely a means of keeping the Jews together. It's needless to say that such a religiousness would hold no appeal for anyone. On the other hand, Hillel Zeitlin was a deeply religious man whose religious convictions mounted with the years. Hillel Zeitlin was a genuine mystic, a man who perceived the vanity of vanities that made up the world as well as its contradictions and illusions. He bore within him the religious fervor of the Jews of yore. It's a fact that the extreme Orthodox didn't look up to him. To them, he was a heretic. Hillel Zeitlin had studied philosophy and had published a book in Yiddish, *The Problems of Good and Evil*. I found more philosophy in this book than in all the other books of this kind put together. He didn't quibble over details but went straight to the essence of things. Even the ice-cold philosophers turned hot in the glow of his light. His son, Aaron Zeitlin, was a great religious poet, in my opinion one of the greatest in world literature. Like his father, he was a mystic and a cabalist; he actually formulated his own concept of the cabala. I had read his poems while still in Bilgorai and had grown enchanted by them. In his early years his style was a bit too muddled and "modernistic," but later on he realized that one can be both deep *and* clear. Although Aaron Zeitlin had received a modern education and knew languages and world literature, he remained essentially a yeshivah student, a bookish man and an intellectual in the truest sense of the word. We became acquainted at the Writers' Club. There was a windowless room there where the lights were always on, one wall always stayed warm. It was connected to the oven of a restaurant that was kept constantly heated. In winter I often sat by this wall and read. I apparently suffered from low blood pressure, since I often felt cold even in the summer. The Gemara has a word for it: "A donkey stays cold even in the month of Tammuz."

One day in spring as we both stood by this wall warming ourselves, we struck up an acquaintance which soon turned into a friendship that was to last a lifetime. Zeitlin was some six or seven years older than I and by then already a well-known, mature poet and essayist, and I was an unknown beginner. It's obvious why I should have been eager to know him, but I can't understand to this day why he should have taken an interest in me. We were very much different in character, and this difference intensified over the years. I saw his faults clearly, as he did mine. I liked women; from the very first I wrote about sex in such a way as to shock the Yiddish critics and often the readers, too; he was decidedly monogamous and a romantic. Books were only a part of my life, but to Zeitlin a book was virtually life itself. As restrained as he was in his own behavior, so wise was he to all the human passions. I waged a private war with the Almighty, but Zeitlin always defended Him. He might have easily been a recluse or a monk. We disagreed occasionally, but we remained friends.

The Yiddish writers who for years were nearly to a man infected with leftism castigated the Zeitlins, both the father and the son. When I grew older and they read my writings, it sent them into a rage. Neither Aaron Zeitlin nor I fitted into Yiddish literature with its sentimentality and clichés about social justice or Jewish nationalism. Both Zeitlin and I were deeply interested in psychic research. We both (actually all three—the elder Zeitlin, too) realized that the writers whom the Yiddish and Hebrew critics considered major figures and classicists were in fact often inept provincials. It didn't take us long to realize that what prevailed in Yiddish literature held true in all the world literatures, too. Every true talent was an oasis in a desert of tastelessness. When he is still young, he assumes that he can push back the sands and transform the desert into a paradise, but as he grows older, he realizes that he should thank God that the desert didn't swallow him up the way it already had many others. What's more, since God had created the desert, the desert had every reason to exist. Where did it say that green grass was more important or even prettier than brown sand? . . .

We often sat for hours then—and years later, too—conversing. We both believed in God, in demons, evil spirits, in all kinds of ghosts and phantoms. In those days Aaron Zeitlin was deeply concerned that the Yiddish critics cut him to pieces, and he often railed against them bitterly. I observed with shame that when a critic occasionally did praise him, Zeitlin changed his opinion of the critic virtually on the spot. This, as far as I know, was Zeitlin's only fault. I had many other, bigger faults, but I couldn't tolerate this particular weakness in Zeitlin, even though he made no mention of *my* shortcomings.

That spring I also met a woman who in her own fashion was a mystic, too, and who came to influence my life and my writing. By then I had already had some doings with women—but always in a hurry and in an atmosphere of fear. I might say that I snatched a taste of love here and there which inevitably left me unfulfilled, confused, and occasionally ashamed as well. Older people often said they envied my youth, but I knew that there was nothing to envy. A day didn't go by that I didn't contemplate suicide. My biggest torment was my lack of success in my writing. I would write something that seemed to me good, but I soon picked it apart and tore it to pieces. I searched about for a criterion by which to judge literature, but I couldn't find it. I frequently awoke filled with doubt and went to bed in the same state of mind. I often had the feeling that someone had bewitched me. I wanted to write one thing, but what emerged was something else altogether. I formulated a plan for a story, but the plan slipped through my fingers.

Spring had come and balmy breezes blew outside. I had to find another place, since the people from whom I subleased wanted the room for themselves. I spent weeks looking for a place, but the rents were too high all over and the rooms seemed cold, damp, insufficiently lighted. My feet hurt from climbing endless flights of stairs. I might have laid the whole burden on my brother's shoulders, but it's not in me to whine. Besides, my brother had problems of his own.

On that particular day I didn't go looking for a room. I got up late and went to the Writers' Club. On the way there I bought a bagel, and I ate it right in the street. The sun was shining, but I felt cold and shivered. I sat down by the warm wall and began to read some book on hypnotism, occultism, magnetism, or however the author described the hidden powers. It told of a man over whom his dead mother had been keeping watch for many years. Each time he faced danger he heard her voice warning him. She gave him advice, even brought him together with the woman he married. The man told this story himself and provided names and addresses of

witnesses who corroborated everything he said. If this story was
true, I told myself, it behooved me to lead a different kind of
life. I had to dedicate myself to disseminating these truths, to
convincing mankind that there was no such thing as death. That
being the case, it made no sense whatsoever to commit suicide. . . .

Someone came over and tapped me on the shoulder—it was
one of the young poets.

He said: "You still read this nonsense?"

"Do me a favor and read just this page!"

He took the book and glanced at it.

"Old wives' tales, hallucinations, crap! Opium to lull the
masses!"

We talked awhile, and he said: "Are you still looking for a
room?"

"Yes, very much so."

"I know of a woman who wants to give up a room. She's a
distant relative of mine, a granddaughter of rabbis. If the room
isn't rented yet, you'll fall into paradise. She's one of your kind,
a bit touched. She sits at a tilting table all night and tries to look
into the future. Her father was a rabbi who went off his head.
She tries to write, to paint. She's gone through three husbands
already."

"How old is she?"

"She could be your mother, but she likes young fellows. Wait,
it seems I've jotted down her address somewhere."

He took out a notebook which was filled with addresses and
with poems inscribed in tiny letters. He found the address and
gave it to me.

I asked whether the woman had a telephone, and he replied:
"She used to, but it's been shut off. She would have been
evicted, too, but the landlord is a Chassid of her uncle."

The woman lived somewhere on Gesia Street near the Jewish
cemetery. "I won't get involved with her," I promptly resolved.
I abhorred dissolute females. I longed for a woman who would
be pure and chaste and would learn about love only from me.

Still, I headed straight for Gesia Street. The closer I came to the house, the more funerals I saw—one hearse after another, some followed by weeping women, others without mourners. Here I was looking for a room, but these people had already finished living, hoping, and suffering and were being transported to eternity. The horses took step after deliberate step. They were draped in black cloths with holes cut out for eyes, and these holes were filled with pupil. I imagined that those horses knew what they were transporting and that they were making an accounting of their own souls. If the cabalists were right that everything is godliness, the horses were part of God, too. . . .

I entered a courtyard with peeling walls and a huge garbage bin in the center much like on Krochmalna Street where my family used to live. A huckster with a sack over his shoulders cried: "I buy clo'! I buy clo'! I buy clo'!" and cast his eyes upward toward the topmost windows. The sun stood fixed in the center of the sky and poured gold down upon the cobblestones, the gutters, the raggedy children, the huckster's reddish beard. A spring breeze blew carrying the smells of blossoms and the manure used to fertilize the fields. I even thought that I detected the stench of the corpses. I climbed three flights and came to rest before a door that thirty years ago might have been red but was now a faded brown. The door handle dangled listlessly; the number on the door was half off. I knocked, but no one answered. "I knew that I was wasting my time," I told myself. I was filled with envy for the dead, who were provided with perpetual quarters and with everything else a corpse didn't need. . . . I knocked again and again. I was too exhausted to go on looking for rooms. Suddenly I heard a woman's voice behind me. I looked backward and saw the lady of the house. She appeared to be in her late thirties or possibly forty. Although it was a weekday, she wore a silk cape and a black dress that wasn't fashionably short but hung almost to the ankles. Over her red hair—also unstylishly long and combed into a chignon—sat a black silk hat, the kind that was worn forty years prior. Her face was white, her eyes a blend of green and yellow. One glance sufficed to note that she had once been a beauty.

In one hand she carried a purse, in the other a basket of groceries. She had apparently just been shopping.

"May I know, young man, whom you're looking for?"

I took out the piece of paper on which the young poet had scribbled her name and address and said: "Mrs. Gina Halbstark."

"I am Gina Halbstark."

The woman (I'm not giving her right name here) stopped, and we confronted each other. She appeared both girlish and prematurely aged, like someone who has just gotten up from an illness. Her cheeks were sunken, her chin was narrow, her nose thin, her neck long, her red hair faded. Earrings were dangling from her lobes. For all her fancy dress there was a kind of genteel seediness about her. Her eyes reflected curiosity as well as a familial intimacy as if by some mysterious instinct she would have known who I was and why I had come. I moved aside, and she unlocked the door and led me into a corridor and from there into a big room. The apartment exuded the same genteel air of neglect as its owner. She asked me to sit down and opened the door to a tiny cubicle, an alcove with apparently no windows, since it was dark in there. She went off and tarried a long time, then came back wearing a house coat, her hair combed and her face powdered—all this before I even told her the reason for my visit. I asked her if she had a room to rent, and she said: "Yes, but only for a bat who doesn't need light."

"I'm a bat," I said.

"You don't look it," she countered, "but you can never tell what a person is."

We began to talk, and literally within minutes there evolved between us a kind of intimacy that astounded me. One moment we were strangers and the next we were chatting away as if we had been friends for years. She recounted her genealogy to me, and I learned all about her grandfathers and great-grandfathers, the books they had written, their honorable lives and piety. She told me who her first husband had been—I had heard of his father. She herself had grown "corrupt" early in life and had turned to worldly Yiddish and enlightened Hebrew books by such authors as Isaac Joel Linetzki, Mendele Mocher Sforim, Abraham Mapu, Shalom Aleichem, Peretz, as well as Yiddish translations of Tolstoi, Dostoevski, Lermontov, Knut Hamsun, Strindberg, and such Polish writers as Mickiewicz, Slowacki, Wyspianski, and Przybyszewski. Not only had I read exactly the same books but I was thoroughly familiar with their appearance, the number of pages they contained, and who their publishers and translators were.

Gina Halbstark had read my brother's works, and she even knew about me. I asked her how this could be, and she retorted: "Warsaw is a small town."

As if of its own volition the conversation drifted to the occult powers, and when Gina heard that I was interested in such things, her face grew animated and youthful. In that very dark room that she was trying to rent she kept a whole library of books and magazines devoted to these topics. She took me into the room and switched on the light. I saw a caseful of books on theosophy, spiritualism, hypnotism, and animal magnetism, in Polish, German, and French, and stacks of magazines.

I asked her how much the rent would be, and she said: "You'll pay whatever you can afford."

And she smiled with rabbinical amiability and said that she would prepare lunch for me.

"What have I done to deserve this?" I asked, and she replied: "Because I like you."

I followed her out, and in the corridor I embraced her and we began to kiss with the fervor of reunited lovers. She kissed and bit me. "I know you from an earlier life. . . ."

Eleven

GOD IN HEAVEN—WHAT A GREAT
stroke of luck had befallen me! I had been prepared to throw
back to God His gift in a rage, but I was obviously destined to
still live, suffer, to wrong myself and others. I sprawled now on
the very same bed where I had lain with Gina, and I slept, probably like Esau did after he sold his birthright for a mess of pot-
tage. In my dreams I was in Warsaw, in Bilgorai, and in the town
where my father was rabbi. Gina and Todros the watchmaker's
daughter merged into one and at the same time became my
mother and my sister Hindele. "What's happening to me?" I exclaimed in my sleep. "I'm losing the world to come!"

Someone within me—my father? my grandfather? a head of a
yeshivah?—conducted a sermon and admonished me: "You've
desecrated your soul. You are defiled! You've copulated with
Lilith, Naamah, Machlat, Shibta! . . ."

This dream was a continuation of the reality. In bed with me
Gina spoke like both a holy woman and a whore. She screamed
so loud I was afraid the neighbors would come running. She
sang, wept, quoted passages from the Song of Songs, called herself Rahab the harlot. It was she who had saved the spies that
Joshua son of Nun had sent out to spy on Jericho, and they had
lain in her arms. I, Itchele, was one of them. In other reincarnations I was Abraham and she Hagar, I Reuben and she Bilhah,
I Boaz and she Ruth, I David and she Bath-sheba. . . . She whispered secrets and licked my ear. She promptly began to instruct

me in new positions, variations, and in her own mad caprices. I
questioned her about her former husbands and lovers, and she
bellowed: "I long for them all! I'd like to have them all at the
same time so that they would tear me to pieces and leave nothing of me to bury! They should spit upon me and drown me in
their saliva. . . ."

I had read Forel and maybe Krafft-Ebing, too, and I already
knew about sadism, masochism, fetishism, and a number of
other such *isms,* but all that which was paper and ink there
turned here into throbbing life, savage lust, a singing and la-
menting madness. She roused both desire and revulsion within
me. We had spent a spring day in a wakeful nightmare and now
the dream added its own absurdities.

I opened my eyes, and it was dark not only here but in the
other room, too. Instead of making lunch for me, Gina prepared dinner. The smells of meat, potatoes, onion, garlic, carried from the kitchen. She sang there and poured water into
sizzling stew. I had awakened thirsty, hungry, tired, yet eager
for new larks and adventures. "Am I happy?" I asked myself, and
someone within me replied: "No." "Why not?" I countered, but
the other remained silent. I cocked my ears and listened to myself. My ideal had always been a decent Jewish daughter, not
some whore who had wallowed in every slime. I partly loved
this Gina, partly hated her. The preacher from my dream seized
upon this and argued: "It's because of such abominations that
the whole human race suffers. The Canaanites and Amalekites
committed such outrages. It was her kind that caused the damnation of cities. Wars and violence stem from adultery. It was
her kind that gave themselves over to the enemies of Israel, and
it was their children who made pogroms upon the Jews. . . ."

My head fell back against the pillow, and I lay there in mute
bewilderment. I had promised my father that I would conduct
myself as a Jew in Warsaw. On the way here I had even related
my philosophy of protest to Jewishness. The Jew personified the
protest against the injustices of nature and even those of the
Creator. Nature wanted death, but the Jew opted for life; nature
wanted licentiousness, but the Jew asked for restraint; nature

wanted war, but the Jew, particularly the Diaspora Jew (the highly developed Jew), sought peace. The Ten Commandments were in themselves a protest against the laws of nature. The Jew had taken upon himself the mission of vanquishing nature and of harnessing it in such a way that it served the Ten Commandments. Because the Jew went against nature, it despised him and took revenge upon him. But the victory lay on the side of the Jew. Even if he had to wage war against God, the Jew would not desist. According to the Talmud, even a voice from heaven should be ignored if it is not on the side of justice. When the Jew knew that something was right, he dared oppose the Almighty Himself. . . .

These had been my thoughts on the train when the hooligans ordered the Jews to sing "Come, My Beloved." At that time the faces of the Jews had shown a resoluteness that was not of this world. Well, but this kind of strength lay only within the Jew who observed the Torah, not in the modern Jew who served nature like the Gentile, was subservient to it, and placed all his hopes upon it. . . .

I heard footsteps. Gina stood in the doorway.

"Are you asleep?"

"No."

"You dozed off like an infant at my breast. Are you hungry?"

"No. Yes."

"Come eat. Come, I need you. You are my last hope. I was ready to die already, but suddenly you came and—"

She switched on the light, but I asked her to put it out again. I was ashamed before her. She had put on a costly robe, but I had nothing besides the clothes I had come in. In the course of the single day my cheeks had sprouted a sharp stubble. Gina went back to the kitchen while I fumbled with my garments and shoes in the dark.

Later when we were eating, Gina confided that she had anticipated my arrival and had actually been waiting for me. She practiced automatic writing, and one night her hand had written my name perhaps a hundred times. She often posed questions to a table with wooden pegs and to a Ouija board, and they both concurred that her great and last lover would be as red-haired as she was. She told me that she knew some other things about me which she couldn't reveal to me as yet. She tipped her head to the side and studied me sidelong with female expertise and not without mockery, as if she would have played a trick on me which would become apparent to me later. I felt ashamed of myself in view of her sexual experience, and I thought of the many men she had had before me.

She seemed to guess my thoughts because she said: "You've wiped them all away. From now on, you're my whole life."

We drank tea, and stories poured from Gina's lips. She had caught typhus during the war and been taken to a hospital where the doctors tried to poison her. She wouldn't be alive now but for her dead grandmother who came to her in a dream and warned her not to take the medicine. This same grandmother had saved her from death several other times. Once when she lay all alone in the house ill with influenza and without any food (it was after her second divorce), this same grandmother brought her a glass of warm milk.

Gina stood up and solemnly vowed that she was speaking the truth. The glass on her night table had been empty. Suddenly, it had filled with milk, and she had heard her grandmother's voice: "Drink!" As soon as she drank the milk, her fever subsided and she recovered.

"Believe me or don't—what does it matter to me what you believe? You won't give me your millions in any case, but I swear on my dead mother and father, may they rest in peace, that I'm not lying to you. If I'm lying, may I not live to—"

"I believe you, I believe you, but it could have been a hallucination that came from the fever."

"I knew that's what you would say. It was no hallucination. My temperature was only 98.6°. Even when it rises above 104°, I remain fully conscious. I once had an operation for my appendix, and the doctor couldn't put me to sleep with the chloroform no matter how he tried. He gave me the biggest possible dose, and still I remained conscious. I felt the pains when they cut into me, and I heard every word he said to the nurses. Incidentally, in the middle of the operation I suddenly began to fly in the air. I glanced down and saw my body, the surgeon, the nurses, and all the rest. This was the first time I went into the astral plane and you can imagine my terror when I saw my own body lying there. I was sure that I was dead. All of a sudden something trembled within me, and I re-entered my body and felt the pains anew. The doctor told me later that my heart had stopped for a while and he had thought I was done for. Why am I telling you all this? Yes, to prove that I don't lose consciousness so easily. I sleep and at the same time I hear every rustle and think wakeful thoughts. I didn't have even a lick of milk in the house at that time. I had nothing at all. Suddenly a glass of milk stood there before me. When I drank it, it tasted as if it had come fresh from the udder. Each sip brought a surge of strength with it. I also heard my grandmother's voice as clearly as I hear you now. What do you say to this, eh?"

"If the dead live and can milk a cow in a hurry and bring a glass of milk through a closed door, then our whole science isn't worth a fig. In that case—"

"Yes, they do live and they can do many things. Not all the souls remain below—most of them go off to other worlds. But my grandmother was terribly close to me, and she didn't want to be parted from me. She knew my accursed nature and crazy ways and how easy it was for me to risk my life. If not for her I wouldn't be here now. Don't laugh, but my grandmother even told me about you. One time she spent half the night with me. I said: 'Grandma, I don't want to live anymore. I've had enough of the disappointments, of men's falsehood and all the rest. So long as there is another world,' I said, 'a prettier world without evil and boorishness and all the unhappiness and complications. I'd rather be there. I want to be with you, Grandma,' I said. I'm not a crier by nature, but I began to weep furiously, and she said: 'Genendele'—that's what she called me—'it's not our world but God's, and everyone who is sent there has some mission and a time in which to perform it. Your time to leave hasn't come yet. Some good still awaits you.' 'What is it?' I asked. 'Another man?' And she said, 'He is still a child, but he is also a man and he will be your final comfort.' She said something else, but I don't want to tell you what. First you spoke like a believer, and all of a sudden you become a skeptic and look at me as if I were crazy."

"I believe in God, but there are things that are awfully hard to accept."

"Eh? If you will stay with me, you'll see things with your own eyes so that you'll be spared having to believe in them. I was resolved not to tell you what my grandmother said about us—it seems she even warned me against talking to you about her, but she is used to it now that I disobey her. I wish I *had* listened to her—I would have spared myself lots of heartache."

"What did she say about us?"

"She said that we would collaborate on a book."

"What kind of book?"

"I don't know. She didn't give me any details. I want you to know that she has never yet told me anything that hasn't come true. Sometimes immediately, other times years later. But the last time she spoke to me I did begin to feel something like doubt. I had taken a holy vow to have nothing further to do with any other man and certainly not with one younger than I. I had also given up my writing. Whatever I wrote the editors sent back. They often sent back things they hadn't even bothered to read. This, as the saying goes, is a chapter in itself. I have countless enemies. They hate me, first of all because God cursed me with talent, and secondly because they know that I'm wise to all their filthy tricks and intrigues and that I can't be so easily fooled. It's enough for me to glance at a person to know all his secrets. Believe me this is no idle boast. Nor is it a favorable trait either. Actually, it's a tragedy. God capped the brain with a skull so that others shouldn't see what goes on inside it. How can you live knowing what someone else is thinking? Thirdly, they hate me because I come from the finest stock while they are all boors from the very dregs. Why am I telling you all this, eh? Yes, they hate me. They would drown me in a spoonful of warm water, as the saying goes. Therefore, since there was no longer any hope of love or literature for me, what sense did it make for me to go on living? But since my grand-mother said that we must write a book together, we will write a book whether you want to or not."

"How do you go about writing a book together?"

"Eh? I don't know myself. You'll write a page and I'll write a page and between pages we'll kiss. How would you like that?"

"Very much so!"

"Well, you're still completely a child. You're like a young horse with a growing passion who plays up to his own mother. But you mustn't have any bad memories of me."

"What makes you say that?"

"Oh, I won't be around much longer. Eat all your dessert, don't leave anything over."

Twelve

I SOON NOTED THAT GINA WAS OB-
sessed with death. We lay in bed, and she spoke of buying a
plot together at the Gesia Street cemetery. I had to promise her
that when my time came I'd be buried beside her. She demanded that right after her funeral I should sleep with another
woman and think of her, Gina, at the same time. She made me
swear solemnly that I would say Kaddish over her and light a
memorial candle. I knew full well that these words roused her
sexually. Her flesh turned hot, and she grew fiercely exultant.
She cuddled up to me, kissed me, fondled me, and said: "I want
to lie in the ground and rot while you, little colt, enjoy yourself!
That is my will, my goal. I'll rest easier knowing that you're
lying in the arms of women, but one thing I beg of you: Don't
forget me. What my grandmother does for me I will do for
you—guide and protect you. I'll provide you females with blazing souls and burning bodies. I'll cast them into your net like
wiggling fish for you to do with them as your heart desires, but
with one proviso—that you don't get married. Why get married?
Why tie yourself down? A bee must flit from flower to flower
gathering nectar from each. Why should a bee be bound up
with one flower? To me you can be bound because I won't be
around for long. I don't want you to marry me either. Our souls
will remain united forever anyhow. Your pleasure will be my
pleasure. . . ."

We barely eked out an existence. I couldn't even afford a

laundress, and Gina washed my underwear. She herself wore
the old-fashioned clothes because she couldn't afford new
dresses. Her apartment hadn't been painted in years and the
furniture was broken, but what did this matter to us? At that
time there were stores in Warsaw where you could get fantastic bargains. On Old and New Wolowa you could buy a pair of
shoes or even a coat (secondhand) for groschens. There were
markets where one could get black army bread for half price.
Peasant women brought cheese, mushrooms, groats, and onions from the country that one could buy for next to nothing.
Gina and I both enjoyed walking. We could walk for miles
without getting tired. Riding the trolley was for us a luxury. We
rode "Trolley Number 11," which is to say, we walked. We
talked about whatever popped into our minds. Gina always
headed for the cemetery—either the Jewish one near us or the
Catholic one in Powazek; but best of all she liked the Russian
Orthodox cemetery far down Leszno Street beyond Karcelak
Place. Few Russians remained in Warsaw after Poland gained
her independence apart from the Russian refugees, the impov-
erished "used-to-bes" who were nearly all drunks and slept at
the "Circus," an institution for the Gentile homeless. Former
colonels, generals, and country squires wallowed in the gutters. Gentiles weren't used to living in exile. When a Gentile
lost his homeland, he became broken spiritually and physically.

But the old Russian cemetery was fenced in, had expensive
tombstones and old and thickly branched trees, and represented a symbol of the former Russian might. For some reason
the Russians affixed photographs of the deceased to their
tombstones. No one came here on the long summer days besides the birds. Gina didn't tire of looking at the tombstones,
reading the dates, studying the yellowed photographs. People
had died young in the nineteenth century, and many young
men and women struck down in their prime were buried
here. Nearly all the women wore blouses with high collars,
lace, and tall pompadours. A glow of health emanated from
their faces and the lust for life characteristic of a ruling race.

But they had been cut down in their forties, their thirties, some even in their twenties. Gina stopped before every tombstone and probed, reflected, reckoned. Flecks of sun shone down on her face from between the tree branches. After a while I, too, began to take an interest in the deceased. What had they died from? Had an ongoing epidemic reigned in Warsaw in those days? Had they committed suicide? Or had they died out of longing for Russia? The photographs had faded over the years, but the eyes had retained their animation. They smiled at some secret known only to themselves. It was hard to believe that these young ladies—each of whom knew sections of Pushkin or Lermontov by heart and whose faces expressed such an eagerness for life—were now nothing more than crumbled skeletons, dust. I became temporarily infatuated with these women and contemplated the pleasures they might have provided a man.

Gina pointed to a photograph and said: "Isn't she lovely? Pretty as a picture! Twenty-seven years is all she lived! A lieutenant's wife. What did she die of, eh? He probably betrayed her with every soldier's whore until she wasted away from jealousy. Or maybe he drank the nights away, and her blood became consumed by passion. Look at her, peaches and cream. You can see her firm breasts right through the blouse. You wouldn't poison yourself on her, God forbid, if you lived in those times. Where is she now, eh? Can there be such a thing as a Russian paradise? What would Russians do in paradise?"

"There's no such thing as paradise."

"So you're a heretic again, eh? Just yesterday you said that there is no death. Life is everywhere, even in a stone in the street."

"Yes, true, but she is not in paradise."

"Where, then, in Gehenna?"

"In you, in me, a part of all the stars and planets."

"Words, my dear, mere words. Life is memory. If she doesn't remember that she was Andrej Popov's wife and that Grisha Ivanov inscribed love verses in her album and that she danced at a party with Boris Nikolaevich Saratov, then she is dead. The fact that flowers grow on her mound of earth doesn't make her immortal."

"What would be so good if her soul remembered all the wrongs the lieutenant did her?"

"Don't twist my words! If my grandmother lives, all the grandmothers, grandfathers, and great-grandfathers going back to Adam and even before live, too. They remember everything, but they're so happy up in heaven they forgive all injustices. You yourself said that the souls in the other world love each other and bustle about. Those are your very words."

"That's what the cabala says."

"It's true. You'll see it all with your own eyes. I'll come to you from the other world and give myself to you. I'll be with others, too, with all the men I've ever loved. Your religion of protest begins to displease me. I can accept the craziest notions, but not that God is a malefactor. This doesn't make sense. He sends us down here to suffer a bit, then He rewards us many millions of times over. There are such pleasures awaiting us there that even fantasy cannot describe them. That time when I had the operation and later when I lay sick with the typhus I paid a visit up there above, and I heard such singing that no opera or symphony could compare to it. Angels sang and each note answered all the questions and filled me with a joy no words can convey. I yearned to stay there, but three patriarchs considered my case and judged that I go back to earth. Their faces emitted a kind of glow that simply doesn't exist here. I began to cry before them, and they consoled and kissed me."

"In your sleep, eh?"

"Awake, awake! There is no such thing as sleep. You don't sleep—you make believe you're sleeping. You don't die, but make believe you're dying. It's all pretense. Just as I suffer and curse my lot, so do I know that it's all nothing on top of nothing. What is suffering? Who is suffering? It's all a kind of game."

"God has no right to make up such games."

"Well, all right, when you stand before Him you'll tell Him

so. Come, little colt, I'm hungry. I have some dried noodles and an onion at home, and there should be a bit of cocoa butter left. I'll brown the onion and we'll eat."

"You mean we'll pretend to eat just like the angels at Abraham's."

"Yes, we'll pretend and later we'll pretend we're tired and go to bed and pretend we're terribly in love. What do you say to this philosophy?"

"There is such a philosophy already. Its founder is a man named Vaihinger."

"Who is this Vaihinger? Everything exists already. Give me your mouth. . . ."

Thirteen

THE GOVERNMENT APPARENTLY KEPT an eye on me, for suddenly I received a notice to report for conscription. I knew precisely what this meant—spending two or three years among peasants, all kinds of toughs and wild characters, with no time for reading or writing, and each day putting up with countless insults—all that so a few years later I could give my life for the fatherland. But did a Jew have a fatherland? Some ten or eleven years earlier, my brother Joshua had received a similar demand to sacrifice his life for the Russian fatherland. In the interim Poland had become a part of Germany, and he was nearly drafted to serve the German fatherland. I must be frank here and say that even if Poland were a Jewish nation, I wouldn't have had the slightest urge to be a soldier. For me, a barrack represented a much harsher punishment than prison. Running, jumping, marching, and shooting would be for me an unbearable torture and even worse would be to have to be among people. Just as others constantly required company, so did I require privacy. My whole world concept demanded isolation, the right and the privilege to stay away from others, and time to pursue my probings and nurture my creative appetites. From reading the leftist newspapers and from listening to the communists and their fellow travelers at the Writers' Club I knew that leftism wanted to completely abolish privacy and to institute a perpetual public domain. They constantly spoke of the masses, but my nature demanded the freedom to be alone as long and as often as I wished. Going to cheder day after day was to me a burden, nor could I stand the yeshivahs. I doubt that I could have lasted long at a university. At times I envied the peasant with his little plot of ground. I could have been a tailor or shoemaker working in his own shop, but I couldn't for the life of me work in a factory. It's significant to add that despite my strong urge for love and sex, I had remained pathologically bashful.

I resolved that if forced to serve, I would commit suicide first. In the interim I did what many other Jewish recruits had done before me during the Russian occupation—starved myself in order to lose weight and grow weak. I constantly wrangled with Gina. She brought me food even as I was trying to fast. I assumed that the fasting would weaken me sexually, but my libido (a new word that the Freudians had introduced into the daily language) grew stronger instead of weaker. I discovered at that time that the sexual urge is thoroughly bound up with spiritual strength rather than with physical. Love and sex were functions of the soul. The nights were filled with wild fantasies and with an inspiration that negated my pessimistic view of the world. Gina told me that sexual intercourse and particularly the climax evoked visions within her, and I never tired of questioning her about these visions.

She responded: "I see faces, strange countenances."

As loquacious as she was regarding all other matters, she became taciturn when it came to these matters. But why? Did these visions frighten her? Did she lack the words to describe them? As for me, the fasts left me in such a state that the division between sleep and wakefulness just about disappeared. The moment I closed my eyes I promptly began to dream. I saw giants with heads reaching to the clouds. They wore clothes not of our time and perhaps not even of this world. They marched along in what seemed a kind of cosmic funeral procession and grunted a dirge rife with melancholy. Sometimes I saw swarms of dwarfs who sang, danced, and rejoiced in an unearthly rapture. These visions were so real, so magnificent, so richly detailed. True, they quickly faded from memory, but they left me perplexed and with the feeling that sleep erases all limitations of time, space, and causality. At times I dreamed of slaughters, massacres, pogroms, and awoke trembling, yet charged with renewed lust. Gina awoke at precisely the same split second, and we fell upon one another with a hunger that astounded us. What a remarkable mechanism was the brain! How extravagant it became the moment one closed his eyes! I often resolved to write down my dreams, yet at the same time I knew that this would be impossible. The moment I opened my eyes they burst like soap bubbles, immediately dissolved, and vanished. Nor did the words exist in my vocabulary to paint a true picture of a dream.

Most philosophers spoke with contempt of human emotion; others ignored it altogether. Our holy books maintained that evil thoughts emanated from the evil spirit. The *Literary Pages* printed constant articles about Freud, who had begun to take dreams and emotions seriously, but his approach was rationalistic. He tried to analyze something that couldn't be grasped, that lacked substance. He tried to make generalizations in an area thoroughly individualistic, one of unique occurrence, and thoroughly ambiguous. That which the cabalists attributed to God applied to a dream as well—no words could be found to describe it. The best you could do was to keep silent about it.

Spring turned into summer and the heat waves commenced in Warsaw. The days stretched endlessly, the twilight lingered seemingly forever, and the sky stayed light until 10 P.M. I ate a spare supper. Gina played awhile with her table and tried to write automatically. I stood at the open window staring down at Gesia Street. The funerals kept on all day. Not far from here rested the old corpses and the new. Balmy breezes wafted up to my nostrils, and I kept thinking that they bore the stench of rot and decay, along with the secrets of birth and death. The street was dark and stars twinkled over the tin rooftops. At times it seemed to me that I could make out the white sash called the Milky Way. Everything was near—death, the universe, the enigma of dreams, the illusion of love and sex. Dogs barked, cats meowed. Gina's apartment swarmed with moths, gnats, and beetles. Insects flew in through the open windows to make a final flutter before dying. Gina and I both sought to unite with the forces that guided the earth and to come to some kind of accounting and conclusions regarding the world, but these forces would have none of it. We were condemned to remain sunk forever in chaos.

Although Gina didn't conduct herself according to the laws of the Shulchan Aruch, she still mumbled her nightly prayers. I mentally begged God to save me from the barracks and at the same time prayed for those forced to stay there. So many dangers and problems lurked for everyone! A moment didn't go by without some kind of trouble. People themselves caused one another grief. All the jails were jammed with criminals. At times I heard gunfire in the night, screams and blows, cries for help. The communists in Warsaw sought every means of fomenting a revolution and turning Poland over to the Bolsheviks. Hitler and his Nazis had already formulated plans to take back Upper Silesia and the "corridor" that the Versailles Treaty had stripped from Germany. Polish anti-Semites agitated against the Jews. The Jewish political parties wrangled among themselves. The Lithuanians yearned to seize Vilno. The Ruthenians and White Russians waged a struggle against Polish rule. Hobbes was right—everyone waged war against everyone else. Every peace was rife with new wars. The leaders themselves were at each other's throats. I couldn't live in this world—merely smuggle myself through life slithering like worms and mice, actually like all the creatures. Each day I got through was—and has remained to this day—a miracle. Jewish history in particular was one mighty travail of smuggling and sneaking through nations and laws that condemned us to death. Before going to sleep I took a last look at the starry sky. Was it this way up there, too? Was there an island of peace somewhere in the universe? . . .

I went to bed, but Gina went on bustling a good deal longer. She washed the dishes, darned and washed her and my underwear. I lay there in the dark with my ears cocked. Maybe God would speak to me. Maybe my great-great-grandfather in the cemetery would tell me something. Maybe I would come up with something like a second Newtonian formula which would unravel the mystery of life. This revelation was likely to be much simpler than one might imagine. It might consist of one sentence. I even had a notion in what direction the formula would go—there was no death. The "I" was a thoroughgoing illusion. Sufferings were pleasures. Today, yesterday, and tomorrow were one and the same. I, Rothschild, the mouse in its hole, the bedbug on the wall, and the corpse in the grave were identical in every sense, as were dream and reality, male and female, thoughts and stones, feelings and atoms, love and hate. Well, but it wasn't enough to say this—it had to be proven. Leibnitz couldn't do it. Spinoza's geometric method wasn't convincing. This formula had to be written not in words and numbers but in some other medium that I would first have to invent. It was altogether possible that it had already been invented on some distant planet. . . .

I began to doze off, and the formula came to me in a dream: that which we called death was life, and that which we called life was death. The stone in the street lived and I was a corpse. The stone didn't hope nor suffer; for it, time, space, and causality didn't exist. It didn't have to eat; it needed no apartment; it was part of the mighty, extensive life that was the universe. That which we called life was a scab, an itching, a poisonous toadstool that grew on old planets. The earth suffered from an eczema of its skin. From time to time it scratched itself causing an earthquake or a flood, but there was no danger of this eczema penetrating deeper or of infecting other planets. The prognosis was a favorable one. All that was required was that for a few minutes the earth should grow a few hundred degrees hotter or colder on its outer surface. The earth could easily manage this, but the eczema was so light and the earth so involved with its activities that she neglected to do this since the eczema might one day vanish of its own. The symptoms of this eczema were quite familiar to the cosmic medicine—a little dust on the surface became ill and transformed into conscious-

ness, which in God's dictionary was a synonym for death, protest, goals, suffering, doubting, asking countless questions and
growing entangled in endless contradictions. . . .

I had fallen asleep and Gina woke me. She had washed up in
the kitchen and her flesh felt damp and cool. We embraced and
lay silent for a long time, then Gina said: "Little colt, I made a
decision today that may change my whole life and maybe yours,
too."

"What kind of decision?" I asked, and she said: "I want to
have a child with you. . . ."

A Young Man in Search of Love

One

1

I HAD MORE OR LESS SETTLED IN Warsaw, the city of my dreams and hopes. I was a proofreader for a literary magazine, which gave me an opportunity to be in contact with writers and intellectuals. My mistress, Gina, was perhaps twice as old as I but a woman whom I could love and from whom I could learn. In a moment of exaltation I had promised her that we would have a child together, but the forces that rule the world didn't want Gina to be the mother of my child. We lived together, but she didn't conceive. I quickly realized that she was even older than I thought. Among her things I found photographs showing her dressed in fashions prevailing before I was even born. She still had her periods, but not regularly. Yes, this woman might easily have been my mother, but not the mother of my child.

My literary and my other troubles were such that I no longer fretted about my romantic complications. I had presented myself for conscription and had been given a "B" classification which under the Russians had been called a green ticket. This meant that I had to present myself again a year hence. During the few hours I spent with the conscripts I got a taste of the army. Some soldiers ordered us around as if we were already part of it. The Christians already cursed the Jewish conscripts and called them all kinds of names. The Jewish youths tried to curry favor with the Gentiles, paid them compliments, offered them cigarettes and chocolate, and even pressed coins upon them. Stripping naked in front of a crowd was to me an ordeal. My skin was unusually white, and my hair as red as fire. Someone gave me a slap in the rear, another flicked my nose, a third called me "slob, jerk."

The soldier who was temporarily my superior measured me head to toe and from toe to head, made comical gestures, and remarked: "Woe to the Polish nation if this has to be her defender."

This evoked a burst of wild laughter. The notion that I might be spending two years among this crew drove me into despair. I looked on with amazement as the other youths somehow made peace with their situation and did their best to adjust. They quickly assumed a military tone; they even made fun of me on their own initiative. A tall youth with a heroic physique came up to me and said: "Are you a mama's boy? The army will make a man of you. Have a cigarette."

I grew so befuddled that I stuck the wrong end of the cigarette in my mouth, which brought a new howl of laughter and applause. The boys had already tagged me with a nickname: *Ofermo,* which was applied to an inept soldier. I sidled over into a corner and mentally vented all my complaints, not against the people who insulted me but against God. What resentments could one hold against these youths? They had been raised in the streets, and nature had endowed them with the ability to adapt to difficult situations instead of breaking. But the creator of the universe should have had more decency than to subject young men of my nature to such degradations. I had made a firm resolution that if I were taken, I would commit suicide despite the fact that this would forever darken my mother's years, she whose bashfulness, pride, and rebelliousness against the laws of life I had inherited. I also toyed with the notion of killing her first before putting an end to myself.

The two military doctors who examined me didn't concur. One was of the frank opinion that I had intentionally starved myself which had brought about my weakened condition. The other waved his hand as if to say: "Let him wander around a bit longer." After I had dressed and the other conscripts learned that I had been deferred for a year, they seemed astounded. In their estimation I should have been classified "D," which meant rejection even during a time of war. One of the wise guys who had already begun to fraternize with the soldiers and speak their jargon had been freed with the classification I should have gotten.

When I came out into the street and glanced into a mirror in the front window of a furniture store, I was frightened at my own appearance. I looked emaciated as if from consumption, pale, and like someone who has just narrowly escaped death. I felt light, hollow, and it seemed to me that my feet were racing as if of their own accord. Now that I was temporarily freed from the fear of military service, I began to agonize about my literary efforts. I had already been writing for several years but sooner or later I had thrown my manuscripts into the wastebasket. The themes employed by Yiddish writers and the writing itself struck me as sentimental, primitive, petty. Too often it had to do with a girl whose parents wanted an arranged marriage while she really loved someone else. Quite often the girl came from a wealthy family and the youth was the son of a tailor or shoemaker. Would it be possible to describe in Yiddish the kind of relationship I had with Gina? Although Yiddish literature flirted with socialism and more recently with communism, it had remained provincial and backward. Besides, Yiddish—the language itself—had become repugnant both to Gentiles and to a great number of modern Jews. Even such Yiddish writers as Mendele Mocher Sforim, Shalom Aleichem, and Peretz called Yiddish a jargon. The Zionists considered Yiddish the language of the Diaspora of which the Jews had to divest themselves along with the Exile. I knew enough Hebrew to attempt writing in that language but at that time few people spoke Hebrew. It lacked words used in day-to-day conversation. Ben Yehuda was just on the verge of creating the new Hebrew. Writing in Hebrew meant constantly consulting dictionaries and trying to recall sentences from the Scriptures, the Mishnah, and the Gemara. Both the Yiddish literature and the Hebrew avoided the great adventures inherent in Jewish history—the false Messiahs, the expulsions, the forcible conversions, the Emancipation, and the assimilations that had created a condition in which Jews became ministers in England, Italy, and America; professors in large universities; millionaires; party leaders; editors of world-famous newspapers. Yiddish literature ignored the Jewish underworld, the thousands and tens of thousands of thieves, pimps, prostitutes, and white slavers in Buenos Aires, Rio de Janeiro, and even in Warsaw. Yiddish literature reminded me of my father's courtroom where almost everything was forbidden. True, Sholem Asch had in a sense created a minor revolution and had taken up themes that till then had been considered taboo, but he was and remained a rustic, at least that's how I saw him then and still do to this day. His stories personified the pathos of the provincial who has been shown the big world for the first time and who describes it when he goes back to the town where he came from.

The problem was that in order to write with skill about people of the world, one needed to know the world, and I only knew a small segment of Jewish Warsaw, Bilgorai, and two or three other small towns. I only knew Jews that spoke Yiddish. Even then I knew a writer can only write about people and things he knows well.

I had promised to let Gina and my brother Joshua know what had happened to me but neither he nor she had a telephone at that time. I went to the Writers' Club and everything there was just as usual. Several journalists played chess. Others read newspapers that came there from all over Poland and from abroad. I knew everyone here and each of his idiosyncrasies. One of them, an old writer named Saks who came from Lodz and who had lived for a time in Central Asia, waged a private feud against the Allies for having wronged Germany. He hurled fire and brimstone upon the Versailles Treaty for taking Upper Silesia away from the Germans and creating the corridor between East and West Germany. In prophetic terms he predicted that Germany would one day rearm and take everything back. By this time Hitler had already conducted his famous *Putsch* and perhaps also published his *Mein Kampf,* but this Lodz Jew knew nothing of this, or maybe he ignored it. I would occasionally ask him:

"What did Germany ever do for you that you take up for her so? After all, we're Polish citizens, not German."

He would glance at me with bewilderment and reply:

"You can't take a great nation, a pillar of civilization, and dismember it."

If I'm not mistaken, this same journalist later died in a Nazi concentration camp.

I recalled Spinoza's words to the effect that everything could become a passion. I had resolved beforehand to become a narrator of human passion rather than of a placid life-style.

Nearly everyone here at the Writers' Club bore some passion and was blinded by it. The young writers all aspired to become literary geniuses and many of them were convinced that they already were except that the others refused to acknowledge their genius. The Communists waited impatiently for the social revolution to start so that they could exact revenge upon all the bourgeois, Zionists, Socialists, petit bourgeois, the lumpenproletariat, the clergy, and most of all, the editors who refused to publish them. The few women members were convinced that they were victims of male contempt for the female sex. One of the hangers-on here was an actor named Jaque Levi, who had made guest appearances with a troupe in Prague in 1911 and had become a close friend of Franz Kafka there. He often spoke of this Kafka of whom I had never heard. Jaque Levi walked around with pockets stuffed with yellowed letters from Kafka.

I would ask him: "Who is this Kafka?"

And he would point a finger and say:

"One day he will be world-famous!"

I did not want to discuss either the evils of the Versailles Treaty or Kafka's greatness, but Levi and Saks had to talk to someone. At that time, an actress used to come to the Writers' Club with whom Kafka was allegedly in love—a Madam Tchizhik. She had performed with Jaque Levi in Prague. It was hard to believe that anyone could be in love with this woman, but I told myself that the passions—like Leibnitz's monads—had no windows.

Gina never came to the Writers' Club for I had forbidden her to do so. I was too shy to be seen with her by the older writers. I felt that everyone would be able to tell from my face that we were having an affair. Most of all I was ashamed before my elder brother with his knowledge of life and sense of irony. My shyness at that time assumed the character of a neurosis.

2

Sitting that day at the Writers' Club, I took yet another accounting of my life. I had barely missed being conscripted that day. I had seen this clearly in the doctors' eyes. A year hence, I would have to present myself again and I lacked the strength to subject myself to further weeks and months of deprivation. My brother suggested that the best solution for me would be to go to the Land of Israel. Maybe I could obtain a certificate from the Palestine Bureau in Warsaw which issued the few certificates that the English Mandate Authority allotted for Jewish immigrants. But what would I do in Palestine? Physical laborers were needed there, not a young man who was trying to write stories and in Yiddish besides. I had met several youths and girls who had gone to the Land of Israel and had come back disillusioned and sick with malaria. They told frightening stories about the privation, the unhealthy climate, the bureaucracy of the English as well as the Jewish officials, the exploitation by the contractors who did the hiring, and the dangers posed by the Arabs. In those days, Yiddish was an anathema in Palestine. Hebraist fanatics invaded meetings in institutions where Yiddish was spoken.

My own concerns were promptly transformed within me into consideration of the world condition. I no longer believed that

God had issued the Torah on Mount Sinai along with all the innovations and restrictions that commentators and exegetes had added in every generation. Whether God was a substance with infinite attributes, or the absolute, or blind will, or whatever the philosophers chose to call Him, one couldn't depend on His justice and mercy. I could never forget the tens of millions of people who had perished in the World War, in the Bolshevik Revolution, in the pogroms, the famines, the epidemics. Millions of peasants in Russia had been labeled kulaks and exiled to Siberia. Whole villages had been starved out. There was fighting in China, in Manchuria. In generation after generation people sacrificed their lives in battle, but nothing was ever realized. How did one become a writer in such a universal slaughterhouse? How could I write about love while millions of innocent creatures writhed in the clutches of slaughterers, hunters, and vivisectionists of every ilk? I imagined that I heard the sound of all the living through all the ages. I had been freed for a year but countless other young men had to begin learning to kill and be killed while enduring the insults and blows of those a rank higher.

I knew full well that Gina was waiting for me but I somehow didn't feel like going home. I owed her months of back rent. I had begun to grow weary of her pathos, her endless assurances that she was in constant touch with the dead, her hunger for love that I could never manage to satisfy. However many compliments I paid her, she still demanded more. She suffered from a terrible inferiority complex (a term I had first heard a short time before). She constantly demanded my avowals of eternal love. She kept saying that she was ready to lay down her life for me—as well as with me—but I neither needed her to die for me nor was ready to enter into a suicide pact with her. During the months that I had been depleting myself I had given in to all her sexual desires. This had been a means of losing weight and strength. Now I was so sated with sex that I longed for a night when I could sleep alone. I was overcome by a fatigue and a feeling that my end was near.

With my last groschen I had ordered something to eat from

the buffet at the Writers' Club. I was joined at the table by several fledgling writers, each with his own plans, complaints, vex-
ations. One had been left out by a critic who had compiled a
list of prose writers of the younger generation in a literary journal. A second had been promised to have his poem printed by
an editor but months had gone by and the poem still lay in the
editor's drawer, or possibly he had lost it. A third needed an
operation and was getting ready to enter a hospital. A fourth
told a joke about a man who went to a brothel, found himself
impotent, and was scolded by the Madam for coming on a Sabbath when the house was so full of patrons.

I chewed my sausage, mused that a cow or steer had paid
with its life for it, smiled at the joke, tried to console the writer
whose prestige had been so neglected, and wished the sick colleague a speedy recovery knowing all the while that the writer
lacked talent and the sick man had no chance of recovery. We
all clutched at something that a knife, a drop of poison, or a
rope could curtail in less than a minute. We were all cursed
with that self-love that no blows or disappointments can dimin-
ish, and of which one is freed only with one's final breath.

On the way home, I stopped before the window of a bookstore. I was preparing to write books yet the world was inundated with books. Thick, dusty volumes lined the store from
floor to ceiling. I had bought a Yiddish newspaper in which a
writer waged a polemic against the Polish anti-Semites who accused the Jews of trying to dominate the world. The chief anti-
Semite, Adam Nowaczynski, had tried for countless times to
prove to his readers that the Elders of Zion, the Masons, Stalin,
Trotsky, Leon Blum, the Rabbi of Gora, Weizmann, Mussolini,
and Hitler were part of one big conspiracy to dismember and
again partition the newly founded Polish nation. Nowaczynski
also included Pilsudski in this cabal, he who a few years earlier
had won the war against the Bolsheviks. The Yiddish newspaper
demanded logic. I had read this writer on more than one occasion. He had such an ability to arouse the emotions that reading him, I myself grew as if temporarily hypnotized by his style,
his passion, his paranoid suspicions.

When I came home, Gina assailed me with recriminations. Where had I been all day? Why hadn't I let her know the good news? True she knew that I was free since her dead grandmother had revealed herself to her and informed her, but where had I been all these hours? My behavior had given Gina a headache and she had to take aspirin or some other pills. She had prepared lunch for me but it had grown cold. She kissed me and scolded me. She accused me of unfaithfulness and predicted that I would treat her the same way the other men before me had done. She was ready to forgive me everything and conduct a sexual orgy with me but the moment I lay down I fell into a sleep from which no caresses or quarrels could rouse me.

TWO

1

FOR A WHILE IT APPEARED THAT YID-
dish and Yiddish literature were making progress. Great numbers of pious youths in the small towns had laid aside their
Gemaras and begun reading Yiddish newspapers and books. A
number of new publishers and magazines had cropped up. In
every sizable city a Yiddish weekly or monthly now appeared.
The literary magazine where I was proofreader had been taken
over by a big publisher—the house of Kletzkin. The proprietor,
Boris Kletzkin, a wealthy man and a patron of Yiddish literature,
had rented quarters in Simon's Passage at 52 Nalewki Street
which included a book warehouse, Yiddish typewriters, telephones, bookkeepers, a cashier, a director, and other employees. My salary was raised slightly and I could now give Gina
something toward the rent as well as pay for my meals. As if
this weren't enough, my brother Israel Joshua enjoyed a sudden
windfall—he was appointed Polish correspondent for the American Yiddish newspaper *The Jewish Daily Forward.* In the period since the World War the Yiddishist movement in America
had flourished. A whole literature had evolved there. The *Forward* was the largest Yiddish newspaper in America and had
about a quarter of a million readers, which for a Yiddish newspaper was an enormous circulation. The Yiddish Theater presented a number of better plays. The editor of the *Forward,* Abe
Cahan, who also wrote in English and was considered something of a classicist in American literature, ruled the paper with

an iron hand. The *Forward,* which was closely connected with
the Workmen's Circle and with many trade unions, had its own
ten-story building on East Broadway. One day, Abe Cahan happened to read my brother's collection of short stories entitled
Pearls and was inspired by the writing. He promptly invited my
brother to publish his literary works in the *Forward* and soon
afterward, he appointed him its Polish correspondent. My brother's salary came to about fifty dollars a week, but in those days
fifty dollars was a considerable sum when exchanged into Polish zlotys. Literary and journalist Warsaw seethed over my
brother's success.

In the first years following the Revolution, the *Forward,* a
socialist newspaper, had expressed sympathy toward communism. But Abe Cahan quickly realized that he had erred and the
Forward became sharply anti-Communist, actually the most important anti-Bolshevik newspaper in America. The *Forward*
writers, most of whom were experts on all the radical move-
ments in Russia, uncovered Stalin's murders long before the
democratic world became aware of them. The *Forward* would
arrive at the Writers' Club and I read it. America was enjoying
"prosperity" (one of the English words that American-Yiddish
adopted). Jews grew wealthy from real estate, from stocks that
kept ever climbing, and from various other businesses. The *Forward* printed stories and novels by the best Yiddish writers as
well as articles written by prominent non-Jewish socialists and
liberals in Europe. The people at the Writers' Club laughed at
the somewhat anglicized Yiddish employed in the *Forward,* yet
they all strove to work for this affluent newspaper which paid
generous fees.

A second child had been born to my brother—Joseph, or Yosele (who is now the translator of most of my works). My
brother had rented a comfortable apartment at 36 Leszno Street.
One day he was a pauper; the next, he was considered rich by
the indigent literary community. He wanted to help me, but I
had resolved to live on my earnings. I actually avoided him, and
the reason for this was my shyness. Known writers and young
women who were admirers of literature used to congregate at

his home. Most of these young women came from wealthy
homes, were fashionably dressed, smoked cigarettes, spoke a
good Polish, laughed loudly, and kissed the men, and I was
ashamed before them with my cheap clothes, my broken Polish,
and my yeshivah-student-like bashfulness. They were all older
than I and they discussed me as if I were some curiosity. They
would point their manicured fingers and ask: "Wherever did he
get such fiery red hair? Do you notice how blue his eyes are?"

It was enough for a woman to merely glance at me to make
me blush deeply. At Gina's house I was a mighty lover, but here
I again became a child, a cheder boy. This double role confused
me and evoked astonishment among others, since it was known
that I wrote and had a mistress. In some book or magazine, I
had stumbled upon a phrase, "split personality," and I applied
this diagnosis to myself. This was precisely what I was—cloven,
torn, perhaps a single body with many souls each pulling in a
different direction. I lived like a libertine yet I didn't cease praying to God and asking for His mercy; I broke every law of the
Shulhan Arukh and at the same time I read cabala books and
Chassidic volumes; I had spotted the weaknesses in the famous
philosophers and great writers yet I wrote things that emerged
naïve, awkward, amateurish. Now my potency was beyond belief—suddenly I became impotent. Some kind of enemy roosted
within me or a dybbuk who spited me in every way and played
cat-and-mouse with me. As soon as I read of some phobia or
neurosis, I immediately acquired it. All the afflictions psychia-
trists and neurologists described in their works assailed me one
after another and often, all at the same time. I was consumptive,
had cancer in my intestines, a tumor in my brain, I was growing
blind, deaf, paralyzed, insane. I suffered from nightmares and
compulsions. Some maniac uttered crazy words inside my brain
and I could not silence him. At the same time I held myself in
such check that not even Gina knew what I was going through.
Older writers at the Writers' Club often told me they envied my
youth and I said: "Believe me, there is nothing to envy."

I sought in books a solution to my distraction (and to all
other enigmas). I constantly browsed through bookstores and

libraries, but the books nearly all disappointed me, even the works of masters. The philosophers all made claims whose truths they couldn't substantiate. What's more, even if what they said were true, I found no new data there and certainly no solace. The literary works, the novels, all concurred that a man could love just one woman at a time and vice versa. But I felt that they lied. Rather than literature denying men's laws, the laws had seized literature in a trap and kept it there. I frequently fantasized about writing a novel in which the hero was simultaneously in love with a number of women. Since the Orientals were allowed to practice polygamy and to maintain harems (if they could afford it), the European could do the same. Monogamy was a law established by legislators, not by nature. But an artist had to be true to nature, human nature, at least in his descriptions regardless how wild, unjust, and insane it might be. Somewhere I had the suspicion that what was going on in my head went on in many other heads as well. Not only Yiddish literature but many other literatures struck me as too inhibited. Already then I had the feeling that every kind of censorship did great harm to literature. When I read *Anna Karenina,* I thought how good it would have been if Tolstoi could have described Anna's sexual relationships with her husband, and later, with her lover. All the details about Anna's dress, her visits, her friendships, and her journeys did little to reveal her situation. How much better it would have been to learn of her erotic relations with the two men; the crises and inhibitions that emerge in bed, when the person doffs not only his or her physical clothes but some of his spiritual ones as well. The sexual organs expressed more of the human soul than all the other body parts, even the eyes. To write about love and exclude sex was a useless labor.

Rummaging through the bookstores and libraries, I encountered a number of books that steered me in the direction I was to follow later. I found Professor Kraushaar's works about the False Messiah, Jacob Frank, and his disciples. I read whatever I could about the era of Sabbatai Zevi, in whose footsteps Jacob Frank had followed. I ran across many books that described the punishments imposed upon witches in Europe and America, the Crusades and their mass hysterias, as well as various accounts of dybbuks both Jewish and Gentile. In these works I found everything I had been pondering—hysteria, sex, fanaticism, superstition. The fact was that in our house these subjects had always been discussed and analyzed.

My father thought the world of Rabbi Jonathan Eibeshutz and bore a grudge against Rabbi Jonathan's enemy, Reb Jacob Emden. Rabbi Jonathan's book *Tablet of the Testimony* almost always lay on the desk in my father's study. Father often discussed with Mother (who was a scholarly woman) the fact that Rabbi Jonathan had been a just and pious man and that the accusations made against him by Reb Jacob Emden alleging that he, Rabbi Jonathan, was a secret follower of Sabbatai Zevi and that he issued amulets with allusions to Sabbatai Zevi and that he had brought down an epidemic and other misfortunes upon pregnant women, were false. Father constantly brought up Reb Jacob Emden's "Torat ha-Kenaot," "Edut beyaakob," "Shebirat Luhot ha-Aron," and his other tracts. Disputes between rabbis going back some two hundred years had more substance in our house than current events in the daily newspaper. Father believed every word written by the cabalists and waged a private war against those who openly or covertly contended that the Zohar hadn't been written by Rabbi Simon Ben Yohay but by Reb Moshe de Leon. One of the most outspoken opponents of the cabala had been the Italian scholar and exegete Reb Aryeh de Medina, and his name was anathema in our house.

Because my brother Joshua had become enlightened and Father was terrified lest the younger children follow his example, he constantly plied us with tales of transmigrated spirits, dybbuks, and miracles performed by various wonder-rabbis and saints. Somewhere inside Father nursed a resentment against Mother, who was inclined toward logic and science and had even been slightly infected by the Enlightenment. Her father, the Bilgorai rabbi, my grandfather Reb Jacob Mordecai, thought highly of Jacob Emden and was a bit of a *misnagid,* or anti-Chassid, and Father occasionally erupted with angry words against his father-in-law. From childhood I had been steeped in Chassidism, cabala, miracles, and all kinds of occult beliefs and fantasies. After lengthy stumbling and groping I rediscovered what I had been carrying within me the whole time.

2

Somewhere, I had heard or read the expression "the reappraisal of all values" and it was clear to me that this was what I had to do—reappraise all values. I could not rely on any authority. I still hadn't published a single word and at the Writers' Club I was known only as "Singer's brother." Just the same I waged contentions with God, the Prophets, religions, philosophies, as well as with the creators of world literature. Was Shakespeare really the genius he was made out to be? Were Maxim Gorki and Andreyev pillars of literature? Were Mendele Mocher Sforim, Peretz, Shalom Aleichem, and Bialik really as great as the Yiddishists and Hebraists wanted them to be? Had Hegel really said anything new in philosophy? Had the species really originated as Darwin claimed they had? Was there any substance to the assertions of Karl Marx, Lenin, Bukharin? Was democracy indeed the best system? Could a Jewish State in Palestine really solve the Jewish question? Did the words "equality" and "freedom" really mean something or were they mere rhetoric? Was it worthwhile to go on living and struggling in this world or were those who spat upon the whole mess right?

I was surrounded on all sides by the faithful who all believed in something: the Orthodox and the Zionists, the Chassidim and the *misnagdim,* the writers of the editorials in the Yiddish press and the anti-Semites in the Polish press, those who defended the League of Nations and those who opposed it. The brides and grooms who were congratulated in the newspapers apparently believed in the institution of marriage and in bringing forth new generations. I had often heard educators discussing the problems of rearing the young. In his letters to me, my father constantly warned me to live like a Jew and not—God forbid—forget or disgrace my heritage. Mother, on the other hand, pleaded again and again that I guard my health, not catch cold, God forbid, eat on time, go to sleep early, and not overwork. She wished me long life and hoped that I would make a good match and provide her with grandchildren. My sister-in-law Genia, Joshua's wife, often consulted with her sister, Bella, and with neighbors about which would be best for Yosele—to breast-feed him or give him a bottle, to use this formula or that? But something within me asked: "What for? Why? Why slaughter chickens, calves, and kids and bring up people? Why slave and stay up nights so that there would be a Yosele, an Isaac, or a Gina?"

As skillful as Tolstoi was in portraying individual types, so naïve did he seem to me when he tried to give advice on how to solve the agrarian problem in Russia or to expedite the teaching of the Gospel. All this babble about a better tomorrow, a rosier future, a united mankind, or equality was based on wishes, delusions, and sometimes merely on lust for power. It was clear to me that after the First World War there would have to come a second, a third, a tenth. Most faces expressed callousness, supreme egotism, indifference to everything outside their own ken, and, quite often, stupidity. Here they prayed and there they slaughtered. The same priests who preached love on Sunday morning hunted a fox, a hare, or some other helpless creature on Sunday afternoon or tried to hook a fish in the Vistula. The Polish officers who strutted about displaying their medals, brandishing their swords, and saluting each other hadn't the slightest chance of defending their country if it were attacked by Russia or Germany. And it was just as hard to believe that England would surrender her mandate in Palestine or that the Arabs would allow the Jews to establish a nation there. By now, I knew that atheism and materialism were just as unsubstantial as the religions. All my probings led to the same conclusion— that there was some scheme within Creation, someone we call God, but He had not revealed Himself to anyone nor was there even the slightest indication that He desired love, peace, and justice. The whole history of man and beast; all the facts pointed to the very opposite—that this was a God of strength and cruelty Whose principle was: Might makes right.

Oddly enough, this total skepticism or agnosticism led me to a kind of private mysticism. Since God was completely unknown and eternally silent, He could be endowed with whatever traits one elected to hang upon Him. Spinoza had bestowed Him with two known attributes and an endless array of unknown ones. But why couldn't one fantasize many other attributes? Why couldn't creativeness be one of His attributes? Why couldn't beauty, harmony, growth, expediency, playfulness, humor, will, sex, change, freedom, and caprice represent divine attributes too? And where was it written that He was the only God? Maybe He belonged to a whole army of gods, an infinite hierarchy. Maybe He procreated and multiplied and brought forth billions of angels, seraphim, Aralim, and cherubim in His cosmic harem as well as new generations of gods. Since nothing was known about Him and nothing could be known, why not confer upon this divine X all the possible values? The cabalists had done this in their own fashion, the idolators in another, and the Christians and Muslims in another still. I personally was fully prepared to crown Him with all kinds of possible attributes except benevolence and compassion. To ascribe mercy to a God who for millions of years had witnessed massacres and tortures and who had literally built an entire world on the principle of violence and murder was something my sense of justice wouldn't allow me to do. In my mind I created a kind of pecking order between us. I, a dust speck trembling with fear and filled with a sort of sense of right based upon my own silly urges and convictions; He, a universal murderer, a cosmic Genghis Khan or Napoleon—eternal, infinite, omnipotent, so wise and mighty in knowledge and technique that He could keep track of every electron, every atom, every gnat, fly, and microbe. It was even possible that one could phone Him directly with a request through the medium of prayer but with no guarantee whatsoever of an answer. I had actually appropriated

Spinoza's God but I had extended Him, anthropomorphized Him, bestialized Him, and reworked Him in my imagination to suit my moods. Incredibly enough, I "phoned" Him my requests and hoped somehow that He *could* answer me if the notion struck Him to do so. At that time my most urgent request was that my stories be printed and that I could have a room of my own. Being together with Gina had begun to grow tiresome for me.

Why? Because Gina grew ever more attached to me. She had seriously begun to demand that I marry her. She had grown jealous. She wanted to build her whole life upon me and even hoped that in time I would support her. I had no yen whatsoever to take a wife at least twenty years older and one that had already gone through who knows how many husbands and lovers before me. I didn't want to assume any burdens. Somehow, almost overnight, Gina had turned solemn. I no longer dared remind her of her past and she began to deny the affairs of which she had once told me. She now nagged at me to work and to be disciplined. In short, she became that which I didn't want—a wife.

3

Again I went around looking for a place to live. Again I climbed stairs and temporarily intruded into the lives of those who wanted to give up a portion of their living quarters.

Most of the advertisements read: "For a gentleman only." Others frankly specified that the lodger must be a bachelor. Those who rented rooms were nearly all women. I rang, they opened, and we contemplated each other. After a while they asked what I did and when I told them that I worked for a publication they were instantly won over. Our glances met and mutely asked: perhaps? I had become a connoisseur of faces,

bosoms, shoulders, bellies, hips. I speculated how much pleasure these various parts could provide if it came to an intimacy.
At times, within the space of a few minutes I gained insight into
a life. Men had died leaving widows. The rich had grown im-
poverished. Husbands had stayed on in Russia, fallen at the
front, gone off to America, or run away with other women. For
a while it would appear that fate had steered me to the right
place but soon the problems would begin to emerge—the rent
was too high or the room was half-dark. Some of the rooms had
no stoves to heat them. Actually I couldn't afford even the
cheapest room but if I was going to write I needed a room of
my own. My publisher had promised to get me to do Yiddish
translations of German, Polish, and Hebrew. Even as I talked to
these women I formed conceptions of their character and intelligence. Some pouted and grew sarcastic when they heard that
I wrote in Yiddish. Others asked if there really was such a thing
as Yiddish literature. They had apparently never heard of
Shalom Aleichem or Peretz, or they only made believe so.
Those that agreed to rent to me for a small sum were ugly,
neglected, with a houseful of children and rooms that stank of
pesticide. Their kitchens exuded the smell of onions, garlic,
washing soda. To go to the toilet one had to pass through the
living room. My eyes wearied of looking at closets, chairs, rugs,
credenzas, beds, sofas, wall clocks, samovars, portraits, and
knickknacks dating back to King Sobieski's time. I inhaled the
scent of perfumes, soaps, bodies. If I could have afforded a
hundred zlotys a month I might have picked and chosen, but I
couldn't even consider paying more than fifty.

I had written down many addresses, telephone numbers, and
prices in my notebook but I hadn't found what I wanted. It was
late in spring but the weather was cold and damp. I left the last
apartment of the day and my brain felt dulled from all the talk,
all the impressions, and maybe even from hunger since I hadn't
eaten any lunch. I hadn't yet told Gina that I was leaving and I
had to make up some lie to cover my whereabouts all day. I
walked down half-dark streets and I wasn't sure where I was. I

glanced up at illuminated windows. Other people had somehow managed to settle in, to eat dinner with their families, and
to hold down more-or-less stable jobs but I roamed through the
wet city like a phantom. I had awakened that morning with
plans for a novel, for stories or even a play, but it had all evaporated. Night had fallen. A deep melancholy settled over me.

I smelled the waste that was carried out from the refuse bins
in the evenings and I inhaled the aromas of trees, blossoms,
and turned-over soil. I passed a house gate where streetwalkers
lurked calling out to passers-by. Certainly it would be crazy,
having Gina, to go with one of them and risk venereal disease.
I barely had enough in my pocket to pay for a meal if I decided
to eat out. But somehow, my pace slowed. I was seized by a
desire for a strange body, for unheard words spoken by a different voice. "Why fear syphilis?" a voice within me asked.
"You're not long for this world anyhow."

I stood there and beneath the shine of the gas street lights examined the live ware. One was small and thin with a narrow face,
sunken cheeks and big black eyes that exuded a Jewish fear as if
she had just escaped a pogrom or had skipped over the few
hundred years from Chmielnicki's massacres. She was huddled
in a shawl of a type rarely seen in Warsaw. She looked straight at
me and her glance seemed to say: "You're the only one who can
drag me out of this mire into which I have fallen."

The second was tall, stout, wearing a yellow dress and green
boots. Her hair was as red as fire. A man had stopped near her
and seemed to be bickering with her about something but she
apparently had no patience for him and looked away. This was
probably not a patron who used a girl and paid her, but some
pest who came just to gab or to try to get something for nothing. In one hand he held a box of the kind laborers sometimes
carry to factories or workshops. The red-haired whore had spotted me and she winked to me to save her from the pest. She
even amiably showed me the tip of her tongue.

A third stood off in a corner not looking at anything. Her face
was red from rouge or perhaps she had rubbed it with red
paper. I had the feeling that she neither wanted to nor was able

to compete with the others. She was obviously waiting patiently till the other two were engaged and her turn came.

I could decide neither to choose one of them nor to keep going. What I now felt wasn't lust but an urge to demean myself, to convince myself once and for all that all my hopes were for naught and that I was already at the end of my road. "If you catch syphilis," my inner enemy went on, "you'll have to commit suicide and that will put an end to all the foolishness."

My feet crossed the street as if of their own accord. I had intended to take another one but instead I went over to the skinny one with the frightened eyes. She trembled.

"Me?"

"Yes, you."

She cast a glance at the redhead which expressed both surprise and something akin to triumph. She ducked inside the dark gate archway and I followed—"like a sheep to slaughter," I told myself. Only yesterday I had concluded that man's resemblance to God lay in the fact that both possessed freedom of choice, each in his own fashion and according to his ability. But here I was doing something that mocked all my ideas. The girl walked downstairs and I found myself in a hallway so narrow only one person could pass at a time. Blackened walls loomed heavily on either side ready to come together and crush me. The floor was bumpy and pitted. A smell of earth, rot, and something moldy and greasy assailed my nostrils. Suddenly in the shine of a tiny kerosene lamp a huge individual with a black patch instead of a nose, a face pocked as a crater, and dressed in rags, materialized. His eyes reflected the laughter of those who have looked down into the abyss and found it less frightening than comical. He walked with a waddle and blocked our path. He stank like a carcass. I started to run backward and my ears rang as if from bells tolling. My mouth filled with nauseating bile. The whore shouted and tried to run after me. The giant began to bellow, guffaw, clap his paws. I groped for the stairs but they had vanished. I heard a meowing of cats and the muffled sounds of an accordion.

"God in heaven, save me!" the believer within me cried.

I turned around and the stairs emerged. I raced up them and in a moment was outside again. The red-haired whore shrieked words I only deciphered later:

"Fool, cheat, dead beat! . . ."

It was all like a nightmare or one of those trials by Satan described in holy volumes or storybooks. I had intended to surrender myself to the powers of evil but the forces that rule the world had interfered. I was drenched with sweat. My heart pounded and my throat was parched. I was overcome by a deep feeling of shame and the silence of one who has just extricated himself from mortal danger. I prayed to the God with Whom I waged war to forgive me. I vowed never to defy Him again.

4

I had found what I had been looking for—a room with an old couple on Dzika Street, part of which the Warsaw City Council now called Zamenhof Street after the creator of Esperanto. The owner of the apartment, Dr. Alpert, an eye doctor, had actually been a friend of the late Dr. Zamenhof, who had lived and practiced two houses away. I had studied Esperanto in Bilgorai. I had even tried writing a sketch in this international language and I considered it an honor to live at the home of a colleague of its creator. Although I had sinned, Providence had granted me what I wanted—a clean room, not expensive, decently furnished, sunny, with a window overlooking the street, and located on the fourth floor so that the outside noises weren't too disturbing. I realize now that the couple wasn't as old as they seemed to me at the time. They had a son of twenty-three or four but Dr. Alpert was completely gray and toothless, and spoke in the thin voice of an old man. He was small, stooped, had a weak heart and a half-dozen other ailments. He no longer had any connections with a hospital, and few patients came to see him. Those who did were all poor and paid accord-

ing to their means. From time to time the doctor himself became sick and had to be taken to a hospital. His dull eyes beneath the bristly white eyebrows exuded the tranquillity of
those who have given up all ambition and have accepted the
coming of death.

Husband and wife both spoke Polish even though they knew
Yiddish. Mrs. Alpert was younger than her husband, no taller
than he, with hair that had begun to thin, a pointy chin that
sprouted a gray womanly beard, and brown eyes that expressed
all the worries and suspicions burdened spirits carry from cradle to grave. From the very first moment she opened the door
to me, she appeared frightened. She measured me sidelong,
inquisitively, and began questioning me before she even allowed me inside the foyer. She told me quite frankly: Although
she could have used the extra money toward the rent, she had
seldom taken in a roomer. What could you know about a
stranger anyway? He might be a thief, a murderer, a swindler.
He might also be a Communist, an anarchist, or a syphilitic. You
read of so many terrible things in the paper that no matter how
careful you were, you could still fall into a net. Under no cir-
cumstance would she take in a woman lodger. Women wanted
to wash out their stockings and underwear, to cook themselves
meals in the kitchen. They also began to take an instant hand in
the running of the household. I assured Mrs. Alpert that I
wouldn't wash or cook anything, merely sit at my table and
write.

After an extended interview she asked me into the living
room and also showed me the doctor's reception room, the
kitchen, and even her bedroom. Everything was old but clean. I
needed but one glance at the son, Edek, to tell that he was
sickly. He was tall, lean, and pale as a consumptive, with a high
forehead, a long neck, narrow shoulders, a sunken chest, a
crooked nose, and bulging eyes. His arms were as thin as sticks.
He listened to his mother's talk and made no response. From
time to time he coughed. A whole stack of newspapers and
magazines lay before him on a table and I noticed that they
were all old and creased. Articles or ads had been clipped out

of some. A scissors lay on top of the pile just like on an editor's desk.

The maid, Marila, had a high bosom and round hips. Her calves were broad and muscular, her pale blue eyes exuded a peasant strength. Mrs. Alpert introduced us and said that if I ever needed anything, a glass of tea, breakfast, or whatever, Marila was always at my service. She would make up my bed, sweep up, and keep the room in order. The girl nodded and smiled showing a mouthful of wide teeth, and dimples.

When Gina heard that I was moving out, she became hysterical. She screamed, wept, tore the hair from her head, and swore that she would take poison, hang herself, or throw herself under a streetcar. She warned me that in the other world, where she was heading, she would kneel before the Throne of Glory and tell the Almighty all the evil I had perpetrated down here on earth. She assured me that the punishment was imminent both for me and for the woman who was snatching me from her. I took a solemn oath that there was no one and that my reason for moving was so that I could work in peace, but Gina whined:

"It's true that I'm a fool but I'm not the dunce you take me for. You found a younger and maybe a prettier one than me, but I gave you my heart and soul, and she, that whore—may she burn like fire, dear Father in heaven—will only give you what you can get for two zlotys on Smocza Street. The trouble with men is that they don't know the difference. They're all a bunch of damn idiots, dullards, madmen, low-lifes—down to the very last one. Mama of mine, look what they're doing to me! Sainted Grandmother, come and take me to you! I can no longer stand so much shame and anguish. I'll be with you, Grandma, and with all the holy women. This phony world disgusts me. Oy, I have to vomit!"

And she dashed into the toilet where I heard her retch, cry, and like Job, curse the day she had been born. After a while it became unnaturally quiet in there. I began to pound on the door but she didn't answer. I tried to break the door down but the lock or the chain wouldn't give.

I cried: "Gina, come out! I'll stay. I'll stay with you as long as I live! I swear on all that is holy!"

The door swung open.

"Beast, don't swear! Take your bundle and go. I don't want you here any more. Oy, Holy Father of mine!"

And she went back into the toilet and resumed throwing up.

When Gina came out again I got the strange feeling that she had suddenly aged. This wasn't Gina but someone else perhaps ten years older, sallow, with bags under eyes grown dim and an expression about the mouth I had never seen on her. A bitterness hovered about her lips and something akin to mockery over her own ill fortune. For the first time I grasped the fact that love was no game. Love killed people. Again and again I offered to stay with her, but she said:

"No, my dearest, you are just beginning and I'm on the verge of closing the book forever."

Three

1

THE REVIVED POLISH NATION WAS barely seven years old, but within that short time it had already gone through a war with the Bolsheviks, an assassination of a president, and a great number of political crises. One spring day as I sat in my room trying to write a story, the door opened and Mrs. Alpert came in. She appeared more frightened than usual.

She said, "You sit there and write and outside a revolution has broken out."

"What kind of revolution?"

I expected to hear that the Communists were about to do to Poland what Lenin, Kamenev, Zinoviev, and Stalin had promised to do to all Europe, but Mrs. Alpert replied: "Pilsudski has taken over the power."

I had been prepared to toss my manuscript in the basket and run to wherever my legs would carry me, since the Communist hacks at the Writers' Club had all assured me that when the Revolution came, they would hang me from "the nearest lamppost" along with all the rabbis, priests, members of the Polish Socialist party, Zionists, Bundists, Poale Zionists both the right and the left, and all other counterrevolutionaries. But I had nothing to fear from Pilsudski. The party politicians at the Polish parliament, the Sejm, had forgotten that Pilsudski had established the new Poland and they ignored him. Every few weeks a new government crisis erupted. All poetic hopes that a liberated Poland would bring with it new spiritual values and a Messianic spirit for all mankind had been dashed. Now it appeared that the army with Pilsudski at its head would set up a dictatorship. For Jews in general, and for someone like me in particular, this would make no difference whatsoever. I had read somewhere that Pilsudski had criticized the Polish Ministry of War for allowing the conscription of inept and unfit recruits. I was scheduled to go before a military commission again and it occurred to me that this revolution might somehow help me avoid the draft.

It happened like this. My brother had persuaded the Palestine Bureau in Warsaw to issue me a certificate of immigration to Palestine, but since such a certificate was good for a whole family, the office made a stipulation that I marry first—whether actually or in name only. This meant going through a ceremony with a girl in Warsaw, then getting a divorce once in Palestine. Such counterfeit marriages were a frequent occurrence those days. They served to bring more Jews to the Land of Israel and also helped poor pioneers who couldn't afford the fare. The alleged "wife" would pay the travel expenses for herself and for her "husband." The whole thing smacked of fraud but Poland wanted to get rid of Jews and England didn't care if a few more Jews settled in Palestine. A large number of those that immigrated suffered disappointment, unable to adjust to the climate and the hard work, and after a while they turned back to either Poland or wherever they were admitted.

There couldn't be even the slightest thought of my getting married for real. I had read Otto Weininger's *Sex and Character* and had resolved never to marry. Weininger, Schopenhauer, Nietzsche, and my own experiences had transformed me into an antifeminist. I lusted after women yet at the same time I saw their faults, chief of which was that they (the modern, not the old-fashioned kind) were amazingly like me—just as lecherous, deceitful, egotistical, and eager for adventures. Some frankly declared that marriage was an outdated institution. How could you make a contract to love for an entire lifetime? they asked. What could be a greater contradiction than love and a contract? The novels these girls read, the magazine articles, the plays they saw, all mocked the husband who worked hard, raised his children and was deceived, and at the same time they glorified the lover who got everything for free. My experiences with Gina and with those that I met later only confirmed this conviction. Well, and what about the things I observed at the Writers' Club! In my own writings the husband emerged an object of scorn.

Even a marriage in name only frightened me somewhat. What would I do if the girl changed her mind later and refused to divorce me. I was ashamed to accept money from a woman. I didn't know where to find such a woman in the first place. My shyness was apparently obvious to the people at the Palestine Bureau, and one of the officials there recommended a girl who was ready to go through such a clandestine marriage. He told me about her in detail. She was engaged to an engineer in Warsaw, a graduate of the Warsaw Polytechnic Institute, and the wedding had been imminent when the fiancé committed some folly and was forced to flee Poland. After long wanderings he had illegally entered Palestine but he wasn't able to bring his fiancée over. Panna (Miss) Stefa came from an affluent home and was deeply in love with her fiancé. She had already met several youths with certificates of immigration but one promptly fell in love with her and urged her to enter into a real marriage with him; a second changed his mind about the whole thing since he had a girl of his own who had somehow managed to scrape together the fare for them both; and a third had tried to swindle money out of her. Miss Stefa had grown so despondent that she had given up on the entire notion. The official urged me:

"Above all, you have to convince her that you have no ulterior motives. I'll call her right now. Her father was once a very rich man but Grabski ruined him with the taxes. The daughter studied at the university, knows languages, and who knows what else."

Everything happened quickly. The official telephoned and apparently spoke well of me, for Miss Stefa asked that I come right over. I told the official that I would like to shave first and put on a better suit but he argued that the more shabby I appeared, the better my chances would be. Miss Stefa's parents lived on Leszno Street in a house built in 1913 just before the war. It had an elevator and all the modern conveniences. The official spoke of this Miss Stefa with such high regard that I was overcome with childish fear and shame at the prospect of meeting her.

Although I didn't walk quickly, I became drenched in sweat. I had knotted my shoelaces but after each few steps they came untied as if by some unseen hand. As usual whenever I grew embarrassed, the imps began to toy with me. I sneezed and my collar button fell off. I searched for it on the sidewalk but it had vanished. A button popped off my overcoat. I suddenly noticed that my trousers were hanging loosely and trailing. I tried to hitch up my suspenders but the loop holding up the trousers had snapped. I tried to apply self-hypnosis à la Coué, told myself to be bold and not allow myself to be cowed by some female no matter how rich or educated she might be, but to no avail. Crossing the street I was nearly run down by a droshky. I walked past a store front with a mirror and caught a glimpse of myself. I looked pale, drained, disheveled. I walked inside the building gate where the janitor was lounging. When I told him whom I wanted to visit he measured me arrogantly and asked:

"For what purpose?"

I didn't know how to answer him and he snarled through clenched teeth:

"Best get out of here! . . ."

2

After a while I got permission to go up and I began to climb the stairs because the elevator was for tenants only. The steps were of marble. I stopped before a massive carved door painted red. A brass name plate bore the inscription: Isidore Janovsky.

I rang and it took a while for the maid, a woman with a red

face and white hair, to answer. The foyer was big and wide with
many doors leading from it. The maid went off to announce me
and I had to wait a long time. There wasn't a stick of furniture
in the foyer. The walls bore traces of removed paintings like in
a vacated apartment. A chain used to hold a lamp hung from
the ceiling, but without a lamp. I suddenly recalled the official's
comments that Grabski had brought Miss Stefa's father to ruin.
Grabski was the Minister of Finance who had imposed such
taxes upon the Jews that they were unable to pay, and after a
while a wagon or wagons would come from the tax collector's
office and remove all the householder's belongings. These wagons had been nicknamed "hearses."

A door opened abruptly and Miss Stefa came out. She wore a
knee-length dress and her blond hair cut boyishly short. She
was tall for a woman, light-skinned and snub-nosed, and her
face had the expression of one who is deeply preoccupied and
had been called away from an important task. She looked me
up and down and asked:

"Were you sent here by the Palestine Bureau?"

"Yes, the Bureau."

She glanced at the slip of paper which I handed to her and
pronounced my Jewish name in a Polish accent.

She asked: "Have you a birth certificate? A passport? Are you
registered here in Warsaw? Are you ready to go to Palestine in
the next few weeks? Are you deferred from conscription?"

I answered all her questions briefly. She stood away from me
as if anxious to get the whole interrogation over with right then
and there. Her gaze was stern and it occurred to me that she
behaved not unlike those bureaucrats who had ruined her father.

After a while, she asked: "Is it true you write in the jargon?"

Her calling Yiddish a jargon irked me. Usually in such cases I
would try to impress upon the other that all languages had been
so disdained at first. French, Italian, and English had been
branded as the vulgar languages of the rabble while the upper
classes had employed Latin. I would point out that as long as
the language of the aristocracy in Russia and Poland had been

French, the Poles and Russians hadn't produced a single work of art in that language. But as soon as they started writing in Russian or Polish, there had emerged a Pushkin, a Mickiewicz, a Slowacki, and many others. But I simply replied:

"Yes, in the jargon."

"What do you write about?"

"Oh, about Jewish life here in Poland."

"And what do you intend to do in Palestine? Also write?"

"If they'll let me."

"Do you know Hebrew?"

"I can read it and write it, but not speak it fluently. I've never spoken any Hebrew."

"When I was a child, a rabbi used to come to the house and teach me a little Hebrew—how to read from a prayer book— what is it called? 'I give thanks.' But I've forgotten everything. I no longer even know the alphabet. Such strange characters— they all look alike to me. Well, and the reading from right to left is bewildering. I'm afraid I'll never get used to it. But it has turned out so that I must get to Palestine. Come in. Why do you stand there in the doorway?"

She opened the door for me and I followed her into a room which contained a folding cot, a small table on which a few books and papers lay, and two kitchen chairs—one white, one blue.

She looked around as if she herself were startled by the changes wrought here. She indicated to me to take one of the chairs while she herself sat down on the cot, which was covered with a faded bedspread. She lit a cigarette, crossed her legs, and it struck me that her knees weren't round as most girls', but pointed.

She asked: "That young man—what's his name? Margolis— explained the situation to you?"

"Yes, more or less."

"I must get to Palestine and the sooner the better. My fiancé and I were supposed to get married here in Warsaw. Everything was already set for the wedding when suddenly something happened that spoiled our plans. The Palestine Bureau won't issue a certificate for a single person. They generally discriminate against the so-called weaker sex. In this respect, they are full-fledged Asiatics."

She went on. "I know languages—French, German, even a little English, but I know no Yiddish and not a word of Hebrew. I'll be frank with you, but don't tell Margolis—I have no intention of staying in Palestine for long. Margolis is a fervent Zionist. If it were up to him, every Jew in the world would pack his bag and head for Palestine. When it comes to Poland, he may well be right. But Poland isn't the world. What will the Jews do there? It's still half desert. You're undoubtedly a Jewish nationalist, but to me the whole Jewishness is a paradox. What does my Jewishness consist of? I don't believe even marginally in God or all those miracles described in the Old Testament. I haven't the slightest notion of what's in the Talmud and all the rest of it. I was raised in the European culture but the World War has stirred up a kind of nationalism—that is beyond me. No, I don't want to stay there but it's hard to get a visa to a European country, and America has closed her gates. You've certainly read about what's going on in Russia. Did you say you were free of your military obligations?"

"I've been given a 'B' classification. I have to present myself again in a few months."

Miss Stefa snatched the cigarette from her lips and crushed it in the ashtray on the table.

"Oh really? But according to Margolis you were freed for good."

"No. He knew I must present myself again shortly."

"Has he lost his mind or what? Already he has sent me three or four candidates and each turns out worse than the last. I'm really beginning to suspect he's acting out of spite. But why would he? What are your chances of being rejected?"

"I hope they won't take me; I'm not altogether well."

"What's wrong with you?"

I wanted to say something but the words wouldn't leave my lips. Miss Stefa measured me with a sidelong, mocking gaze.

"You don't want to go in the army, that's all. Not that I blame you. I wouldn't want to myself if I were a man. What kind of pleasure is it? But someone has to defend the country in case of attack. My fiancé, Mark, is Jewish but he served in the army and worked his way up to officer. He fought in the war against the Bolsheviks and was highly decorated. He is an outstanding horseman and marksman. He once took part in a military horse race and he received a commendation. Were you born in Poland?"

"Yes, in Poland."

"Your pronunciation sounds foreign. The Polish-Jewish press keeps fighting anti-Semitism but the Jews here behave in such a way that the anti-Semitism must exist. Thank God not all Jews are like this. You were undoubtedly raised in the cheder and in the yeshivah, on those ancient, moldy volumes. I believe you when you say you feel sick, but it's only because you've never breathed any fresh air and never done any physical labor. You're barely twenty-one or two but your spine is bent like an old man's. Why are you so pale? Are you anemic?"

"Yes. Maybe."

"What does your father do?"

"He's a rabbi."

"A rabbi, eh? Every third Jew is a rabbi. They walk the streets in their long caftans, disheveled beards, and flying earlocks and when I see them and their wild gestures I'm ashamed that we share a heritage. They are total savages."

"You're wrong, Miss Stefa, they are highly civilized."

"In what sense?"

"They want to live, not to be heroes. What the Christians merely preach, they have been practicing for two thousand years."

"Oh, you're a strange young man. I'm beginning to believe that this Margolis from the Palestine Bureau is having fun at my expense. You know what? Since you're here you can show me the Hebrew alphabet. At least I'll be able to read a sign when I am there. Wait, I have a Hebrew book. I left it in the living room. I'll be right back."

3

From the way Miss Stefa spoke I gathered that her parents were thoroughly assimilated, but a moment after she left, the door opened and in minced a tiny individual with a minuscule white goatee and brown eyes smiling with Jewish familiarity. He had a pinched, hooked nose, a high forehead as wrinkled as parchment, and sunken cheeks. He wore a stiff collar and a black silk tie.

He said: "I hope I am not disturbing you. I am Isidore Janovsky, Stefa's father."

He spoke Polish in the very same accent as I. He smiled, revealing a mouthful of yellow teeth. I hurried to say that he was in his own house and that it was my pleasure to meet him, but Isidore Janovsky countered in singsong:

"What's the big pleasure? These days a father is no authority. There has grown up a generation that's ashamed of its own parents. You're undoubtedly one of the bridegrooms Margolis from the Palestine Bureau keeps sending us. Forgive me, I don't mean to sound insulting. Since my daughter has elected to drop everything and go to Palestine, she has to go through all this. There is a saying: 'Once you say A, you must also say B.' But who told her to say 'A' in the first place? . . . So, you're actually going to the Land of Israel? What will you do there? You have to work hard there and the climate is harsh. I'm not just talking through my hat—I've been there. I visited the colonies and all the rest of it. Before the war I was a rich man and could afford to travel. When it gets hot there and the chamsin starts blowing you can go mad. I became very sick there. The colonies, Rishon le Zion and Petah Tikvah, are certainly an accomplishment, but outside of the piece of bread they provide nothing, and when the crops are meager they don't even provide that. The Zionists claim things are better now— but I'm no heretic if I choose not to believe them. At one time a lie was a lie. Today, they've given the lie a fancy name— propaganda. May I ask your profession?"

"I'm a proofreader for a literary magazine."

Isidore Janovsky clapped his ear.

"From this you make a living?"

"Yes."

"And what will you do in the Land of Israel? Be a proofreader too? What's the name of the magazine? What is it in—Hebrew or jargon?"

"In Yiddish."

"Over there they look down on Yiddish. My dear young man, since you're a proofreader you are probably something of a writer too. I used to read the older writers—Mendele, Shalom Aleichem, Peretz, Dinesohn. It had a kind of flavor. Once, one of the current crop of writers gave me his book. I didn't understand a single line. Such difficult words and one had no connection to the next. They're all Communists. In Russia it's hell—people are starving to death and if one utters a word against their rulers they send him to Siberia. Here it's bitter too. Without the Russian market Poland is like a head without a body. They want their taxes paid but how can you pay taxes when the factories have no customers to supply? What's the name of that magazine?"

I told him its name.

"Never heard of it. I shouldn't say this to you but I'm going to say it anyway. We have one daughter who is very precious to us. There was another, a younger, a girl of seventeen, wonderful child—pretty, smart, devoted to her parents, a treasure, but she got the crazy urge to dance. She danced and danced till her appendix burst and before the doctors, those quacks, could diagnose her ailment it was too late. It's no tragedy when a girl dances but everything has to have a limit. There has evolved a generation that knows no restraints. They want to drink in all the pleasure all at once, and if you tell them that this isn't the way, they're ready to tear you to shreds. Anyhow, she passed on and took our hearts with her. It almost killed her mother. Her every moment is torture. How she goes on living is one of God's miracles. I say this in connection with the fact that Stefa—her real name is Sheba Leah—is all we've got left now. Once she leaves, her mother won't last a month. The story is this: If she were only going to someone worthy of her, it would be at least some consolation for me. It's accepted that a daughter has to be given away. We wouldn't want her to remain an old maid, God forbid. Maybe we would even follow her to Palestine or wherever she might settle. But she's mixed up with the worst charlatan in Warsaw. To begin with, he had a wife who refused to divorce him and it cost a fortune to buy her off. He had a rich father who left him a large inheritance but he, Mark, lost it all. Yes, he literally gambled it away at cards, roulette, and other such games whose names I don't even know. He has a gambling mania. He'll bet on anything and he hasn't won a bet yet. I discussed this with a doctor, a psychiatrist, and he told me that this is a sickness. He must constantly be risking something. He became a regular big shot in the Polish Army, a real hero. Each time they needed someone for a dangerous job he was the first to volunteer. He has jumped horses over fences and he has already killed several of them. It was a miracle he didn't kill himself or become crippled. How a Jew could be born so reckless is beyond me. Such lunatics existed among the old Polish gentry. They would risk their fortune on the turn of a card or in lawsuits that dragged on for years and bankrupted both the litigants. I didn't know his father, he died during the war, but he has an old bitch of a mother who is just as crazy as he is. She was left a lot of money but her son got it away from her, although they say she still has a bundle salted away somewhere. She never leaves her house since she lives in constant fright of thieves. He, that Mark, had to flee Poland because—"

The door opened and Stefa appeared holding a book.

"So, Papa, you're baring your soul to him? You're confessing already? The moment a person walks into the house he assails him with his tales of misery. Papa, if you ever again—"

"Hush, daughter, hush, I'm not doing anything to harm you. Believe me, you don't have a better friend than me. . . ."

"God protect me from such friends."

"You should be ashamed to talk this way to your father,

daughter. We gave our lives for you and look how you repay us."

"What am I doing to you, Papa? What harm am I causing you? I love someone and I want to be with him. Is that such a crime?"

"You know very well that your going to Palestine thousands of miles away will finish your mother. About me, you needn't worry. I've lived long enough as it is. What else can life offer me—that the 'hearse' come again and snatch the pillow from under my head? But I can't stand to watch your mother suffering and I feel for you too, daughter, because the man you're going to will—"

"Papa, be quiet!"

4

Isidore Janovsky went out and Stefa said:

"He's my father and I love him but he is an exhibitionist. He likes to bare all wounds and not only his own but my mother's, mine, and everybody else's as well. Is this a specifically Jewish condition? Why deny it? We're a shattered family in every respect, but we aren't yet beggars to display all our sores in public. Show me the alphabet and how to read it."

Stefa opened the book and I showed her the alphabet.

She interrupted to complain: "Why did they make the *nun* and *gimel* so much alike? Also the *mem* and the *tet* . . . and the *daled* and the *resh?* I can't understand this. It's the same in the Gothic script too. In English, on the other hand, you never know how a word should be pronounced. In Hebrew it's even worse. I was already reading Hebrew, but I've forgotten it. I'm beginning to believe that those who developed scripts and languages were all idiots. I'd like to hide on some island without culture and languages and live like a bird or an animal. But where do

you find such an island? Is there really such a thing as
Yiddish literature?"

"Yes, there is."

"What is it?"

"A literature like all the others—ninety-nine per cent bad and
one per cent good."

"You're a funny young man—you speak the truth. I've
turned into a half anti-Semite. I can't stand Jews. They're always running, bustling, mouthing endless complaints against
everyone and only striving to create a better world. Mark is
that way too. I love him, yet I see all his faults. Why am I
telling you these things? I never talk to anyone, but since you
are a writer—or wish to be a writer—you should possess
some understanding. My father undoubtedly blabbed everything to you. He does this with whoever comes into the
house, even the man who collects the money from the gas
meter. Let's read on."

We resumed and it didn't take Stefa more than fifteen minutes to begin reading faultlessly. She had already gone through
this book with someone else before. She read and smoked. She
even remembered the meaning of some of the words. She read
to the bottom of a page and said:

"You lack strength because you don't eat. It's just that simple,
and you don't eat because you don't want to be conscripted.
But that won't help you. The doctors are on to these tricks.
When they classify a person 'B', it means he is organically
sound. Why can't you smuggle yourself across into Germany or
Rumania and catch a ship from there to Palestine?"

"I don't know how to go about this."

Stefa closed the book.

"Listen to me. I must depart as soon as possible. I can't put
things off for the future. My fiancé is waiting for me with impatience. Neither can I stay away from him. Each day without him
is for me like hell. According to the letters with which he showers me, he yearns for me too. My father probably managed to
malign him, but he is the most interesting person I've ever met.
I have the exact amount needed to pay the fare for two people.

We must get to Constantsa and board a ship there. That's the cheapest route. I have everything figured down to the very last groschen. If they get the notion to raise the fare, it's all over for us. We have relatives and so-called friends here, but no one can nor wants to help us. What did Father say about Mark?"

"Nothing bad. Only that he likes to gamble and take risks."

"Yes, that's one of his aberrations. Do you at least have a domestic passport?"

"I don't even have a birth certificate."

"We can go to Danzig. You don't need a foreign passport to go there since it's a free city. No, that wouldn't do. It's too far from there to Rumania. We must go to Zaleszczyki in Galicia and from there cross on foot into Rumania. There are smugglers everywhere who will guide you across the border for a few zlotys."

"They wouldn't let me aboard ship without a foreign passport. I couldn't get the certificate without it either," I said.

"What? A regular foreign passport costs four hundred zlotys. To receive a concession on this price you have to present all kinds of petitions, and the *starosta* and the government commissariat set up delays and obstacles. They might even levy taxes against you or at least demand proof that you don't owe any. Do you have such proof?"

"I have nothing."

"You have nothing. . . . Where do you live anyway—on the moon?"

"I wish I could."

"Well, I see how things are. Margolis only sends me young men to waste my time so that it will all come to naught. He is my enemy but I don't know why. Are you hungry?"

"Hungry? No."

"You look hungry. I don't want you to pass out in my room. I know of a young man who starved himself for so long that he dropped dead. We have a maid; that one who let you in. But we can't pay her a salary so she has become like the mistress of the house. If she feels like it, she cooks, if she doesn't, we eat dry food. She's been with us since I remember and she's like part of the family. She adored my younger sister but she spites me at every turn. My sister is dead."

"Yes, I know."

"So he told you everything, the old chatterbox. Totally lacking in character. If he weren't my father I'd call him a dishrag. But I know he wasn't always like this. There are troubles that can change a person's character. Be that as it may, our maid hates visitors, particularly mine. Come, we'll go down to a café and grab a bite. I see that all my plans will come to nothing, but I do believe that your intentions are good and in my situation even a little goodwill helps. Come."

"Really, I'm not hungry."

"You'll eat, you'll eat. I won't order too much for you anyway since I must literally count every groschen. It's come to it that when I have to go somewhere, I walk to save the few groschen trolley fare."

I got up to go but at that moment there was a knock on the door. It was Isidore Janovsky. He said to Stefa:

"You're wanted on the phone."

"Who wants me?"

"Since you're wanted—go!"

"It's Treitler, eh?"

"Yes, Treitler."

"Papa, I'm not at home to him."

"Daughter, I told him you were home. Don't make me out a liar."

"I've told you countless times that I don't want to talk to him."

"Tell it to him yourself. I'm not your errand boy."

5

There was no restaurant in the immediate neighborhood and Stefa took me to a café on the same street. She spoke to me, but she kept her face averted giving the impression that she was talking to herself.

She asked: "What kind of name is Treitler? Jews have such odd names."

"It comes from Treitle. Perhaps a German name."

"And what's the meaning of Treitle? And how is it my father is called Janovsky? It just so happened that this name came in handy when I was attending the Gymnasium, and even more so at the university. Janovsky is a true Polish name but my birth certificate lists me as Sheba Leah. These are all trifles, but one suffers because of them. When my Polish teacher pronounced the name Sheba Leah he did it with such venom, such irony! I never wanted to be Jewish, but to accept Jesus—another Jew and martyr—that wasn't to my liking either. Must people belong to a group and drag along all its burdens of superstition and discrimination behind them? Why can't there be one united mankind with one language?"

"Dr. Zamenhof tried this too. I actually live on the street named after him which used to be part of Dzika Street. People don't want to belong to a united mankind."

"Why not? In Palestine I'll probably become Sheba Leah again. Jewish nationalism has reared its head there. They return to a land they left two thousand years ago. They want to revive a language that was dead even then. The Jews spoke Aramaic and Greek in the time of Jesus. I've read Graetz, I've read him. I thought he would solve the Jewish enigma for me but he himself was a fervent nationalist and committed to all its dogmas. Here we are."

We had come to the restaurant. We went in, took a table, and Stefa said:

"I'm not religious, actually, I'm an atheist, but there *is* some hidden force that directs people's lives. It's an evil force, not a good one. I was prettier than my sister, a better student, taller too. She took after Papa. But the men pursued her, and for some reason, ignored me. When she lived, the telephone never stopped ringing. A day didn't go by without her getting some invitation. She left behind whole stacks of love letters, a regular archive. My affairs—if they took place at all—were brief and always filled with misunderstandings that embittered everybody. Mark came into my life after my sister's death and I had the eerie feeling that it was she who had kept the men away from me. This was silly nonsense but all kinds of crazy notions flit through one's brain. When Mark did what he did and had to flee, I got the strange feeling that my sister's ghost—or whatever you might call it—had revived after the shock of death and that she had resumed her silent war against me. Deep inside we are all rooted in the Middle Ages or maybe even in prehistoric times. This Treitler is actually the only man outside of Mark who is in love with me. But he's old enough to be my father, in his late fifties if not sixty. And I'd sooner let myself be hacked to pieces than marry him. No one has ever repelled me like he does. Nor can I understand what he sees in me. There couldn't be two more opposite types than we are. Why am I telling you all this? It's not entirely without a reason. I want a favor from you. You are my last straw."

"I am ready to do everything for you."

"Why, of all things? Because I am buying you a glass of coffee?"

"Not because of that. But—"

"It doesn't matter. Once you hear what I want, you'll have a change of heart and I'll understand. The story is this. It's already clear to me that I won't be leaving on that certificate in the near future. There were several other young men before you and each of them brought his own complications. I'm convinced that this Margolis not only doesn't want to help me but actually wants to place obstacles in my path. Even if he did want to help me, it would all be too late. I'll be perfectly honest with you—Mark left me pregnant."

Stefa uttered these last words as if in a single breath. Just then the waiter came up.

Stefa ordered two tomato soups, rolls and butter, and coffee. After the waiter left, she said:

"Oh, you can still blush. That's good. I had assumed this was no longer possible these days. You're still young. I'm five years older than you and in my case, it's as if I were twenty years older. He didn't seduce me. You might even say that I seduced him. I desperately wanted to have his child and when it became clear that he would have to flee and we might never see each other again, I demanded that he leave me his child. You probably can't understand such things because you're a male. My parents don't know a thing about it. If they ever found out it would cause a terrible row. They're so old-fashioned—you might even say backward—they could be living two centuries ago. It would kill them both as surely as it's day now. I'm not the hysterical sort but I've thought seriously about killing them both and then doing away with myself. After what they went through with my sister, I can't subject them to a new blow. I still hope that Mark and I can be reunited. Even if he came back to Poland and stood trial it wouldn't be the end of it. He didn't murder anybody, merely forged a piece of paper. Nor would I want to destroy his child. My parents still nurse hopes that I'll provide them with a half-dozen grandchildren. What they need with grandchildren only God knows. The situation of the Jews here is desperate. The Poles have had quite enough of us and I can see their side of it. We've lived here for eight hundred years and have remained strangers. Their God is not our God, their history is not our history. Most of us can't even speak a proper Polish. One time I watched a huge Zionist demonstration with blue and white flags and Stars of David and the whole falderal. They stopped the trolleys and shouted slogans in Hebrew or Yiddish. The Gentiles stood around staring as if at a freak show. Just the same my parents want grandchildren. If I choose not to destroy them and myself as well, I must go through with this phony marriage ceremony regardless whether we can leave at once or must first go through the thousands of formalities. So long as I bear someone's name the humiliation won't seem as great to them. Your soup is getting cold."

"May I ask what month you are in?"

"Surely in the fourth and maybe even the fifth. Don't look so alarmed. It was I that sinned, not you."

"I'm not alarmed. . . . You're not showing at all . . . not even a trace."

"Soon it will show. I lace my corset so tightly now I can barely breathe."

Four

1

AT FIRST IT SEEMED THAT PILSUD-
ski's coup would be bloodless. Pilsudski the marshal and
Wojciechowski the president met on some bridge, and after Pilsudski called the other a name, Wojciechowski capitulated. That
was what Mrs. Alpert had heard on the radio and that's what she
had passed along to me. But presently the shooting commenced
and news came of dead and wounded. People had already paid
with their heads or been maimed. A civil war threatened. It was
in the interests of many elements that a blood bath erupt. The
Ruthenians and White Russians who, following the Brest-Litovsk
Treaty, had been left under Polish rule awaited the opportunity
to break away from Poland. Russia had lost the war with Poland
in 1920 but by now she already possessed a strong army and
she wouldn't have minded regaining her lost territories or simply seizing all Poland and instituting her order there. The Germans would have been delighted to take back Upper Silesia.
The Communists at the Writers' Club whispered conspiratorially
and held clandestine meetings. Zinoviev and Kamenev were
plotting the world revolution. They had their functionaries in
Poland who came to the Writers' Club with their directives.
Nor was there a lack in Poland of those eager to exploit this
opportunity to beat Jews. I wanted to do what Jews had done
for two thousand years—flee or hide somewhere until the
danger passed. But there was no place to run or hide. My enemies were Jewish youths, fledgling writers who lauded the

Russian revolution, already glorified Comrade Stalin, wrote
odes to the Cheka and Comrade Dzerzhinski, and demanded
death for all rabbis, priests, bourgeois, Zionists, and even Socialists who didn't follow the Moscow line.

I was shocked to see how bloodthirsty Jewish boys and girls
had become. Two thousand years of exile, ghetto, and Torah
hadn't created a biological Jew. All it took was a few pamphlets
and speeches to erase everything the books of morals had tried
to imbue in us throughout the generations. Within me asceti-
cism warred with the urge to give in to all the passions. I reminded myself a hundred times a day that all was vanity; yet a
friendly girlish glance or a compliment about my writing would
be enough to arouse me. This inner lack of consistency both
astounded and shamed me.

I lay in bed in my room holding a book of the sort used by
storekeepers to mark down their debts and credits and a pencil,
ready once and for all to take an accounting of the world, to
come to some firm conclusion and commence a life based on
my convictions so that my conduct could serve as an example
(or a maxim as Kant put it). On a chair nearby I had placed a
history of philosophy and a number of other books which
might help me restore order to my disturbed spirit. From Bresler's Library I had borrowed a collection of Tolstoi's moral stories and essays, Spinoza's *Ethics*, Kant's *Critique of Practical Understanding*, Schopenhauer's *The World as Will and Idea*,
Nietzsche's *Thus Spake Zarathustra*, a book by the pacifist For-
ster (I've forgotten its title), Payot's *The Education of the Will*,
and several books on hypnotism, autosuggestion (Coué, Charles
Baudouin), and who knows what else—all of them works that
touched on the essentials. I had even bought *The Path of the
Righteous,* by Rabbi Moshe Haim Luzzatto, and the Book of Deu-
teronomy, which I had considered the wisest work ever created
by man. I was ready to reappraise all values even as I heard
shooting outside and was involved in an adventure that could
bring me only grief.

What didn't I scribble into this account book that I had

bought from a pushcart of remnants? Regimens for behavior, themes for stories, novels, plays; rules of physical and spiritual hygiene I had learned from this same Payot; all kinds of aphorisms which might have been my own or dimmed memories of something I had read and forgotten; sketches that I couldn't finish since they lacked plots; and nothing less but a rewrite of the Ten Commandments. Bits of these revised commandments (I think they grew to twelve under my direction) I still recall to this day. "Do not kill or exploit the animal, don't eat its flesh, don't flail its hide, don't force it to do things against its nature. . . ."

To "Thou shalt not kill," I added: "Control the birth of man and beast—He who said, 'Thou shalt not kill,' should have also said: 'Thou shalt not overly procreate.' . . ."

To "Thou shalt not commit adultery," I added that no marriage should last longer than fifteen years. Right next to this piece of audacity I drew a creature with the antlers of a deer, the scales and fins of a fish, and the legs of a rooster. Contemplating what I knew of history and my own nature, I had already come to the conclusion that human beings are in constant need of adventure, change, risk, danger, challenge. The fear of boredom is as great as and often greater than the fear of death. But is there a base for ethics in the face of that biological necessity? Aren't all commandments just wishful thinking? Can there be as much adventure in curbing the emotions as in letting them have their way? Can there be as much hazard in building as in destroying? Can man ever learn to indulge in the whims and excitements of his nature without hurting other people and animals? Many times I had decided that this was impossible, but I kept on returning to this problem of all problems which has been bothering me from my childhood. I still hoped against hope that science, art, technological advance, and permanent study of how to have fun without doing evil to others may replace the lust for murder, rape, treachery, revenge, and all the other destructive passions for which mankind pays such a terrible price. I was dreaming not only of a new philosophy, a new religion, a new social order, but also of new ways of amusing people and giving them the tension which they must have to be themselves.

Whole pages of the book were filled with figures. Since my job as proofreader of the literary publication wasn't secure and I was liable at any day to be left without an income, I tried to calculate the minimum amount I would need to avoid starving to death, sleeping in the streets, or asking my brother's help. Now that he had the job with the *Forward* he offered me money at every opportunity but I was resolved not to accept it. I had seen so much sponging by the young writers at the Club that I had sworn to myself never to seek help from anybody. I figured out how much starch, fat, and protein one needed to survive and how much this would cost. As for vitamins, I probably didn't know anything about them or didn't believe in them.

The net in which I entangled myself consisted of the fact that I had promised to marry Stefa, in name only, of course. Nevertheless, I intended to stand under the wedding canopy with her and even sign documents in such a way that her parents would be taken in. Thus, even if she didn't manage to make it to Palestine in time it would mean that she had a husband and a father for her child—at least to the neighbors and distant relatives. The whole scheme was insane since the child would be born some four and a half months hence and no one would be duped into believing me its father. By this time already, I realized that in moments of desperation people forsake all reason. The question merely was why I had agreed to this.

The answer was that first of all, I was desperate myself—unable to sleep nights for fear of the draft. Secondly, I somehow couldn't refuse such an elegant and educated young lady. And thirdly, I yearned for some of the suspense found in the works of Balzac, Victor Hugo, Tolstoi, Dostoevski, Flaubert, Alexander Dumas, and Strindberg. Yiddish and Hebrew literature both suffered from a lack of suspense. Everything in them centered around some yeshivah student who had gone astray, sought worldly knowledge, then suffered the consequences at the yeshivah or at his in-laws'. But I had already grasped the fact that suspense was the essence of both life and art. Mere description wasn't enough. What was needed was tangled situations and genuine dilemmas and crises. A work of fiction had to draw in its readers. In later years the suspense in my life and in my writing fused in such fashion that I often didn't know where one began and the other ended.

The maid, Marila, knocked on my door to announce that I was wanted on the telephone. I asked her who was calling and she countered.

"A pretty young miss."

2

It was Gina calling. I was supposed to come to her for dinner that night and naturally, to sleep over. I was reconciled to the fact that Gina would talk about death. She often spoke in the tone of one gravely ill and whose days are numbered. I never took her words seriously since she often interspersed these conversations with plans leading months and years ahead. She intended to collaborate with me on a book, a play. I had long since perceived that talk about her death stimulated her sexually. Often in the nights she extracted my promise to attend her funeral and demanded declarations of how and with whom I would spend the time immediately following her death. She went into details that struck me as mad, but it was obvious that they aroused her desire. Even then I knew that one could not question the emotions and that the division between sanity and insanity was remarkably slender. Within every brain and nervous system lurked cells of madness and criminality. Well, but ever since I had moved out of her place I had been haunted by the suspicion that Gina was really sick. She had lost her appetite and lost weight. Her complexion had turned yellowish. She had begun to address me in a strange mixture of irony and maternal concern. She often reminded me that I had promised to say the

Kaddish over her even though I had broken the laws of Jewishness and had communicated to her my outlandish theory concerning religious protest.

Everything had grown remarkably complicated, but I needed
these complications and sought others. At the Writers' Club I
met one of those girls who were called in jest "literary supple-
ments." They came to the Club to partake of the literary and
journalistic gossip, to strike up acquaintance with the writers
and launch illicit affairs with them. At times it came out that
these girls—there were some married women among them as
well—wrote poems in Yiddish or in Polish. Some were Zionis-
tically inclined and wanted to go to Palestine; others were Communist sympathizers who one day might cross illegally into the
Soviet Union. Some came from wealthy families, and the literary
Don Juans got small loans from them. The management of the
Writers' Club made frequent resolutions to bar these women. It
was voted that no one but members and their wives or husbands would be admitted. A number of special guest cards were
printed and a woman was stationed by the door to keep strangers out. But somehow it was impossible to get rid of these hangers-on. They claimed to love Yiddish literature, they admired
the writers' talents. Some offered to translate the writers' works
into Polish. Although the Yiddish actors had their own union,
many actors and actresses were standing guests of the Writers'
Club—painters and sculptors as well as potential producers of
Yiddish films who were merely waiting for the right screenplay
and money. The proprietor of the buffet and the waitresses often extended credit to these uninvited guests.

Miss Sabina was small and plump, with a high bosom, a short
neck, a hooked nose, full lips, and a pair of brown eyes that
reflected the merriment of those who have little to hope for.
She made jokes, smoked cigarettes, told spicy anecdotes. She
owned a Yiddish typewriter and the writers occasionally gave
her a manuscript to type. She worked in a library part-time and
supported a widowed mother and two younger brothers. Sabina
claimed to be my age but she looked older. She dressed poorly
and with a touch of the Bohemian. Someone had told me that

she had been the sweetheart of an old writer with one lung and one kidney who had been impotent besides. He had just recently died.

Sabina talked a lot and told me stories that seemed to be lies, but I subsequently became convinced that for all their strangeness they were true. The impotent old writer had had a whole harem of mistresses. He spent every penny he earned on them. He had indulged in all kinds of quirks and perversions. He slept days (after swallowing enormous quantities of sleeping pills) and stayed up nights. He had stopped writing fiction in his last years and lived from the one *feuilleton* he published every Friday. He would write the piece at the last minute, at the same time consuming so many cigarettes that once a dense smoke began issuing from his window and the policeman outside called the fire department. L. M. Preshburger, as I call him here, had lost the talent or the urge to write, but he had concentrated all his art in his tongue. He would repose on the couch, smoke, drink, and utter words that evoked amazement, shock, and awe from his female admirers. The doctors had long since given him up—he lived in defiance of all the laws of medicine.

Sabina liked to walk, unlike Gina, who had stopped taking walks since she complained of pains in her legs. Sabina would accompany me for miles. After Pilsudski became the dictator, we went to see the damaged buildings where the fighting had taken place. We bought rolls from a street vendor and munched them as we strolled along. Sabina had told me her life story in all the details. She was descended from rabbis and merchants. Her father had died of typhoid fever leaving nothing but a large apartment of six rooms plus a kitchen. Because of the rent control the rent was cheap and her mother rented rooms to elderly bachelors and cooked lunch for them. One time, the mother rented a room to a female cousin, a rabbi's daughter who turned out to be a Soviet agent. One night the house was surrounded by police, the cousin was arrested and sentenced to death. However, the Communists managed to free her and smuggled her into Russia where she became a highly placed official in some ministry and a leader in the Comintern. Beside her passion for communism, this cousin had a wild appetite for men. It later came out that she had had doings with all the old bachelors in the apartment, and following her arrest, one of them (after learning that he hadn't been her only lover) attempted suicide.

Yiddish literature had remained naïve and primitive and even its radicalism was provincial, but from Sabina's lips poured tales of high adventure. After nearly two thousand years of ghettos and extreme segregation from the Gentile world, there had been awakened in the emancipated Jew an enormous yearning for worldliness coupled with a boundless energy. In Poland, this transformation had evolved later than in the other lands, but with incredible rapidity. Yiddish literature with its sentimentality and slow pace wasn't ready for such a transformation. The same writers who told astounding stories at the Writers' Club trembled the moment they took pen in hand lest, God forbid, they slip into melodrama. Among the Communist writers it had become fashionable to fling mud at the *shtetl* and to contend that its time had passed. But even this they did in provincial fashion. From reading the world literature I had realized that the Gentile writers too lacked the perception to describe the epoch in which they lived. They were also rooted in a literary tradition which discouraged them from writing what their eyes saw.

There had appeared such works as *Jean Christophe,* by Romain Rolland, and *The Magic Mountain,* by Thomas Mann. I had translated this latter work into Yiddish and I had had the opportunity to analyze its construction so to say "from the inside." Both these works represented long essays spiced with description. Neither Jean Christophe nor Hans Castorp were living beings but mouthpieces through which the authors spoke. Both books lacked the suspense and vitality that great literature evokes in a reader even if he is a simple soul. These were works for intellectuals seeking a purpose, a sum total, a cross section of culture, an indication for the future, and other such fine things that no art (and actually no philosophy) is capable of supplying. These were works for critics, not readers. They bored me, but I was afraid to say so since all so-called aesthetes had seized on them as if they were treasures. Already then I realized that there was emerging in the world the kind of reader who sought in a book not the synthetic but the analytical. They dissected the books they read and the deader the corpse, the more successful the autopsy. I liked much better Thomas Mann's *Buddenbrooks* and Romain Rolland's *Colas Breugnon*, works full of the zest of life.

3

I had written a story and submitted it to the editor of the magazine of which I was the proofreader. He promised to read it and if it pleased him, to publish it. After a while he informed me that he had read the story and even though he found it flawed, he would print it. I asked him what these flaws were and after some deliberation he said that the piece was too pessimistic, that it lacked problems, and that the story was negative and almost anti-Semitic. Why write about thieves and whores when there were so many decent Jewish men and devoted Jewish wives? If such a thing were translated into Polish and a Gentile read it, he might conclude that all Jews were depraved. A Yiddish writer, my editor argued, was honor-bound to stress the good in our people, the lofty and sacred. He had to be an eloquent defender of the Jews, not their defamer.

I didn't have the opportunity to answer him since the telephone rang at that moment and he stayed on it for a long time, but his comments irked me. Why did a story have to be optimistic? What sort of criterion was this? And what did it mean that it "lacked problems"? Wasn't the essence of the existence of the world and of the human species one enormous problem? And why must a Yiddish writer be a defender of his people? Was it the Yiddish writer's obligation to conduct an eternal dialogue with the anti-Semites? Could a work written in this vein possess any artistic value? The Scriptures on which I have been raised didn't flatter the Jews. Quite the contrary, they constantly spoke of their transgressions. Even Moses didn't emerge pure. I didn't have too high an opinion of this editor and his contentions. I had observed his politicking. Now he was a Communist and now an anti-Communist. Now he was for Zionism, now against it. He published and praised bad things by known writers and often rejected good things by unknown writers. Might was right always and everywhere—in literature, in the universities, in the community office that appointed rabbis, in the Vatican, even among those who demanded justice for the exploited and oppressed. As soon as two people met, one assumed the dominant role.

In America, a faction had formed among Yiddish writers called Die Junge (The Young). In their little magazines they poured vitriol upon "the old." The Yiddish newspaper publishers in Warsaw had engaged persons of little taste to be critics. My friend Aaron Zeitlin told me that some vandal of an editor had permitted essays written by his father, Hillel Zeitlin, to be altered, cut, and often corrupted. Hillel Zeitlin was a deep thinker, a cabalist, and an exceptionally capable journalist besides. God had granted power to every bully to annoy and destroy animals and people as well. I noted with sorrow that I was no exception. In my chance opportunities to write reviews I had already denigrated writers whose works had displeased me. No matter how weak one was there was always someone weaker upon whom he might vent his fangs and claws.

I managed to do this with Gina. The more she was drawn to me, the more drawn was I to others. Although I felt no love toward her (who knows what love is anyway), I started up with the maid at the house where I boarded. Marila and I had already kissed and made clandestine plans for me to come to her in the kitchen when the household was asleep. I had also promised to go through with the wedding ceremony with Miss Stefa, an act which Gina would consider treacherous. Stefa had sent off a long letter to her fiancé and everything depended upon his reply.

I had become a thief not for money but for love. I had discovered how easy it was to inveigle oneself into a woman's heart. I had even tried to start something with Stefa. I did it all with the quiet desperation of one who is aware of how senseless his deeds are. I often felt as if I were two people—one young, full of ambition, passion, and hope; the other a melancholic indulging in a final frolic before being lowered into the grave. Oddly enough, all the Jewish funerals wound beneath Gina's window while all the Catholic passed beneath mine on Zamenhof Street. I constantly heard the dirges of priests, and sometimes Chopin's Funeral March as well. Each time I glanced outside I caught glimpses of a coffin bedecked with garlands (real or tin), a priest in a cassock with lace at the sleeves and a miter, men carrying halberds and lanterns, and women with black-veiled faces and hats draped in crepe. The female Jewish mourners shouted their laments, clawed their cheeks, and howled in chorus while the Gentiles bowed their heads silently. Death notices plastered all the walls, and the newspapers were filled with obituaries. Every second, people passed into eternity. But what was the eternity? So long as I couldn't find the answer to this, all I did was sheer futility.

Was this state of mind hypochondria or a true foreboding of death? I often went to sleep with the certainty that I would never get up any more. When I went to buy razor blades and the storekeeper asked if I wanted two blades or five, I always answered: "Two."

I still groped in books hoping for an answer, but I knew beforehand that none would be forthcoming. I even became disappointed in psychic research. The dead who supposedly materialized at séances spoke as foolish as the living. One had to be an idiot to believe in their authenticity. The philosophers' commentaries all led to the same conclusion: We neither know nor could know the essence of things. I believed in God anyhow, but there wasn't, nor probably would there ever be, any proof that He preferred Gandhi to Hitler, Stalin, or Genghis Khan.

I often heard people say: I believe in Zionism, in socialism, in a better world, in the endurance of Jews, in the power of literature, in democracy, and in many other such beliefs. But on what did they base their faiths? I could never forget the twenty million people who had perished in the war almost before my very eyes, this one for Russia, that one for Germany, some for the Revolution, others for the Counter-Revolution, this one while capturing some village, the other while retreating from the same village. Where were they, all those murderers and all those murdered? Did they share the same paradise? Were they roasting in hell together?

The telephone rang and Marila came to announce that it was for me. She smirked and winked. I had already given her the right to be jealous. Her cheeks were red, her eyes blue. They reflected both strength and curiosity. It was Stefa calling. I barely recognized her voice. She sounded hoarse and choking, like someone gravely ill.

She said: "Something has happened. Come right over! Don't leave me waiting. When will you be here?"

"What's happened?" I asked.

"Nothing good. Come at once!"

And she hung up the receiver.

I started right off for her house. I wasn't too concerned whether the news was good or bad. I needed momentarily to forget myself with something. What could have happened? Had someone in the family taken ill? Had someone died? Hurrying along, it struck me how light I felt. From not eating I had lost weight. I would wake up in the middle of the night and my brain would be churning like a machine. I suffered from nightmares. Sometimes my fantasies evoked laughter even in myself. I had conquered not only earth but all the planets in all the galaxies. God had endowed me with powers He possibly didn't possess Himself. Through some miracle I conducted affairs with all the beauties of all the ages. Since time and space were merely points of view and even existence itself was, as Salomon Maimon and the neo-Kantians clearly brought out, a category of thinking, perhaps miracles were more real than the laws of nature. Either everything that had ever been existed or nothing existed. You could roll back time like the hands of a watch. Since the world of deed and matter was energy and perhaps spirit, all impossibilities were nothing more than temporary inhibitions. I often felt myself being transported within seconds from depression to exultation and vice versa. I consulted the psychiatric textbooks and was fully cognizant of the symptoms.

I rang Isidore Janovsky's bell and Stefa opened the door instantly, as if she had been waiting for me on the other side of the threshold. I barely recognized her. In the few days I hadn't seen her she had grown pale, emaciated, sallow. She looked disheveled, like someone who had just left her sickbed. She wore an old bathrobe and frayed slippers. She gazed at me a moment numbly as if she didn't recognize me, then seized my wrist and led me to her room. She virtually dragged me along.

Stefa's room was in disarray as if she had been packing to go on a trip. Dresses, underwear, and stockings lay scattered across the floor along with books, magazines, and papers. The bed was unmade and toothbrushes, vials of perfume, jars of salves, and toothpaste lay strewn over the sheet. For a long while Stefa stared at me with the disoriented gaze of one who primed herself to say something but has forgotten what it was she wanted to say. Finally, she blurted:

"He got married, that idiot! Ran away with some whore from England! Nothing is left me but to die!"

"How do you know this?"

"Eh? I know. I have a girl friend there and she telegraphed me. He is no longer in Palestine either. Left with her for England or the devil knows where. Maybe India."

"In that case, he is really a criminal."

"Eh? A charlatan, a madman, a scoundrel. We shared a great love but now he has killed it. It's my fault, mine! My father was right. He needed but one look at him to know what he is. But he bedazzled me, hypnotized me. Well, what's the difference? I must die and that would be a minor tragedy. That would actually be a release for me from all my misfortunes. But I simply can't pass such a blow onto my parents. They lost one daughter, and now the other? Unless I took an ax and chopped off their heads. Yes, that's it!"

"No, Miss Stefa, we are still Jews."

"Eh? What kind of Jews are we? Maybe you are a Jew but what does my Jewishness consist of? I never wanted to be one. I was as ashamed of it as if of a scurf. He, Mark, ran from it too. But after he forged that promissory note and had to flee, he ran straight to Palestine. I helped him with my money, otherwise he would be rotting in jail this very minute. He had lost forty thousand zlotys to a colonel who threatened him with a revolver. That other was a drunk and a degenerate. What about your promise? Are you still ready to go through with that phony marriage with me? I have no more reason to go to Palestine. But what shall I do with my bastard?"

And Stefa indicated her belly.

"We can still go to Palestine," I said without thinking.

"What will we do there? Yes, so be it. We'll find some kind of work. All I must do is wait till my parents die which I hope will be soon. My mother is sick from head to toe. Nor will my father drag around for long once she is gone. All they ever wanted was a little satisfaction from their children—some satisfaction they got! Why Jewish parents require so much satisfaction from their children is something I'll never understand. They don't have lives of their own. All their hopes are pinned on children and grandchildren. A crazy race. A sick race. Maybe it's not too late for an abortion. I'm in my fifth month. If I should get blood poisoning it wouldn't be any great loss either."

"No, Miss Stefa, don't do that to your parents!"

"Don't play the saint with me. You're not so holy yourself. All men without exception are the worst kind of egotists. They'd trample on corpses to gain their merest whim. Why would you want to do this? You can be frank with me."

"There is still the chance it might save me from the draft."

"No, not even the slightest chance. I told you you'd have to get papers, but so far you haven't done a thing. Without documents you won't get a passport. I offered to pay your expenses to go to your father's town so that you could obtain an excerpt from the permanent population register, but you kept putting it off. Each time you made up a different excuse. The *starosta* here in Warsaw is in no hurry to issue passports to someone like you who is due for conscription. Especially a discounted passport. Everything proceeds at a snail's pace with these bureaucrats. Don't interrupt me. Somehow, you're just like Mark. You're completely lacking in will. A portion of your brain is paralyzed. You told me about a woman who is twice your age. What is there between you two? Are you in love with her? Is it that you can't bear to leave her? If that's the case, why are you wasting my time? One charlatan is enough—I don't need two. Give me an honest answer."

"If I'm conscripted, I'd have to leave her anyhow. She is sick besides."

"What's wrong with her? Well, it's all the same. You won't be conscripted and even if you are, you'll soon be discharged. You can as much be a soldier as I can be a rabbi. I'll give you a thousand zlotys to marry me, then after my bastard is born you can divorce me."

"I won't take any money from you."

"What is it with you—a sort of philanthropy?"

"I want to do it for you."

"The situation is such that I can't be in Warsaw when the child comes. I'll have to go away somewhere and I'll let them know about the child a few months later so that they can nurse the illusion that everything is in order. God cursed the female gender. He is an even greater antifeminist than Otto Weininger and Strindberg. You don't look like an actor, but you must try to play the role that the fiction has become a reality for you. I'll tell you something: After you came here the first time, my father said: 'This young man appeals to me more than that rogue Mark. I wish you were marrying him for real.' I laughed at the time but fate has a way of playing funny tricks. Are you ready to go away with me for a few weeks? We have to arrange it so that the farce is carried through one hundred per cent."

"I hope I can get leave from the magazine."

"Eh? You must know that you'd be saving the lives of my

parents. True, not for long, but it's a *mitzva* anyhow. As you see I know the word *mitzva*. I'm not a complete ignoramus. I'm in such a spot now that anything can happen. You're yet liable to become a widower a day or a week after the wedding. I want to ask you something, but answer me truthfully. Do you love anyone? Did you ever love anyone? What about that woman who could be your mother—do you love her?"

"Yes, but—"

"What *buts* are there? Where you love there are no *buts.*"

"The but is that I can love someone else too."

"Get him—a yeshivah boy and he talks like a regular Don Juan. How many lovers have you had so far?"

"Only the one, Gina."

"At least you're honest, or so it would seem. Mark was a liar, a dreadful liar, a pathological liar. All the while he was writing me those burning love letters—they sizzled between my fingers—he was selling himself to some snob from England, probably a spinster that no one else wanted. If people can be such liars then life isn't worth a fig. You told me you were interested in writing and all that. Why are people such liars? What's the reason for it?"

"The reason is that laws are formed that are lies from the very start. Your Mark might have loved you and six other women at the same time. He couldn't sign a contract to love you all your life. He obviously had others all the while. I only wonder why you can't understand this."

"I do understand it, I understand, all right. I can understand everything—every thief, every murderer, every degenerate. But I can only love one person. From the day I met him I loved only him, thought only of him, and all my dreams were of him only."

"It's not his fault that his nature is different from yours."

"No, it's not his fault. You don't know what love is, that's why it's easy for you to defend him. Why you would want to play out this farce is something I can't understand either, but when one is drowning, he'll clutch at any straw and to me you are that straw. Go to my father and tell him you want to marry me. We won't do it here in Warsaw. We'll go somewhere else. We have relatives here and people who consider themselves our friends and I can't play out this comedy in front of a whole crew. You say you have a brother here. Someone told me he's a very talented writer."

"Yes, that's true."

"You'll have to keep this a secret from him. From your parents too. We'll go to Danzig and hold the ceremony there. The next day you'll come back to Warsaw as if nothing had happened. I'll stay there, as the saying goes, to drain the bitter cup. Only one hope is left to me—that I die in labor and he, my son, dies with me. You still believe in God?"

"Yes, I still do."

"If He exists, then He is a comedian. This whole world is one big joke. Has any philosopher or theologian yet described God as a comedian?"

"It says in the Scriptures: 'He that sitteth in the heavens shall laugh.' "

"Everything is in the Bible and if it's not in the Bible, it's in Shakespeare. Go in to my father. I have to laugh too."

And Stefa erupted in a laugh, then her face grew quickly grim.

4

I had asked for a leave of absence from the magazine and it had been granted at once. I promptly regretted having done so for the editor's tone seemed to imply that the magazine could get along without a proofreader. To begin with, I overlooked many errors. Secondly, the editor and the writers could read their own proofs. The readers in the provinces could no longer afford to pay for their subscriptions and the postcards dispatched to dun them cost more than what they owed. A dreadful poverty reigned over the villages. The young people all strove to go

abroad but the consulates of all the nations seemed to have conspired to grant no more visas to Jews. It was easier for Polish
peasants to obtain them. There was a need abroad for coal min-
ers, farm workers, heavy laborers, not for study-house striplings
who took to commerce or tried to enter the universities. Besides, many of the young Jews were infected with Marxism and
communism and they instigated the local workers to strike. A
number of leftist-oriented Jewish youth had smuggled themselves into Soviet Russia, but rumors spread that they had been
imprisoned or sent to slave camps in Siberia. In any case, they
were never heard from again. The Trotsky opposition had already emerged in Russia and the Party and the population were
being purged of deviators, both left and right. A number of
Trotskyites who had fled the Soviet Union to Poland told tales
of horror. All the prisons were jammed with political prisoners,
people were dragged from their beds in the nights. Hundreds
of thousands of kulaks and plain peasants had been exiled en
masse to Siberia. At the Writers' Club, Isaac Deutscher, the editor of a Yiddish Stalinist magazine, was suddenly transformed
into a Trotskyite and published an attack against Stalin. The
Stalinists at the Club labeled him a fascist, an enemy of the proletariat, a counterrevolutionary, and an imperialist lackey.

I knew this Isaac Deutscher and often had heated debates
with him. He had called me the very same names with which
he was now being assailed. He told me with brutal frankness
that on the day of the revolution there could be no neutrals.
Whoever didn't line up on the side of the masses would be
treated as an enemy of the people. He, Isaac, was an expert on
Marxist literature, a 100 per cent materialist. Compared to me,
he was wealthy and worldly. He had a well-paying job on the
Jewish-Polish paper *Nasz Przeglad.* He came from Cracow and
spoke an excellent Polish. Nor did he tremble at the thought of
the draft as I did. When his time came, he went off and soon
earned corporal's stripes even though—as I suspected it—he
disseminated the Communist propaganda among the soldiers.

To return to Stefa. It happened like this. That day Stefa asked
me to go in to her father and ask for his daughter's hand, Isi-

dore Janovsky had gone off somewhere, I believe to his ex-partner who had been bankrupted along with him. I was supposed to phone Stefa the next day but when I rang, no one answered. I called again and again and it turned out that there was no one at home, not even the maid. This seemed to me puzzling. Mrs. Janovsky, a sick woman, hardly ever left the house. Had some tragedy occurred? Had Stefa tried to commit suicide? I went there and knocked on the door but no one came. Another day went by and still no one answered the phone. I had taken leave from the magazine and had risked losing my job because of this phony marriage, but my bride had vanished along with my prospective in-laws.

I stayed awake nights trying to arrive at some solution of the puzzle but I knew that no brain can foresee the surprises life can invent. Almost a week went by and still no one came to the door or answered the phone. I sought out the janitor and asked him what had happened.

He said: "Seems they went away somewhere."

"All of them?"

"Seems so."

And he turned abruptly away from me to talk to the mailman who had brought a registered letter. The janitor appeared to me to be acting in a suspicious manner and I harked back to the volumes of Sherlock Holmes and Max Spitzkopf I had read as a boy. I took a walk down the street. I had sought suspense, and fate had provided it to me. Stefa had spoken about murdering her parents and then killing herself and in my imagination I pictured the family lying in a puddle of blood.

Stefa had marked down my address in her notebook and the suspicion of the crime was yet liable to fall on me. The police might somehow discover that I had been planning to marry her. I pictured myself in the courtroom as the prosecutor described my depraved character. I had lived with a woman twice my age, I had tried to get out of serving my country, I was about to marry fictitiously the murdered Stefa. My writings were brought into court and the prosecutor showed them to be rife with sadism, eroticism, demonology. One of the witnesses for the prosecution was Sabina. She admitted in court that I had made love to her. The prosecutor asked her:

"Is it true that your cousin who lived with you was a Soviet spy?"

"Yes, it's true."

And I was condemned to death.

The day was warm and Leszno Street was crowded with pedestrians, mostly women. At the Writers' Club I had often heard women speak about spring fever. They all agreed that spring in Warsaw could make one crazy with longing. Today was just such a day. The air smelled of lilac blossoms, cool breezes from the Vistula, and the Praga woods. The scents of the fields and orchards lying around Warsaw blended with the odors of newly baked bread, rolls, and bagels, roasted coffee, and milk fresh from the udder. The sky loomed clear and perfectly cloudless above the rooftops and although it was still early in the day, it reflected the deep night-blue of those climates where the sun doesn't set during the summer months. The women, looking elegant in their new dresses and hats, carried bunches of flowers and parcels bound in colored ribbon. They stretched in swarms, just as during Rosh Hashanah when they gather at the stream to cast their sins upon the waters. I looked each one over and they looked back with frivolous glances and something like silent consent.

Suddenly, I saw Isidore Janovsky approaching in a long black coat and matching derby. He took mincing steps and leaned on his cane. He apparently didn't recognize me since he looked straight at me without a change of expression.

I stopped him and he seemed to come awake. I said: "Mr. Janovsky, how are you?"

He hesitated a long while, then said: "I know you. You're the young man with the certificate."

"Yes, right."

Isidore Janovsky wavered again. "Stefa no longer needs a certificate."

"May I ask why not?"

"Stefa is getting married this week."

I felt myself blush. I wanted to ask to whom, but all I said was:

"Well, congratulations."

"Thank you."

And Janovsky placed his cane a step forward.

I got out of his way and he went past me, the father of a bride and proud in-law-to-be. I stood there and stared after him. Then I headed for the Writers' Club.

Five

1

FATE PLAYED WITH ME AND I PLAYED along. I could see clearly that it was leading me to disaster but I told myself that I was ready for this. Everyone lost to it anyhow. The mystery regarding Stefa had been cleared up. She had married Leon Treitler, a wealthy man, a father of two married daughters, a landlord, a partner in a textile factory in Lodz. Leon Treitler owned a villa in Michalin, a resort on the Otwock line, and all the while I had been trying to reach Stefa, the whole family had been visiting there. Soon after the wedding the couple left on a trip around the world. They were scheduled to return only after the Days of Awe. How this change had suddenly occurred was something I could not fathom. Did Treitler know that she was carrying another man's child and had forgiven her? Or had she tried to deceive him?

None of this had anything to do with me now. The Palestine Bureau had withdrawn my certificate and it appeared that I was fated either to serve in the army or commit suicide. I lived in a state of suspension. I both played with fate and at the same time observed the game, or kibitzed, as they called it at the Writers' Club.

Following my leave of absence I was given my proofreader's job back but both the magazine and the publishing house that backed it hovered on the brink of bankruptcy. The authors had rebelled against me and issued an ultimatum that if I overlooked any more errors they wouldn't contribute any more articles. They accused me of spite and indifference. I promised fervently and even took a solemn oath to be more careful, but things deteriorated from week to week. I read without knowing what I was reading. If I made an effort and managed to grasp their meaning, the writings seemed to me trivial and false. The reviewers would praise a book but I couldn't figure out why. When they condemned one, the condemnation seemed without basis too, often rife with personal antagonism. The poetry was full of rhetoric and banality. Many poets only strove to please the Communist party leaders and their cultural activists, who no matter how much they were fawned upon could never be appeased. The stories struck me as boring and written in one vein. Although the number of industrial workers among Jews in Poland was comparatively small—most Polish Jews being merchants, brokers, cheder teachers, and employed in various handicrafts—the authors kept writing about Jewish factory workers and even peasants, a species that hardly existed.

Correcting this trash became for me a physical torment. I suffered headaches from reading and sometimes the lines began to leapfrog over one another or turn green, gold, or fiery and I feared going blind. Everything with me proceeded awkwardly and I clearly saw that this state of affairs was no mere aggregation of accidents but part of a somber design.

Gina began to ail and hint that her months or weeks were numbered. I begged her to see a doctor but she found a new excuse not to each time. I watched with alarm as she grew thinner, weaker, unable to eat. Her sexual urges had dissipated and were replaced by a kind of maternal or sisterly affection toward me. She began to act modest around me and wouldn't let me see her naked. She'd lie in bed with me and not utter a word. Lying beside her, I lost my power of speech too. Although I had never mentioned a word to her about Stefa, I had the suspicion that she somehow knew about her and bore me a grudge. But how could she have learned about it? Unless her late grandmother had told her.

Spring had passed and the heat waves started. My brother Joshua had gone to Svider for the summer along with his wife and children, Yasha and Josele, or Joziek, as his mother called him. My brother had rented a villa from the Yiddish writer Alter Kacyzna. Other Yiddish writers and journalists were also vacationing in the area. From earliest childhood I had felt a powerful desire to be with my brother. Now that I had begun to write I was anxious to show him my work and consult with him. My brother was more than willing to help me but I was ashamed to face him both on account of my dealings with women and because of my writing.

I also knew that my brother couldn't agree with my world outlook. He was far from an optimist but he wasn't as pessimistic as I. He had a wife and children. Like many other liberals he hoped that despite all its insanities, mankind would move forward not backward. But I spoke like a nihilist and a suicide and more than once I evoked his anger.

He had invited me to spend the whole summer with him in Svider but I couldn't mix with the writers, nor did I want to cause him embarrassment with my pessimism. I knew that the writers' wives whispered about me and slandered me among themselves. Such were the contradictions within my character that I could neither be alone nor stand others or manage to keep perfect secrets about my conduct. I waged a kind of personal conspiracy. In a sense, I practiced my theory that one could not proceed in a straight, direct fashion through the world but had to constantly smuggle himself through, or muddle through.

Around that time I had written a story called "In the World of Chaos." Its hero was nothing less than a corpse who didn't know that he was dead. He wandered across Poland, attended fairs, called on rabbis, even allowed himself to be proposed for marriage. He could not understand himself nor did others understand him until he came to a rabbi, a cabalist who resolved his mystery for him—namely, that he was dead and must lie in his grave rather than make a fool of himself with the ambitions of the living. The story ended with the rabbi telling him: "Unbutton your gaberdine and you'll see that you're wearing shrouds."

I never had this story translated, but I wrote a number of variations on it, such as the story "Two Corpses Go Dancing."

"In the World of Chaos" might have provided me my first direction as to style and genre. Somehow I identified with this hero. Just like him, I lived yet was ashamed to live, ashamed to eat and ashamed to go to the outhouse. I longed for sex and I was ashamed of my passions. I always felt that the story in Genesis in which Adam and Eve eat of the fruit of the Tree of Knowledge then grow conscious of their nakedness expressed the essence of man. Man is the only creature who is ashamed to be what he is. The whole human culture is one mighty effort to cover and embellish itself; one huge and complex fig leaf.

As far as I knew, Gina had never gone away on vacation, but that summer she told me that she had rented a room with a kitchen in a villa lying between Otwock and Svider, and if I wanted, I could come to stay with her.

This put me in a quandary. It was one thing to be secluded with Gina in a third-story flat on Gesia Street where no one visited or looked in through the door or windows. It was something else altogether to be with her at a summer resort where you lived on the ground floor, where the door and windows stood open, and where you spent most of your time outdoors surrounded by neighbors.

The villa where Gina had rented the room lay close to Kacyzna's villa where my brother was staying. To go out to a resort I needed a special summer wardrobe. Gina informed me that her place was close to the Svider River where the vacationers bathed and sunbathed along the shore. But this was hardly an attraction for me. I hated the nudity and noise of a beach. I was shy to undress even in front of men. Besides, my skin is so white that if I stay out in the sun for even a short while I burn and blister. Nor can my eyes tolerate the sun's glare. I asked Gina if the doctor had told her to go away for the summer and she replied:

"Yes, no, it makes no difference."

2

My musings brought me no closer to any conclusions regarding the world nor my own duties toward God and man, but I enjoyed—I might say—philosophical fantasies: variations on Spinoza, Kant, Berkeley, and the cabala, along with my own cosmic dreams. Since time and space were merely points of view; since quality, quantity, and even existence itself were categories of reason; and since the thing in itself remained completely concealed, there was room left for metaphysical fantasizing. My God was infinite, eternal, and possessed of endless attributes, properties of which we humans could only grasp a select few. I didn't agree with Spinoza that all that we know of God are His extension (matter) and His thinking. I was sooner inclined to see in Him other such qualities as wisdom, beauty, power, eternity, and maybe too a kind of mercy that we could never comprehend. The cabalists attributed sex to God, and I more than agreed with them in this concept. God Himself and all His worlds were divided into he and she, male and female, give and take, a lust that no matter how much it was satisfied it could never be sated completely and always wanted more, something new, different.

Since man is created in God's image, man could learn more about God by looking within himself, observing all his aspirations, yearnings, hopes, doubts. I envisioned God as resembling myself. He got much, much love from the Shechina, His feminine counterpart, the angels, the seraphim, the cherubim, the Aralim, the holy wheels and holy beasts, from the countless worlds and souls, but this wasn't enough for Him and He also demanded love from insignificant man, the weakest link in the divine chain whom He exhorted: "And thou shalt love the Lord thy God with all thine heart, and with all thy soul, and with all thy might."

He wants love (as I do) regardless of whether He has earned it. He frequently punishes His creatures but He demands that they forgive Him and acknowledge that all His intentions are of

the best. He Himself keeps many secrets yet at the same time
He demands total candidness and a full baring of the soul.

Now that Gina was in Svider, Stefa traveling with a husband
she didn't love, and I sleeping alone all the time, I would waken
in the middle of the night and give my imagination free rein.

"Think what you wish," I ordered it, "you needn't be
ashamed before me. You can soar to the highest heavens or
sink to the lowest abyss for in essence they are one and the
same."

It wasn't the Logos that was in the beginning, but the oneness,
the unity. In God, everything is united—infinite thought and
infinite passion, the ego and the non-ego, the greatest pleasure
and the deepest despair, all matter and all spirit. The infinite
had filled all space leaving room for nothing else. God was omnipotent, but He suffered from restlessness—He was a restless
God. At first glance, this seems a contradiction. How can the
omnipotence be restless? "Is anything too hard for the Lord?"
How can an all-powerful suffer? The answer is that the contradictions are also a part of God. God is both harmony, and dis-
harmony. God contradicts Himself, which is the reason for so
many contradictions in the Torah, in man, and in all nature. If
God did not contradict Himself, He would be a congealed God,
a once-and-for-all perfect being as Spinoza described Him. But
God is not finished. His highest divine attribute is His creativeness and that which is creative exists always in the beginning
stage. God is eternally in Genesis. Each time He lifts His gaze
He sees chaos and He wants to create order. But creation is
coupling and God must come together with His female aspects
to produce birth. Male and female are contradictions that constantly yearn to unite, but the more they unite the sharper grow
their longings and caprices.

I slept some, awoke, dreamed, and came to again. Although
my dreams were rife with fear, with demons, evil spirits, wild
cruelties, and scenes of horror, I awoke from them with a lust
that astounded me.

I stood by the open window to catch a night breeze. The sky
over the Zamenhof Street rooftops was filled with stars. I liter-

ally felt the earth revolving on its axis, rotating around the sun, wandering in the direction of a constellation which would take it millions of years to reach and at the same time racing along with the Milky Way toward a target and only eternity knew what it was and to where it extended. *I am earth, I am the sun, I am the galaxy, I am a letter or a dot in God's infinite book. Even if I am an error in God's work, I can't be completely erased.* I tried to conceive the trillions, quadrillions, quintillions of planets in space, their individuality and the creatures that swarmed upon them, each with its own evolution, history, and passions. No, there was no death within this cauldron of life. Each atom, each electron lived and had its function, its ambitions, its unfulfilled desires. The universe shouted voicelessly. It sang a serenade to another universe. Not only I but the table in my room, the chair, the bed, the ceiling, and the floor all took part in the drama. A heat emanated from the walls. A shudder zigzagged down my spine.

I tried to speak to Gina through telepathy. "Are you awake too? Do you also stand by a window looking out at the nocturnal mystery? What's wrong, my love, what ails you? Don't die, Ginele, for all death is a lie, a misunderstanding. Besides, I need you and I know that no one can take your place. Our coming together is a page in God's novel and no one can tear it out. No one can ever kiss, attract and satisfy me as you have. I long for you, because we have already met who knows how many times and our lives are intertwined in such a way that it can never be severed. Our love commenced when we were still amoebas. We were fish in the sea, birds in the air, moles in the ground. We kneaded clay into bricks in Egypt. We stood at Mount Sinai together. Later, I was Boaz and you Ruth, I was Amnon and you Tamar. When Jeroboam disjointed the tribes of Jacob, you were in Jerusalem and I was in Beersheba but I smuggled myself across the border to search for you. I worshiped the Golden Calf and in your despair you became a harlot in the temple of King Manasseh. You danced before Baal and Ashtoreth and you bared your nakedness for half a shekel. For your betrayal I beat you the whole night but at dawn when the morning star emerged, we fell upon each other with a thirst that no sin could ever slake.

"Because three thousand years ago you lay with the priest of Baal, Chammor son of Zev, tonight I will lie with the maid, Marila, daughter of Wojciech. She waits for me in the kitchen on a straw pallet. Her belly is hot, her breasts are rigid, her groin is primed for me and for every male who comes her way. I know full well that this act will complicate our accounts even more, bring new reincarnations and maybe prolong the Diaspora, but even though free choice was bestowed upon us, everything is predestined. The divine ledger is manifold. Marila is the eleventh generation of a coachman who seduced the wife of a peasant, and I the thirteenth generation of a milkmaid raped by a squire. It's all noted in our genes. God toys with us; He experiments with us in a test of reward and punishment, omniscience and free choice. A year hence, Marila will marry her fiancé, the soldier Stach, son of Jan, and for me there also awaits somewhere an ovary and a womb that will give birth to my son or daughter. God is the sum total not only of all deeds but also of all the possibilities. Good night, heaven. If you can, have mercy upon me."

3

A letter from my father had arrived at Gina's but since I seldom went there (even though I had a key) I didn't get the letter until days later. The letter read as follows:

To my dear son, the scholar and man of substance, long may he live.

After I've wished you peace, I inform you that I must come to Warsaw to see a doctor since I am, may it not happen to you, not in the best of health. I'm suffering from stomach trouble as well as hemorrhoids and may the Almighty take pity and grant complete recovery to all the ailing of Israel. I've been away from Warsaw so long that I don't know if any of my old friends are still alive since all kinds of misfortunes and plagues occurred during the war, heaven protect us, and I haven't received any letters from them in a long time. "Thou knowest not what a day may bring forth." I heard that a Dr. Sigmund Frankel in Warsaw is a great healer and they are all, as it is known, emissaries of God. I therefore ask you to get me an appointment for a visit with this doctor, and to meet me at the train that will leave, God be willing, on the evening of the 11th day of Tammuz and arrive in Warsaw on the morning of the 12th at 10 A.M. at the Danzig Depot. I'll have to find a room at some inn in the Jewish quarter where the food is strictly kosher and which isn't far from a house of worship. Best would be the old neighborhood where we once lived—on Gnonya or Grzybowska Streets, an area with which I'm familiar. I've written to my beloved son, your dear brother Israel Joshua, but his wife, my daughter-in-law, Gittel, wrote back that he is abroad on business and won't be back for several weeks, and the local doctor feels I should see a Warsaw doctor immediately in case there is some growth, God forbid, that must be attended to. I certainly would like to visit with your brother, my son Joshua, and his family when he returns safely, and to greet them all heartily, and in behalf of your mother and myself I wish you all long life. Your father Pinchos Menachem, the son of the saintly Samuel, blessed be his memory.

I read the letter and shuddered. What day of the month of Tammuz was this? Father had failed to indicate on what day of the week he was arriving. I had gone to Gina's flat to pick up a German-Polish dictionary I had left there and which I now needed for a translation I was doing. I began to search for a calendar knowing full well that Gina wouldn't have a Jewish calendar in the house. She didn't have a calendar at all. Father's letter had rattled me so that I left without the dictionary I had come for. Afterward, I wasn't even sure that I had locked the door behind me.

Once outside, I started looking for a stand selling Yiddish newspapers which would show the Jewish date on the front page. But there were no Yiddish newspaper vendors on Gesia Street or maybe in my confusion I failed to see them. As usual, funeral processions wound along, one after another. At the corner of Gesia and Franciszkanska Streets, I finally got a Yiddish newspaper and to my horror I saw that today was the 12th day of Tammuz! But the clock already showed twenty past noon. Was Father still waiting at the depot or had he wandered off somewhere? And if so—where? A feeling of despair came over me. Although it wasn't far from where I was to the Danzig Depot I tried to flag a cab. But they were all taken. A streetcar came by and I did something I had vowed never to do—I sprang aboard as it was moving and caught a blow on my knee.

The conductor turned to me: "Do you want to kill yourself or what?"

And he added:

"Idiots!"

I began to pray to God that Father would still be waiting, recalling at the same time the saying in the Gemara that praying for something that was in the past constituted a false prayer. On the other hand, if time possessed no objective existence and the past was merely a human concept, maybe this wasn't a false prayer after all. I sprang down from the trolley even before it had stopped and was nearly thrown under the wheels. I began to race toward the depot and near the entrance I spotted Father standing next to a white-bearded rabbi and another man. I ran up all breathless and cried out:

"Papa!"

"There he is!" the rabbi said, pointing to me.

I wanted to hug Father, to kiss him and apologize, but somehow the opportunity never came. He held out his hand in greeting. He seemed perfectly composed. He half-said, half-asked:

"You obviously were delayed."

"I just got your letter ten minutes ago. It came to an address where I'm no longer living. I just happened to drop by there to pick up a book I left behind. A miracle! A miracle!" I exclaimed, ashamed of my own words.

The other man spoke up: "What did I tell you? It's a good thing you listened to us and waited. Upon my word. Well, how does the saying go—All's well that ends well."

"Praised be the Almighty!" Father said. "I didn't know what to do. All of a sudden I recognized the rabbi from Kupiecka Street. It was really a stroke from heaven. We hadn't seen each other for years but I'm good at recognizing people."

He turned to me. "You should remember the Kupiecka Street rabbi. He used to visit our house. It was during the time that Nahum Leib Weingut wanted to take all us neighborhood rabbis into the official rabbinate. This was yet under the Germans."

"How could he remember me?" the Kupiecka Street rabbi demanded. "He was just a child then. My beard has turned completely white since. But I remember him well with his red earlocks. How long is it, eh?"

"I remember you, I remember you!" I exclaimed, overcome with gratitude for the fact that Father hadn't wandered off and I didn't have to go searching for him. "I even recall what you said at that time: 'If heaven wants us to be paupers, nothing Nahum Leib Weingut does will help.'"

The old rabbi's face beamed and his cherrylike eyes grew youthful.

"Is that what I said? Some memory he's got, the evil eye spare him! Yes, I recall now. Like father, like son. You know what, Rabbi? Since we've met, it's a sign that it was fated. In which case, why should you go look for an inn? You'll be my guest. Thank God I have a spacious apartment. So long as the children were still with us, it was somewhat crowded, but the daughters married and the sons left home. That's the kind of world that's evolved. Children no longer want to live with their parents. A father is likely to moralize a bit and who wants to hear the truth these days? The days fly by and there's no one to exchange a word with. Rabbi, where will you find lodgings in Warsaw? Listen to me and come to my house. We'll take a droshky and your son can ride along with us."

"No, no I couldn't!" Father argued. "I'm deeply grateful to you but how does the saying go: 'A stranger is a burden.' The rich people have servants to help them but your good wife—"

As the two old friends bickered, I studied my father. He had aged and seemed to me shorter. The reddish beard was now half-gray and shrunken, his forehead was sallow and wrinkled. His back was stooped and his gaberdine hung loosely on him. I saw in Father what I had seen in Gina a few weeks before— that he was much sicker than he knew. His blue eyes reflected the ponderings of those whose time has come. After lengthy haggling, Father agreed to stay at the Kupiecka Street rabbi's house but only if he would be allowed to pay his expenses. This was for me a blessing. I wouldn't have known where to locate the strictly kosher quarters Father required nor did I have the money to pay for them. I barely had enough to cover the fare for the droshky.

From the depot to Kupiecka Street was a short ride. We crossed Muranow Street, turned into Dzika Street, and soon were on Kupiecka. During the war all the houses had been allowed to go to seed. Some of the walls had to be buttressed with wooden beams to keep them from collapsing. We went into an apartment that reminded me of our own on Krochmalna Street years ago. The kitchen exuded the same familiar smells— chicory, onion, moldy bread, gas. We entered a room resembling Father's old study—almost bare of furniture—containing only a table, two benches, bookshelves, and a lectern. The rebbetzin had gone shopping. Both men began to discuss learned matters. I said good-by to Father and went to arrange his appointment with the doctor. Father apparently sensed that I was broke for he gave me the money to buy the chit for the doctor and threw in a few extra zlotys besides. I didn't want to accept them, but Father said:

"Take, take. I'm your father."

And he nodded his head at a truth as old as the world itself.

4

I had purchased a chit at the doctor's which would allow Father a visit, but not until a week hence. Father had brought along a manuscript and although he was short of money for a printer, he discussed the possibility of its publication with me. Even as a young man he had undertaken the responsibility of defending Rashi on every point on which he had been challenged by the tosaphists. He had been working on this manuscript virtually his whole life. I had heard him discuss it even while I was in cheder. One Purim when Father had had a drop too much, he began saying to me:

"What happens to a person after he is gone? What becomes of his money, his houses, his stores, his honors? But the Torah and good deeds accompany him to the other world. It's the greatest merit to write a book and to glorify the Torah. It is said of an author of a holy book that his lips speak from the grave."

He added: "I'm convinced that when I come to the other world, Rashi will be there to welcome me."

Father would only speak of himself so highly when he'd had a drop to drink. It seems to me that this was the first time that I, his son, felt the urge to become a writer.

Now Father confided to me that since he was already in Warsaw, he would try to publish his "Righteousness of Rashi," as he had entitled his manuscript. Since Joshua had gotten his job with the *Forward,* he had been sending money home every month and Father might have managed to save up a couple hundred zlotys. Still, he now had to pay the doctors, and he hardly had enough to publish the book. He had apparently also forgotten that the number of Talmudic scholars and yeshivah students was declining. The Orthodoxy of Warsaw had involved itself deeply in politics and now issued a newspaper and held conferences and congresses. True, these were politics of religion, but still they had acquired the jargon and style of worldly politics. The Orthodox no longer wanted to send their children to dingy cheders and yeshivahs, but instead built schools and academies complete with all the modern conveniences. The Beth Jacob schools for girls had also evolved, which was a novelty in Jewish religious history. Like all other parties, the Orthodoxy needed funds—huge sums to meet budgets. Father didn't understand the new ways. Why couldn't the teachers go on teaching children at home as they did for generations? Why couldn't a youth who wished to learn simply go into a study house, take a Gemara down from the shelf, and study? And whoever heard of teaching the Torah to girls? Father feared that this was all the work of Satan.

I strolled with him along Franciszkanska Street and we gazed into the windows of the religious bookstores. They were nearly all deserted. The Torah had fallen out of fashion. Who needed so many commentaries, interpretations, exegeses, books of sermons and morals? Who needed justifications for questions posed to Rashi by the tosaphists? Besides, other authors had already answered them. Father was fully aware that his sons, Israel Joshua and I, had become involved with worldly literature. My brother had published several books and my name too had appeared occasionally in a literary magazine or even a newspaper. But Father wouldn't speak of this and it seems to me that he didn't even allow himself to think about it. Father held that all enlightened books regardless whether in Hebrew or in Yiddish, were deadly poison for the soul. The writers were a gang of clowns, lechers, scoundrels. What shame and mortification he felt for producing such offspring from his loins! Father put all the blame on Mother, the daughter of a *misnagid,* an anti-Hasid. It was she who had planted the seeds of doubt, of heresy, within us. Father had one consolation—that we hadn't grown up ignoramuses. We had studied the Torah, and whoever once tasted the flavor of Torah could never again forget that there is a God.

At times, Father made a mistake and stopped before the window of a secular bookstore. They featured such works as *Crime and Punishment, The Polish Boy, Anna Karenina, The Dangers of Onanism, The Jewish Colonization of Palestine, The Role of the Woman in Modern Society, The History of Socialism, Nana.* Some of the book jackets displayed pictures of half-naked females. Father shrugged his shoulders and I could read his thoughts. That Gentiles should surrender to such trash was understandable. They had been and still remained idolators. But Jews? . . .

Father didn't recognize Warsaw. Here came a long column of boys identically dressed in green tunics and short pants displaying bare calves. They carried long poles and wore caps with the emblem of the Star of David. They were followed by girls in short dresses also revealing naked calves. They all sang. These weren't Gentile children but Jewish boys and girls singing in Hebrew.

"Who are they? What do they want?" Father asked in amazement. I explained that these were youths seeking to emigrate to Palestine.

Father gripped his beard. "To Palestine? Why are they holding sticks? Do they mean to hit somebody?"

I told him that they had dedicated themselves to sports or perhaps the sticks were meant to simulate rifles.

"What? They want to fight wars? With whom? And how can Jews fight wars? We are like lambs surrounded by wolves."

"How long can we go on being lambs?"

"What do you mean—how long? Until the Messiah comes."

"Jews are tired of waiting."

"Those that grow tired aren't Jews. 'They that wait upon the Lord shall renew strength.' "

We passed a kiosk featuring a poster which read in large Yiddish letters: *"His Wife's Husband,* an operetta from America." Father stopped.

"What is this?"

"Theater."

"Well, well, well. Everything the Mishnah predicted has come true. High time the redemption came, high time. That which we are seeing are the pangs preceding the deliverance."

We strolled for a long time in silence. We had emerged onto Nalewki Street and passed the prison on Dluga Street, the Arsenal, as it was called. Outside, convicts swept the gutter watched by an armed guard. The inmates had yellow complexions, yellow-gray uniforms, and even the prison walls were of the same dingy dun color. One convict leaned on his broom and studied Father and me with a half-bemused, half-amused expression, his eyes two laughing slits. I imagined that this was no living person but a corpse which instead of being buried had been thrown into jail, and it now laughed at this blunder committed by the living.

"Father, what does God want?"

Father stopped.

"He wants us to serve Him and love Him with all our hearts and souls."

"How does He deserve this love?" I asked.

Father thought it over a moment.

"Everything man loves was created by the Almighty. Even the heretics love God. If a fruit is good and you love it, then you love the Creator of this fruit since He invested it with all its flavor. And if someone is a lecher and lusts for females, it was the Creator who bestowed them with their beauty and allure. The sage recognizes the source of all the good things and he loves that source. When the fruit rots, you no longer love it, and when the woman grows old and sickly, the lecher runs from her. The fool will not give any thought to where everything stems from."

"What about the evil things? What is their source?"

"There are no evil things. Death which man fears most is a great joy and a blessing to the just."

"What about suffering?"

Father was silent a long time and I assumed that he hadn't heard me, but then he said: "That is the greatest secret of all. Even the saints weren't able to fathom it. So long as man suffers he cannot solve the riddle of suffering. Even Job didn't arrive at the answer. Moses himself didn't know it. The truth is that body

and pain are synonyms. How could there be free choice without
punishment for choosing evil and reward for choosing what is
right? Behind all this suffering is God's infinite mercy."

Father paused and then asked: "Is there a house of worship
in the neighborhood? Time to say the afternoon prayers."

Six

1

THE SUMMER HAD PASSED BUT GINA still didn't return to Warsaw. The secret was out—Gina was both consumptive and anemic. The doctors felt that she would be better off in a sanitarium but Gina didn't want to nor could she afford to enter a sanitarium. She had rented a room outside of Otwock, in the woods and away from all neighbors. When I came to visit her there, she told me frankly that she wanted to isolate herself from people and all their affairs. She had come there to die. She had given up her apartment on Gesia Street for which she had received a few thousand zlotys for surrendering the lease. Gina had estimated that she could exist on fifteen zlotys a week. She belonged to a Sick Fund which provided her medicines free. I had helped her move her books, occult magazines, and the few other necessary possessions to Otwock.

My fear of the draft had been removed—I had been rejected for military service. The doctors had found my lungs not in the best of order and Pilsudski had admonished the army to conscript no more weak young men. Rumors circulated that the colonels who now ruled Poland weren't too eager to have too many Jews in the army since many of them were leftists. The leaders of the Polish parties—the NDK, the PPS, and the Peasant party—complained that Poland had become a dictatorship. Pilsudski ordered the arrest of Witos, Lieberman, and a number of others of his opponents and he made them stand trial. For some strange reason, the editor of the Yiddish newspaper *Der Haint* sent me to cover this trial and to write my impressions of it from the standpoint of a literary observer. This had been arranged by my brother, who since obtaining his position with the *Forward* had proven himself an exceptionally able journalist. The reports that he published in the *Forward* under the pseudonym of G. Kupfer (his wife's maiden name was Genia Kupferstok) became famous among Yiddish readers in both America and Poland, where they were frequently reprinted.

I myself nursed ambitions to be a journalist and this assignment was a stroke of luck for me. I was issued a press card by my newspaper and was seated in the courtroom among the journalists facing the accused, who only a brief time before had been ministers of the Polish Government. I felt more frightened here than the accused. The chamber was small and it seemed to me that these well-known political figures gazed at me with mockery. The journalists ignored me. The court proceedings dragged along. They consisted of lengthy, boring readings of charges that no one took seriously. Although I needed both the money and the prestige this assignment offered, I decided one day that it wasn't for me. My brother was a bit disappointed that I was tossing aside such a good opportunity, but he left the decision to me. Politics was not my game.

Nothing had come of Father's plans to publish his manuscript. Dr. Frankel had written one or two prescriptions for Father but from Mother's letters I gathered that they hadn't helped. Father wrote curt notes but Mother's letters were longer. With my younger brother, Moishe, Father was studying such volumes as *The Teacher of Knowledge* and *The Breastplate of Judgment,* and it looked as if—after Father's demise—Moishe would take over his post. It was therefore necessary that he be married, since pious Jews like the Belz Chassidim wouldn't accept a bachelor rabbi. But it wasn't easy to find a match for Moishe. He was too pious. He had isolated himself completely from the world. He hadn't an inkling about business or about any other worldly matters. He shouted during prayer, clapped his hands, sang the chants of Nachman the Bratslav Rabbi, went into religious ecstasy. Describing Moishe to me, Father called him a saint. He said that compared to Moishe, he, Father, was a sinner. But the Galician girls who had nearly all attended Gymnasium and read newspapers and Polish novels weren't too keen about a youth who at nineteen wore a wild beard and earlocks dangling to the shoulders, a gaberdine to the ankles, an unbuttoned shirt, and old-fashioned slippers. Moishe was tall, even taller than my brother Joshua; blond; with a rare white skin, big blue eyes, and well-formed limbs. He looked like the image of Jesus Christian artists had created. The Gentiles in Father's town considered Moishe a holy man and that's what he actually was. Had there existed such an institution as a Jewish monastery, Moishe would have surely become a monk. The danger was that Moishe might remain without a job.

In the letters my parents wrote me, they kept wishing me to get married, but I was no better suited to be a husband than was Moishe. Like Moishe, I neglected my appearance. So long as Gina was around she kept an eye on me, sewed on my buttons, darned my socks, even washed out my shirts and drawers. She referred to me good-naturedly as an idle dreamer, as a scatterbrain. She would complain: "What's the point of fantasizing? You, my little colt, won't change the world. Since God plays hide-and-seek, you'll never find Him."

Now that Gina had departed Warsaw, I went about messy and buttonless, with torn shoes, I went days without shaving. My hair had started to fall out. The stiff collars I wore were either too tight or too loose.

I was still seeking some means with which to penetrate the barrier of the categories of pure reason, to comprehend the thing in itself and to find a basis for ethics. I still rummaged through libraries and bookstores in the hope of encountering some proof as to the existence of a soul, of an astral body, of some remnant that lingered after the heart stopped beating and the brain stopped functioning. I had read a lot of occult literature but more and more I kept hearing how mediums were being caught in swindles. Books came out detailing how professional spiritists duped their victims. I had already heard about Houdini stripping the masks from a number of famous mediums who had made ectoplasm out of cheesecloth, fabricated phony photographs of ghosts, used cheap tricks to fool such serious scholars and psychical researchers as Flammarion, Sir Oliver Lodge, Sir William Crookes, and many others who desperately clutched for every scrap of evidence of the immortality of the soul. I often had the feeling that sooner or later the truth would reveal itself to me if only I didn't cease groping and hoping. My literary work, my interest in the epoch of Sabbatai Zevi and Jacob Frank, had driven me to search for volumes that described various miracles and wonders of nature. My own nervousness gave me lessons in the power of hysteria and in the force of autosuggestion, or self-hypnosis. My inner enemy constantly pressed me and I had to keep formulating ever new strategies to overcome him or at least keep him temporarily at bay. I had begun glancing into the works of Freud, Jung, Adler. If I found less information there than did others, it was only because our own moralists and authors of Chassidic volumes had been keen students of man and had in simple terms revealed the deepest conflicts existent within the human soul. They knew all the symptoms of hysteria and the whole schism of the spirit. Man had to maintain watch over himself all the time since every second posed a danger. The pit of crime and insanity yawned beneath us constantly. The Evil Spirit never grew weary of assailing us with theories, conjectures, half-truths, fears, fantasies, and illusions of pleasures intended to eradicate the greatest gift God had given us—free will. In all the centuries that the Gentiles had waged wars against each other the Ghetto Jew had waged a war with his inner enemy, with that power of Evil that roosts in every brain and constantly strives to lead it astray. The Emancipation had partially (or gradually) put an end to this Jewish war. The Enlightened Jew had himself become a bit of the Evil Spirit thanks to his experience of wrangling with him. He had become a master of specious theories, of perverse truths, of seductive utopias, of false remedies. Since the Gentile

world needed its idols, the modern Jew had emerged to provide
new ones. He grew so absorbed in this business of idolatry that
he came to believe it himself and even sacrificed himself to it.

2

I had chosen but two idols that I would be willing to serve:
the idol of literature and the idol of love, but many of my colleagues both in and out of the Writers' Club invariably served
the idol of World Betterment. They hammered away at me: How
can one be a writer if one isn't ready to fight for a better world,
equality, freedom, justice, a world without competition and of
eternal peace? The capitalist countries fought wars on account
of oil. They kept putting up new munitions factories. The
strongest among them seized huge areas of the earth. Within
the groups, some individuals seized all the power under the
guise of democracy while they preached offering the other
cheek. How could an honest and sensitive person witness all
this and still keep silent?

Well, but terrible tidings emerged from the land of socialism.

Isaac Deutscher, who had become a Trotskyite, revealed
many Stalinist outrages in his little magazine—the slave camps,
the liquidation of the old Bolsheviks, the rigged trials and
purges which had already taken the lives of millions of innocent
people. Was this socialism? Was this the ideal postulated by
Marx, Engels, Lenin? Deutscher had overwhelming proof that
Leon Trotsky would have handled things differently. I attended
a meeting at the Writers' Club at which this Isaac Deutscher was
the speaker. The Stalinists tried to outshout him. They called
him the renegade, fascist, sellout, capitalist bootlicker, imperialist murderer, provocateur. But Deutscher had a powerful
voice. He pounded his fist on the podium and his audience of
Trotskyites encouraged him with thunderous applause. He
hurled sulphur and ashes at Stalinists and right-wing Socialists,

at Fascists, and at such alleged democracies as America, England, and France.

Within the Jewish circles, he castigated the Zionists in all their factions and variations. What madness to want to turn back the clock of history two thousand years! Well, and why had the Zionists concluded that Palestine belonged to the Jews? They gleaned all their information from the Scriptures, a book filled with miracles and legends. Deutscher said that the fact that Zionism could attract millions of Jews merely demonstrated the degeneracy and hopelessness of the bourgeoisie.

Among those who came to the lecture were Sabina and her younger brother, Mottel. Although Sabina was leftist-oriented, she hadn't yet decided whether she was a Stalinist, a Trotskyite, or an anarchist. Mottel was a fervent Stalinist and he had come to heckle and maybe even throw a rotten potato or egg at the speaker. Mottel was short and broad-shouldered, with thick lips, a broad nose like a duck's (he actually was nicknamed Mottel Duck), and small, piercing eyes under bushy brows. Mottel was something of a buffoon. He spouted jokes, and absurdities that evoked laughter. He had a low forehead and a thatch of pitch-black, curly hair. Mottel Duck had already served time at the Pawiak Prison for his Communist activities. His sister told me that he carried a gun. He allowed his sister and mother to support him. He ran around with rich girls who were drawn to communism and he took money from them, allegedly for party causes. He was a big eater and able to quaff numerous mugs of beer and sleep fourteen hours at a stretch.

Sabina frequently complained to me: "How it happened that such a child should come out of our pious family is something I'll never understand. Unless he is a bastard."

I had resolved repeatedly and warned myself not to have anything more to do with this Sabina, but I did the opposite. My earnings were so meager that I could no longer pay for my room at the eye doctor's on Zamenhof Street and Miss Sabina proposed that I move in with her family. A room had become vacant in their apartment and the rent was half of what I was now paying. Sabina's mother would serve me lunches cheaply.

We had already kissed and I knew that once I moved into her house she would become my mistress.

This Sabina didn't speak of romantic love as had Gina or Stefa. Sabina had read the works of such modernists as Margueritte, Decobra, Zapolska, and she had a high opinion of Emma Goldman. She often derided the institution of marriage as antiquated and held that the man of the future wouldn't make contracts for lifelong love but would conduct himself according to the dictates of nature. Sabina had read some of my stories and she believed in my literary powers if I could only find the right direction.

Sabina spoke to me frankly. A young man was after her, ready to marry her, but the little love she had felt for him before had completely cooled within her. He wrote poems in Polish. He came from some town in the Lublin region. He had dropped out of the Gymnasium and gone off to Palestine where he had struggled for two years, suffered from malaria, and come back a dedicated Communist. He had been arrested twice. She couldn't drop him all at once since he was madly in love with her and was, despite his Leninist convictions, capable of killing himself. But if I moved in with her, sooner or later he would remove himself. There was even a chance he might smuggle himself into Soviet Russia or be sent there by the Party.

When Mrs. Alpert heard that I was giving up the room, she fell into a kind of panic. She was ready to keep me on without paying rent, she claimed. Her eyes filled with tears. She told me that I was the best boarder she had ever had. She thought of me as a son. To her, a boarder wasn't someone who merely paid his rent—she had to feel a rapport toward someone with whom she shared a roof. My name had been mentioned in a Polish-Jewish newspaper she read and it was an honor for her to have such a person in her home. How could I treat her this way? Marila the maid also flushed, and turned sulky and tearful when she heard I was moving out.

She complained to me: "What bad did we ever do you that you're running away from us? I always kept your room spotless, not even a speck of dirt. When you wanted tea or whatever, I was ready to get up in the middle of the night to serve you. I took care of your phone calls and all your dates. You're obviously drawn to one of those fancy young ladies of yours, but none of them will be as faithful to you as I've been."

I listened to these reproofs in amazement. It had never occurred to me that I was such a catch. I wasn't tall or handsome, and I spoke a poor Polish. Whenever I glanced in the mirror I always grew half frightened of my own face. The little hair left on my head was fiery red. My face was pale and often as white as that of someone who has just gotten up out of a sickbed. My cheeks were sunken, my ears flaring, my back stooped. Women constantly corrected my Polish, pointed out that my tie was crooked, that my trousers seemed about to fall off at any moment, and that my shoelaces were untied. I suffered from colds and no matter how many handkerchiefs I had, they were always soiled. I felt so touched by Mrs. Alpert's and Marila's reaction that I blurted: "Well, all right. I'll stay with you, my dears!"

In a second I decided to hold on to both rooms! This was pure nonsense since I didn't earn enough to maintain even one room. But somehow I had the feeling that a God Who tolerated my insanities wouldn't forsake me.

3

When Sabina heard what I had done, she said that I wasn't merely deranged but also suicidal. The most important thing for a young writer was to have a clear head, not to have to constantly fret about money. Well, and what would I do with two rooms? I didn't have any possessions outside of my few books and manuscripts. I had nothing to move out and nothing to move in. The whole thing sounded like a bad joke. Sabina was ready to give me back the few zlotys I had given her as a deposit, but I wouldn't hear of it. My only fear was that my brother shouldn't find out what I was doing. He would have scolded me like a father. He would tell his fellow writers and they would have something to laugh at. Well, but I had already had two residences when Gina was still living in Warsaw. It seemed that my type of conspiracy required two addresses.

I awaited a miracle and a miracle came. I walked into the Writers' Club and the woman at the door told me that the editor of the afternoon paper, *Radio,* had telephoned me. He had left a number where I was supposed to call him right back. Had my brother again tried to get me a job? No, this time it wasn't my brother but someone else who had told the editor of *Radio* that I had displayed a talent for writing. He had also mentioned that I could translate from the German. The *Radio,* like the other Yiddish newspapers, printed suspense novels. The editor had just acquired an exciting novel from Germany, where it had enjoyed a huge success. The problem was, however, that the Yiddish reader wouldn't accept a novel with a locale as alien as Berlin with its strange-sounding streets. The novel didn't have to be merely translated but adapted in such a way that the action was shifted to Warsaw and the heroes and heroines became familiar Jewish men and women.

On the telephone the editor proposed this revision to me. He told me to come to his office and I didn't walk but ran. I've forgotten his name, but his image is fixed in my mind—short, stout, with a round face, ruddy cheeks, and amiable, half-sleepy eyes. He was a favorite of the newspaper's owner, perhaps a relative of the owner.

He smiled at me with the geniality of one who wants to grant a favor and rid himself of a burden at the same time. He took a thick German book out of a drawer. It appeared to be a thousand pages long.

He handed it to me and said: "Glance through it!"

I read the first page and asked: "Will my name have to be used?"

"No names."

"Oh, this is a stroke of luck for me!" I gushed, knowing the whole while that it is poor business to show how eager you are for a job. I came from a house which knew of no diplomacy.

The editor said: "We'll give you sixty zlotys a week."

In those days, sixty zlotys came to no more than eleven or twelve dollars, but in Poland this was a big sum. Whole families got by on such an amount.

I said: "Really, I don't know how to thank you."

"Go home and get to work. You'll supply us some ten thousand words a week. Write simply, in short paragraphs and with lots of dialogue. Don't use any difficult words. If you need an advance, you can get one right now."

"As you understand . . ."

"I understand that you can use it. If the novel catches on, you'll get more work from us."

"I'll do everything in my power."

He wrote out a slip of paper for me and showed me where to take it to a cashier, who handed me two hundred zlotys. I had been struggling along as a proofreader and translator and suddenly I had become rich, even if burdened down with work. Although I felt doubts about God, His benevolence and providence, I offered up silent praise to Him. No, the world was no accident, no result of an explosion or something similar, as Feuerbach, Marx, and Bukharin contended. Because I didn't want to disappoint Mrs. Alpert and Marila, God had sent me this source of income. But why didn't He reward deeds nobler than mine? Why did He allow poor people to jump from trolleys and lose arms and legs, or Gina to die of consumption, or innocent children to burn to death by falling kerosene stoves?

Afterward, when I told a journalist at the Writers' Club what had happened, he told me that I was a dunce. The editor was paying me half of what other writers of this kind of work were getting.

"Why didn't you bargain with him?" he asked me. He advised me to call the editor and demand more. He was willing to bet that he would raise me at least forty zlotys a week on the spot. But I was too proud to do something like that. I had been raised to believe that haggling and praising your own work and asking for a raise after a deal had been made was beneath human dignity.

4

We sat around the table with Sabina, her mother, and her two brothers, and we ate dinner. Bryna Reizel, as Sabina's mother was called, told stories of her hometown.

I listened to every word. I had been disappointed in philosophy, I hardly believed in psychology, and not at all in sociology, but I had come to the conclusion that many truths or fragments of truth were buried in folklore, in dreams, and in fantasies. Where thought isn't linked with any discipline, it's able to catch a glimpse behind the curtain of the phenomenon. Bryna Reizel told of some Polish squire who following the failure of the 1863 uprising confined himself to a coffin where he ate, slept, read books, and lived for the next thirty years. When he died, they found inside his straw pallet a fortune in gold ducats and a will leaving his entire estate to an old lecher, a former lover of his, the squire's, wife. She, the wife, had died twenty years earlier. Bryna Reizel spouted stories about dybbuks, werewolves, demons who celebrated weddings and circumcisions in attics and cellars, corpses who worshiped in synagogues at midnight and summoned frightened passers-by to join them.

Bryna Reizel was past fifty and had suffered much grief, yet her face had remained youthful. The words slid out of her small mouth as if of their own volition and she used Yiddish idioms I had not heard for a long time or only encountered in old storybooks. Sabina and her brother Mottel winked to each other and at times even laughed at their mother. They didn't believe in such nonsense, but I and Bryna Reizel's younger son, Haskele, listened. Haskele suffered from scrofula. He had a large

head, "water on the brain." He had been taken from cheder at
an early age and hadn't been able to get a job with an artisan.
He did a girl's tasks around the house—ran errands, heated the
oven, swept, and at times even washed the dishes. His eyes
were whitish and unevenly set. Sabina and Mottel reminded me
at every opportunity that Haskele was a victim of capitalism.

Winter came early that year. Soon after Succoth a deep snow
fell and the frosts commenced. My worries about a living had
ceased so long as the novel would run, but Sabina's brother
Mottel accused me of contributing to yellow journalism. He
read each day's installment and pointed out again and again that
this was opium for the masses to lull them from the struggle
for a just order.

Sabina's fiancé (as he was known in the house), Meir Milner,
only sought to engage me in debates. He was blond, blue-eyed,
snub-nosed. He worked a half-day as an assistant bookkeeper in
a button factory. I had blurted out that I didn't believe in historical materialism and he had promptly become my enemy. He
kept on needling me. In what, he asked, *did* I believe? In the
League of Nations that had immediately after its formation begun to expire? In Wilson's hypocritical manifesto? In the Balfour
Declaration which wasn't worth the paper it was written on? In
the false promises of Leon Blum, Macdonald, Pearl, Diamond,
Gompers?

I reminded him about the number of comrades who had
gone to the land of socialism only to disappear, but Meir Milner
shouted: "False accusations from fascist dogs! Lies fabricated by
the reactionary pigs! Delusions of Trotskyite provocateurs!"

"Let them burn like a wet rag, slowly," interposed Mottel the
wag, "there is one cure for them—to be made a head shorter."

"One death isn't enough for them!" Meir Milner snarled
along.

For the countless time I grew astounded over the bloodthirst-
iness that had been aroused among Jewish youth after two thousand years of Diaspora, after centuries of ghettos. If Lamarck
and his disciples were correct in that acquired traits are inherited, every Jew should have emerged a hundred per cent paci-

fist. Modern Jews and Muslims should be born circumcised. I
read books about biology and was particularly interested in the
debate between the mechanists and the vitalists, the Lamarckists
and the Darwinists.

Late at night I went to sleep. It was a tiny room with a window facing a blank wall. It was half-dark in there even on the
brightest day. There was no electricity in the house, only gaslight. I had taken on so much work that I was constantly behind.

I lay awake thinking about Gina. I had visited her during the
Days of Awe—a sick woman alone in the woods and far from
neighbors, from a store, and without a telephone. She sat there
and waited for death. This was no longer the Gina I knew but
someone else; completely unfamiliar to me. She had almost
stopped talking. I tried to carry on a conversation with her
about the supernatural but she didn't answer. Had she given up
her belief in the immortality of the soul? Had she lied earlier
about her communications with the dead and now no longer
sought to deceive me? Or had she gained access to secrets denied the healthy? I had the feeling that whatever I said to her
would constitute a burden.

I asked her if she wanted to accompany me to the synagogue
to hear the blowing of the ram's horn, and she replied:

"What for?"

And soon there was nothing left to say.

I wanted to come to her bed at night. I hoped to rouse a
passion within her and to make her talkative one last time, but
Gina said that she must sleep alone. Weak as she was, she had
made up a bed for me on a cot in the same room where she
slept. She put out the lamp and grew immediately silent. I didn't
hear her breathing. During the day she occasionally erupted in
a wet cough but that night I didn't hear so much as a rustle
from her. She had apparently swallowed a number of sleeping
pills and had sunk into a kind of coma. I was afraid lest she die
in the night.

Strangely enough, she had formed a friendship with a woman
named Genia who was also consumptive and with whom she
was more open and talkative. Genia's brother was a doctor in

Warsaw. She came each morning to visit and brought food she had bought for Gina. Genia liked to talk. In the two days that I spent with Gina, Genia and I became so friendly that we kissed when I left. She told me that doctors—her brother concurring—had given her a year to live. She lived next door to a friend, a young man who was in the last stages of consumption and could last another six months at best. She confided to me that Gina was hardly as sick physically as she assumed. Doctors who had examined her had agreed that she suffered from anemia, but it wasn't the kind of anemia that necessarily killed. She had been prescribed injections and a diet of liver which she ignored. Gina no longer wanted to live. I knew that it was my fault. My leaving to take a room at Dr. Alpert's had convinced her that all the hopes she had placed in me had been foolish.

My having moved in with Sabina seemed to me even more than foolish. I had light-mindedly broken up a match between two young people. I generally wasn't inclined to marriage and even if I had been, it certainly wouldn't be to someone like Sabina. Although I didn't follow in the path of my pious parents, I had retained an ideal of a wife as my parents conceived it—a decent Jewish daughter, a virgin who after the wedding would serve if not one God at least one man. In brief, a wife like my mother. I should have admitted this to Sabina, but I saw that she was tired of flighty affairs and that she longed with all her womanly instincts for a husband, a home, and children. She might have calculated that in time I might tear myself away from Poland. Since my brother was a correspondent for an American newspaper, I had some connection with America. Somewhere inside, the Polish Jews sensed that they were doomed. I knew full well that playing around with women meant toying with lives, but I lacked the character and the strength to heed the voice of my conscience. I belonged to a generation which no longer believed in free will and which based everything on circumstances, ideologies, and complexes.

That night I had slept an hour or two. Suddenly, I awoke. Sabina was bending over me and her hair brushed my face. She too couldn't live like her righteous forebears. Although she was a leftist and I was considered a rightist, we were united by the same passion—to seize every possible pleasure at any price before we vanish forever.

One day as I sat in my room at Dr. Alpert's trying to stretch the novel in the *Radio* so that I could collect my sixty zlotys another few months, Marila the maid knocked to announce with a smile and a wink that I was wanted on the phone by a "beautiful young lady."

I went to the phone and heard a voice that seemed familiar, yet I couldn't place it. I searched my mind, and the woman at the other end of the wire made fun of my poor memory and tried to offer me hints to help jog it. After a while she revealed her identity: the former Stefa Janovsky and current Madam Treitler.

We were both silent for a long while, then I asked:

"What did you have, a boy or a girl?"

"I had nothing. Forget it."

"Your parents—"

"Mother died."

"Mark—"

"He is dead too. Not really, but as far as I'm concerned. I beg you not to mention his name. I've forgotten him completely. But as you see, *you* I haven't forgotten. Isn't that strange?"

"If it's true."

"Yes, it's true."

LOST IN AMERICA

One

1

AT THE ONSET OF THE 1930s, MY DIS-
illusionment with myself reached a stage in which I had lost all
hope. If truth be told, I had had little of it to lose. Hitler was on
the verge of assuming power in Germany. The Polish fascists
proclaimed that as far as the Jews were concerned they had the
same plans for them as did the Nazis. Gina had died and only
then did I realize what a treasure of love, devotion, faith in God
and in human values I had lost. Stefa had married the rich Mr.
Leon Treitler. My brother Joshua, his wife, Genia, and their
younger son, Yosele, had gone to America, where he would
work for *The Jewish Daily Forward*. Their elder son, Yasha, a
lad of fourteen, had died of pneumonia. The boy's death drove
me into a depression that remains with me to this day. It was
my first direct contact with death.

My father also died around this time. Even though over forty
years have passed, I still cannot go into details about this loss.
All I can say is that he lived like a saint and he died like one,
blessed with a faith in God, His mercy, His Providence. My lack
of this faith is actually the story which I am about to tell.

The status of Yiddish and Yiddish literature was such that
there was no way it could worsen. Kleckin Publishing, with
which I had been connected, had gone bankrupt, ceased oper-
ations. The evening newspaper *Radio* no longer required my
services. The same colleagues who only a year or two before
had chided me for working for a bourgeois newspaper, the so-

called yellow press, thus helping to feed opiates to the masses, were now trying to peddle their own *kitsch* at half or quarter price. The disappointment with communism had imbued a good many radicals with Zionist doctrines. My only source of income now was a Yiddish newspaper in Paris which also was on the verge of suspending publication. The checks from Paris kept arriving later and later. Not only couldn't I keep two separate rooms for my two girl friends, but maintaining even one became harder from month to month.

I owed Mrs. Alpert several hundred zlotys' rent, but she assured me each month that she had complete trust in me. I noticed that Marila, the maid, brought me more rolls for breakfast than she had in the past. She apparently suspected that breakfast was my only meal of the day.

I corresponded with my brother in New York, but I never complained about my lot. Although my plans depended on my brother sending me an affidavit to come to America on a tourist visa and later helping me to remain there, I seldom answered his letters. Writing letters had always been a burden for me and I envied those who found the time and the inspiration for extensive correspondence.

Others bewailed their lot to me, but I never told them about my troubles. Some writers had become experts at requesting and obtaining various grants and subsidies, but I asked nothing of anyone. Gina, may she rest in peace, had nicknamed me "the Starving Squire."

I had often seen men chasing after women, pleading for love, a kiss, an endearment. Young and even elderly writers weren't ashamed to besiege editorial offices imploring that they review their work. They praised themselves and toadied up to the editors and critics. I never could hold out a hand for love, money, or recognition. Everything had to come to me of its own or not come at all.

I denied the existence of Providence, yet I awaited its dictates. I had inherited this kind of fatalism (if not faith) from both my parents. My one consolation was that if worst came to worst, I could commit suicide.

The literary scene in Warsaw, which was so rife with favoritism, clannishness, with "you scratch my back and I'll scratch yours," with sucking up to political factions and party leaders and seeking their patronage, found in me an alien element. Even though I felt that a man cannot go through life directly but must muddle through, sneak by, smuggle himself through it, I made my accounting with the divine or Satanic forces, not with the human.

I had drifted apart from Sabina, who had broken with Stalinism and turned Trotskyite. Her brother, Mottel Duck, had done the same. Brother and sister both hoped that mankind would shortly realize that the true Messiah wasn't Stalin but Trotsky, and that the social revolution in Poland would be led by Isaac Deutscher, not by that obdurate Stalinist Isaac Gordin (who subsequently spent eleven years in one of Stalin's concentration camps).

As for me, since I didn't possess the courage to kill myself, my only chance to survive was to escape from Poland. One didn't have to be particularly prescient to foresee the hell that was coming. Only those who were totally hypnotized by silly slogans could not see what was descending upon us. There was no lack of demagogues and plain fools who promised the Jewish masses that they would fight alongside the Polish Gentiles on the barricades and that, following the victory over fascism, the Jews and Gentiles in Poland would evolve into brothers forever after. The pious Jewish leaders, from their side, promised that if the Jews studied the Torah and sent their children to cheders and yeshivahs, the Almighty would perform miracles in their behalf.

I had always believed in God, but I knew enough of Jewish history to doubt in His miracles. In Chmielnicki's times, Jews had studied the Torah and given themselves up to Jewishness perhaps more than in all the generations before and after. There was no Enlightenment or heresy at that time. The tortured and massacred victims were all God-fearing Jews. I had written a book about that period, *Satan in Goray*. It hadn't yet appeared in book form but it had been published in the magazine *Globus*. I hadn't received a penny in payment. Quite the contrary, I had to contribute toward the cost of the printing and paper.

A person filled with my kind of doubt is by nature lonely. I had only two friends among the Yiddish writers: Aaron Zeitlin and J. J. Trunk.

Aaron Zeitlin was some six or seven years older than I. I considered him one of the greatest poets in world literature. He was a master of both Yiddish and Hebrew, but his enormous creative force was better demonstrated in his Yiddish writings. He was a man of great knowledge, a spiritual giant among spiritual dwarfs. When the Yiddish PEN Club in Warsaw issued my book *Satan in Goray* prior to my departure for America, Zeitlin wrote the Introduction for it. The printed book, with its Introduction, didn't reach me until I was already in America.

We were both lonely men. We both knew that a holocaust was descending upon us. I often visited Zeitlin in his apartment on Sienna Street. We even tried collaborating on a book about the mad philosopher Otto Weininger. Sometimes Zeitlin visited me in the furnished rooms I kept changing. He supported himself by writing articles for the newspaper *The Express*, which occasionally published my little stories.

Intellectually and literarily, we were as close as two writers can be, but we were totally different in character. Zeitlin's number-one passion was literature, especially religious literature and everything pertaining to it. My number-one passion was the adventures of love, the endless variations and tensions peculiar to the relations between the sexes.

Zeitlin was well versed in Russian, Polish, Hebrew, French, and German literature, all of which he read in the original. He discovered writers and thinkers who had been forgotten with time or had never been recognized. For all his erudition, his poetry remained original. He mimicked no one, since he himself was often greater than those he studied. He was a faithful husband to his pretty but cold wife, whom he had married in an arranged match. He dedicated some of his poems to her. He was immensely grateful that a half-assimilated Warsaw girl, the daughter of a wealthy man, had agreed to wed him instead of some doctor or lawyer more suited to her personality. Oddly, she had a job in the burial division of the Jewish Communal Organization and she didn't give up this somber post after the wedding or even after she had given birth to a son, Risia. She spoke Polish to the child, not the language in which her husband wrote. I rarely saw the couple together.

There was an unwritten law among the wives of Yiddish writers and of the great number of so-called Yiddishists that their children should be raised to speak the Polish language. My brother's wife was no exception. The husbands had to accede. Only Chassidim and the poor, especially in the small towns, spoke Yiddish to their children.

My other friend, who was also Zeitlin's friend, J. J. Trunk, was some twenty years older than I, the son of a rich man, an owner of buildings in the city of Lodz, and the grandson of a famous rabbi whom Trunk's nouveau riche great-grandfather had arranged to marry his daughter.

These two forebears, the merchant and the rabbi, waged a war within Trunk the man and Trunk the writer. Trunk had a good eye for people and situations. He also had a sense of humor. In later years he wrote a ten-volume set of memoirs, which are of great value as a document of Jewish life in Poland. He loved literature and he was virtually desperate to make a mark as a writer. But his writing lacked something that prevented him from achieving this. We, his friends, knew it. Chekhov once said about some Russian writer that he lacked those doubts that give talent gray hair. Trunk was and remained an amateur, albeit a gifted one. He was too cheerful, too gullible about all kinds of "isms," too naïve to be a true artist. For the very reason that he came from a rich home he resolved to become a socialist. Yet even his socialism somehow didn't agree with his character and he had constantly to justify himself to both his party comrades and to us, Zeitlin and me.

Trunk's wife, Dacha, shared his heritage of wealth and man-

ner. Generations of Polish Jews spoke from the couple's lips.
Their every word, every tone and gesture exemplified Polish-
Jewish life-style, a Polish-Jewish naïvete. The husband and wife
were as close as a brother and sister, and as distant as a
brother and sister can sometimes be. He was fair, blue-eyed,
stout. A boyish joy exuded from his eyes along with a youthful
mischievousness. Dacha was lean, dark, and her black eyes reflected the vexation of the put-upon wife. Her only consolation
in life was books. The Trunks had one daughter—a tall, slim,
blond girl resembling the Polish aristocratic debutantes who
rode horseback along Ujazdowe Allee and in Lazienki Park. It
is perhaps no coincidence that during the Second World War
this proud maiden converted and became a devoted Catholic.
Her husband, a Christian, died during the Polish uprising in
1945.

Yes, Zeitlin, Trunk, and I were close friends. We published
our works in the same magazines and anthologies of which I,
the youngest, was occasionally a coeditor. I often visited their
homes. But as pressing as my need was, it never occurred to
me to ask them for a loan. I had already become a member of
the Yiddish Writers' Club and even of the PEN Club, but I remained boyishly bashful and I never took any of my girl friends
there. (Zeitlin never asked me about my private affairs. I did
occasionally boast to Trunk of my alleged conquests.) The
Trunks were both much older than I, and they considered me
a half-crazy prodigy who was here one minute and vanished the
next, like one of the demons or sprites I described in my stories. My brother also had given up trying to put my life into
some kind of order. After he went to America, I became a riddle
even to myself. I did things of which I was ashamed. I waged
love affairs on several fronts. They all began casually and they
all quickly turned serious and led me into countless deceptions
and complications. I stole love, but I was always caught in the
act, entangled in my lies, and I had constantly to defend myself,
make holy promises, and take vows I couldn't keep. My victims
castigated me with the foulest names, but my betrayals apparently didn't repel them sufficiently to get rid of me.

2

It was summer again and the heat engulfed Warsaw. Again I managed to have two residences—this time, one in Warsaw and one in the country, between Swider and Otwock. I still wrote for that Parisian Yiddish newspaper that was about to close, and from time to time I published a fragment of a story in *The Express*.

I had moved out of Mrs. Alpert's, but I had promised her and Marila to return at the first opportunity if the room was still available. At the same time I knew that I would never go back since at that time I had already obtained an affidavit to America from my brother and I was waiting for a tourist visa from the American consul. I had also applied for a foreign passport but it turned out that I lacked the required documents. I had a premonition that I would never leave Poland and that all my endeavors were for naught.

The days were long in the summer. It wasn't until ten o'clock that the last remnants of sunset vanished from sight. By three in the morning, the birds already commenced to twitter in my caricature of a dacha. My girl friend Lena and I both slept in the nude since our garret room was baked by the sun all day, roasting our bodies like an oven. It wasn't until dawn that some cool breezes from the pine forests began to blow. The entire villa was one enormous ruin. The roof had holes, and when it rained we had to set up buckets to catch the water. The floor was rotted and infested with vermin. The mice had fled for lack of food. For the sum of one hundred and fifty zlotys, we had rented a room for the whole season. Actually, we had the entire house to ourselves, since no one else would move into this building. The doors to all the rooms stood open. The mattresses on the beds were torn, with rusted springs protruding. Occasionally, when the wind blew, the whole house shook as swarms of demons whistled and howled.

Lena and I had grown accustomed to the evil powers. They scampered over the stairs at night, opened and slammed doors, moved furniture. Even though Lena considered herself a hundred percent atheist and mocked me and my writings about the supernatural, she confessed that she had glimpsed phantoms in the corridors. At every opportunity Lena quoted Marx, Lenin, Trotsky, and Bukharin, yet she was afraid to go to the outhouse at night and she used a chamber pot. The reason she gave was that the outhouse was overgrown with weeds and snakes lurked there. We were given a kerosene lamp by the owner, but we seldom lit it, since the moment a light came on, moths, gnats, and other insects entered through the broken windowpanes. Huge beetles emerged from holes and cracks in the floor. I covered the vat of water I brought in each day from the pump, else dozens of drowned creatures would be found floating there in the morning.

I had inherited Lena from Sabina. They were close friends for a time. They had even spent several months together in Pawiak Prison, in the women's section nicknamed "Serbia." There, in their prison cell, they had fallen out because Sabina had become a Trotskyite while Lena continued to swear allegiance to Comrade Stalin. Lena had been released on bail and was supposed to stand trial, which had been scheduled months before, but she had jumped bail because new witnesses had been found for the prosecution and she would surely have been sentenced to many years imprisonment.

She had come to me in Warsaw requesting a night's sanctuary because she was, as she said, surrounded by police spies. I had only one narrow iron bed in my furnished room and she slept with me not just that one night, but for more than two weeks. She called me a capitalistic lackey even as she clamped her lips onto mine. She complained that my mystical stories helped to perpetuate fascism, but she tried to translate some of them into Polish. She swore to me that she had undergone a gynecological operation that had rendered her sterile, but she was already in her fifth month that summer. She said that she wanted to have a child by me even if the world were destroyed the next day. She assured me that the ultimate struggle between justice and exploitation was coming and, if truth triumphed, she wouldn't need my support. I could go to America if I wanted to escape the unavoidable day of revenge by the Polish masses. The revolution would reach there as well.

It was empty talk. Actually, she wandered through the ruin I had rented like a caged beast. She didn't have a penny and was in danger of being arrested. Lena came from a Chassidic household. Her father, Solomon Simon Yabloner, was a follower of the Gora Rabbi. He had driven his daughter from the house when she got involved with the Communists. He observed a period of mourning over her, as did her mother, three brothers, and two sisters. Solomon Simon was known as a strongwilled fanatic. When his children did something that displeased him, he struck them, even after they were married. In the Gora study house at 22 Franciszkanska Street, it was said that Solomon Simon had defied even the Rabbi himself. Lena (her true name was Leah Freida) told me that she would sooner hang herself than go back home to her reactionary clan. She was tall for a girl, dark as a gypsy, flat-chested as a man. Her hair was cut short. A cigarette always dangled between her full lips. She didn't trim or tweeze her thick eyebrows. Her pitch-black eyes exuded a masculine resoluteness and the frustration of one who, due to some biological error, has been born into the wrong gender. She was anything but my type. She had confessed lesbian tendencies to me. For me to associate with such a woman, and to become father of her child, was an act of madness. But I had already accustomed myself to my queer behavior. For some reason unknown to myself, this wild woman evoked within me an exaggerated sense of compassion. Although she said at every opportunity that I need assume no responsibility for her and that I was free to do as my heart desired, she clung to me. She was a coil of contradictions. One day she swore eternal love to me. The next day she said that she wanted to become pregnant because the court would be inclined to be more lenient with a mother. Now that she was a Trotskyite, she hadn't the slightest urge to do time for having served Stalin.

Our room had a wooden balcony that was rotted and sagging

from years of rain and snow. Each time I stepped out onto it I had the feeling it was about to collapse under me. From there I could see the railroad tracks and the pine woods as well as the sanatoriums where thousands of consumptives slowly gasped out their lungs.

That summer only a few of my sketches were printed in *The Express* and the checks from Paris were delayed for so long that I had lost count of how much was coming to me. Years ago Lena had learned the trade of corsetmaking but for that you needed a special sewing machine, fishbone, scissors, and other paraphernalia.

Our possessions in our refuge consisted of a pot, a pan, some tin cutlery, and several books. The handyman of the villa, a Russian named Demienty, was a drunk. He supplied us with the buckets with which to catch the water when it rained. His wife had left him for another Russian. The landlord had stopped paying him wages. When Demienty wasn't lying drunk, he roamed through the woods with a rifle shooting hares, rabbits, birds. Someone had told Lena that Demienty ate cats and dogs. The villa was due to be demolished soon and used as a site for a sanatorium.

Lena and I both lived for the present. In order to get through the day—and sometimes the miserable nights as well—I fantasized that I was already dead, one of those legendary corpses which, instead of resting in the cemetery, leave their graves to reside in the world of chaos. I had described such living dead in my stories and now in my imagination I had become one of my own protagonists. Since I was a corpse, I told myself, what need had I to worry? What could happen to me? A corpse could even afford to sin.

As I stood on the balcony that night I figured out my plans for the day. I had no real reason for going to Warsaw and spending the few zlotys for the fare, but I had to see the few people with whom I was still connected in this worst of all worlds. No one in Warsaw knew my Swider address. I had no telephone. I never saw a letter carrier enter this has-been villa.

Perhaps the check from Paris had come? Maybe there was an answer from the American consul? Maybe there was a letter from Joshua waiting? It was too early to dress and I went back to bed. Lena was awake too. She was sitting on the edge of the bed smoking a cigarette. For an instant I could see her naked body in the glow of its tip. She asked, "What time are you dashing to Warsaw?"

"Ten o'clock."

"So early? Well, it's all the same. Bring me back something to read, at least. Yesterday I finished Dreiser's *An American Tragedy*."

"Is it good?"

"Neither good, nor bad. There is nothing American about this tragedy."

"I'll drop by Bresler's and bring you a whole stack of books."

"Don't get lost in Warsaw."

I was hungry after last night's meager supper. I was in a mood for fresh rolls, coffee with cream, and a piece of herring, but all we had was stale bread and a package of chicory. The little bit of milk that remained had turned sour overnight. Maybe it's already time to return to the grave? I asked myself. But somehow, I wasn't ready yet. Experience had taught me that whenever things grow extremely bad and I think that the end is near, something inevitably happens that seems a miracle. Though I had refuted God I still believed that somewhere in the celestial register accounts were being kept of every person, every worm, every microbe. I did not expect to fall asleep, but I did when I lay down on my torn mattress, and when I opened my eyes the sun was shining.

Lena lit the Primus stove and it began to seethe and stink of alcohol. She boiled water with chicory and handed me a thick slice of black bread smeared with jam. It seemed to me that she took a thinner slice for herself and less jam. Even though she preached equality of the sexes, a trace of respect for the male inherited from generations of grandmothers and great-grandmothers still reposed somewhere within her. I chewed the stale bread for so long that it began to taste fresh. Even the chicory and water acquired flavor when you drank it slowly. Millions of people in India, China, and Manchuria didn't even have this. Only ten years or so earlier, millions of peasants had starved to death in Soviet Russia.

There was no point in getting dressed, since the sun had already begun to bake the roof overhead. I had a clean shirt for my trip to the city, but I didn't want to get it sweaty. A few weeks before I had started a novel for which I nursed great hopes. Joshua had written that the *Forward* would publish my work if they liked it. Besides, I might be able to sell it to a Warsaw newspaper. But the longer I worked on it, the clearer it became to me that it had lost both its action and form. I tried to describe an ex-yeshivah student who had become a professor of mathematics and later grew senile, became an occultist and a believer in the mystical power of numbers, but I lacked the experience for this type of work. Lena had told me this right from the start.

I had failed in every area. I had actually sabotaged myself and my own goals. I had squandered a lot of energy on this manuscript. Certain chapters had come easily to me—those in which I described the confusion and loss of memory inherent in old age. I often had the eerie feeling that I had been born old and senile. But I knew too little about mathematics and nothing at all about life at a university.

It was too early to go to the station, but I could not spend all morning inside that ruin. Lena accompanied me. I warned her that she might be recognized and arrested and she contended that it would be better for her to be imprisoned. At least she wouldn't have to worry about a maternity clinic and a place to live after the summer was over. We strolled along in the sand, each preoccupied with his own thoughts.

Lena began to speak to me and to herself:

"In what way is this miserable place better than a prison? At the Pawiak I had a clean bed. I ate better too. Before I had the fight with the girls, I also had more company. Here, hours go by that you don't speak a word to me. I warned you to put aside that ridiculous novel but you clung to it like a drowning man to a straw. Simply watching you struggle over this damn manuscript is more painful to me than the toughest jail. At times I feel like stopping a policeman and saying, 'Here I am.' At least, I'd find a place for my son."

"How do you know it'll be a son? It could be a daughter."

"For my part, it could be an incubus."

I tried to comfort her by saying that I would take her along to America, but she replied:

"Do me no favors. You can take your America and stick it!"

Finally, the train came and I climbed aboard. Lena turned around to go back. I had to keep reminding myself that I was a corpse, freed of all human anxieties. I was dead, dead, dead! I didn't dare forget this for even a moment.

After a lengthy wait, the train started off toward Warsaw. The car was empty. Fresh breezes blew in from the resort towns. Some vacationers already lay on folding chairs, sunbathing. In Falenica I saw a Jew standing beside a tree in a prayer shawl and phylacteries, swaying over the eighteen benedictions. He beat his breast as he intoned, "We have sinned . . . We have transgressed." At a long table sat yeshivah students while the master lectured, gesticulating and pulling at his yellow beard.

If no check came for me from Paris today, I was through for good. The only way out would be to jump into the Vistula. I received my mail not at my room on Nowolipki Street, but at the home of Leon Treitler, the husband of the former Miss Stefa and the present Madam Treitler.

I was actually going to her. All my mail came at her address. I could have called her long-distance but this was not less expensive than a third-class ticket. I had reached such a stage of isolation where Stefa and a poor cousin of mine, Esther, had become my only contact with Warsaw. Zeitlin and his wife had gone to the Zakopane Mountains for their vacation. J. J. Trunk went to some spa abroad. The Yiddish Writers' Club was deserted in the summer months.

3

Leon Treitler lived in his own building on Niecala Street, a few steps from the Saxony Gardens. The apartment consisted of eight rooms. Leon Treitler had read my stories in Yiddish and Stefa had tried translating them into Polish. She knew more Yiddish than she admitted. She no longer called it slang; she had ceased believing in assimilation. The Jews could neither become totally Polish nor would the Poles tolerate this weird minority. Stefa had been insulted several times in Polish cafes when she had gone there with her husband; she had been advised to go back to Nalewki Street or to Palestine. The anti-Semitic writers in the Polish press even attacked the converts. Some of these writers had accepted the racial theories of Hitler and Rosenberg—this at a time when the Nazi press was describing the Poles as an inferior race and maintaining that a number of their best families, such as the Majewskis and the Wolowskis, were descendants of the followers of the false messiah Jacob Frank, an Oriental Jew and a charlatan. There was even conjecture that the Polish national poet, Adam Mickiewicz, was of that breed since on his mother's side he was a Majewski, which was the name assumed by all the Frankists who converted during the month of May. The Wolowskis, on the other hand, were the offspring of Elisha Shor, one of Frank's most learned disciples.

Warsaw lay in the grip of a heat wave. I couldn't wait until I got to Stefa's to learn whether a letter had come for me and I called her. Telephone service had already made direct dialing possible. I heard the ringing and, presently, Stefa's voice. Stefa had so utterly rejected the idea of assimilation that she often insisted on being addressed as Sheba Leah, and she called me Yitzchok, Itche, and sometimes even Itchele. She now exclaimed:

"Yitzchok, if you called me a minute before, no one would have answered! I went down to buy a paper."

"What's the news?"

"Bad as always. But I have some good news for you. There is mail for you."

"From where?"

"From halfway around the world—from Paris, from New York, from the American consul. It seems there are two letters from New York. Shall I take a look?"

"We'll look together."

"Where are you?"

"At the station."

"Come over. I'll make breakfast for you."

"I've already had my breakfast."

"Either you eat with me or I'll throw all your letters out the window."

"Sheba Leah, you're terrible!"

"That's what I am."

I had intended to walk to Niecala Street from the station to save the fare, but I now raced to catch a streetcar. What a few words can do to a corpse, I said to myself. I had come as close to Treitler's house as the streetcar would take me and I ran the few remaining steps. The janitor knew me. Even his dog didn't bark at me as he once had. On the contrary, he began to wag his tail when I entered the gate. Each time I paid a visit to this house I marveled at what time and human emotions could accomplish. I could never forget my first meeting with Stefa; how she had questioned me as I stood on the other side of the door; the contempt with which she had spoken of Yiddish and of Yiddishkeit; of how close she herself had been to suicide at that time. Now, Stefa was a rich matron and my Polish translator. A fragment of my novel had been published in a Polish newspaper and, thanks to me, her name had appeared in print for the first time. She had signed herself Stefa Janovska Treitler. Leon Treitler was so proud of seeing his name in print that he arranged an evening in honor of the occasion. Among those invited were Stefa's former friends from the *Gymnasium* and the university, several of her relatives, and Leon Treitler's partners with their wives and daughters. Champagne was drunk and speeches

were made. Leon Treitler had bought a hundred copies of
the paper and had had one of them framed. I had never before encountered such exaggerated respect for the printed
word.

Stefa's former teacher, who was also present, made a toast
and recalled that when Stefa had still been in the sixth grade at
the *Gymnasium* he had predicted a literary career for her. He
now prophesied that Stefa would forge a bond between Polish
and Yiddish literature. The fact was that he had mistaken me for
my brother. Joshua's novel had come out in Polish after he had
immigrated to America and it had received favorable reviews.
Oddly, the most virulent Polish anti-Semite, the infamous Nowaczynski, had written a glowing review of this book, *Yoshe
Kalb*. According to his article, my brother had demonstrated the
extraordinary extent of Jewish energy in his novel, and how
skilled the Jew was at hypnotizing himself and others—also,
how the Pole, who was by nature soft, naïve, and weak in character, could easily be influenced by the Jew and dominated by
him if he didn't resist.

The prophesies made by Stefa's teacher that evening at the
Treitlers' didn't come true. Outside of that single piece, no
other work of mine was ever published in Polish. But a love
awoke between Stefa and me that she didn't bother to conceal
from her husband. We kissed in Leon Treitler's presence. He
was one of those men who actually cannot exist without a
hausfreund. He often called to reproach me for neglecting
Stefa.

Leon Treitler was tiny, with a pointed skull lacking even a
single hair. He had a long nose, a sharp, receding chin, a
pointed Adam's apple, and jutting ears. He couldn't have
weighed over a hundred pounds. He dressed like a dandy, loud
ties with pearl stickpins, buckled shoes, and hats with a little
brush or feather. He had a thin nasal voice and he spoke in
ironical paradoxes. He always began the conversation somewhere in the middle—needling and flattering at the same time.
He would say, "And even when you're a famous writer already,

must you ignore every ordinary person just because he or she isn't versed in all works of Nietzsche and can't remember all of Pushkin by heart? I search for you like with candles and you hide out just as if I were your worst enemy. And even if I am an ignoramus and it's beneath your dignity to associate with one of my kind, how is it Stefa's fault? She simply dies of longing for you and you punish her for the fact that instead of marrying a poet she took a moneybags while her true love, that swindler Mark, deserted her with all his diplomas and medals."

This was Leon Treitler's style. He nipped and he stroked. One eye winked and the other laughed. Stefa said that he was both a sadist and a masochist. He was crooked in business and was forever tied up in litigation, but he also gave money to worthy causes. Stefa swore to me that just four weeks after their wedding he had begun seeking a lover for her. He had a female secretary who knew all his tricks and who had been his lover for over twenty-five years.

Leon Treitler was different from other people in many ways. He never slept more than four hours out of the twenty-four. For breakfast, he had bread and wine; for supper, cold meat and black coffee. His sexual gratification consisted of pinching Stefa's bottom and calling her "whore." He owned a whole library of pornographic pictures.

Stefa said to me once, "What Leon Treitler really is, I'll never know if I live to be a thousand. At times I suspect that he is one of your demons."

I rang and Stefa answered. The maid had gone out to market. Stefa had gained some weight but her figure was still slim and girlish. In protest against being constantly complimented on her Gentile appearance, she had dyed her hair brunette, and she wore a Star of David around her neck.

Right there in the corridor we embraced and kissed a long time. Even though she maligned Leon Treitler at every opportunity, I had long since observed that she had acquired some of his mannerisms. She pledged me her love yet at the same time she needled me. Now she took me by the ear, led me into the dining room, and said, "You'll eat with me even if you'll stand on your head!"

"Where are the letters?"

"There are no letters. I fooled you. I don't want you to go off to America and abandon me."

"Come with me."

"First eat! You're as pale as death. They wouldn't allow a skeleton into America."

I had assumed that I was full. My abdomen was bloated and I felt something akin to revulsion toward food. But the moment I bit into the first roll, I became hungry. I said, "Do me a favor and give me the letters. I swear I'll finish everything."

"Your suit is covered with hair. Wait, I'll brush you off."

She carefully plucked a hair from my lapel and examined it against the light of the sun. "A red hair?" she asked. "You told me she was a brunette."

"It's my hair."

"What? You have no hair. It's not your shade either."

"Sheba Leah, don't be silly."

"You're getting to be more like Mark every day. All you need is to forge a signature. What is it with me? It seems I attract this kind of man. One lunatic worse than the next."

"Stefa, enough!"

"You look like death warmed over and you run around with God knows how many sluts. Once and for all I'll give up all hopes of love. This seems to be my fate and that's how it must remain. You're leaving me anyhow. I see everything clearly—you'll go off to America and I'll never hear from you again. And even if I do get a letter, it'll be all lies. Who is the redhead? Red hair doesn't simply float through Otwock and just happen to light on your lapel. Unless your former wench—what was her name—Gina—rose from her grave and paid you a visit."

"Stefa, what's wrong with you?"

"I can endure the worst betrayals, but I can't stand to be deceived. I told you as soon as we got together—everything yes, but no lies! You swore on your parents' lives—your father was still living. Is this true or not?"

"Yes, it's true."

"Who is she? What is she? Where did you meet her? Tell me the truth or I'll never look at your face again!"

"She's my cousin."

"A new lie! You never told me about any cousins. And what about this cousin? Are you having an affair with her?"

"I swear that what I am about to tell you now is the sacred truth."

"What is the truth? Speak!"

I started to tell Stefa about my cousin Esther, who was six years younger than I. When I came to Bilgorai in 1917, I was past thirteen and she was a child of eight. There evolved between us one of those silent loves that neither participant verbalizes nor even dares to think about. When I left Bilgorai for the last time in 1923, Esther was a girl of thirteen but I was a young man of nineteen teaching an evening course in Hebrew. I had begun to write, too, and was having a platonic affair with a girl. I didn't even recall shaking Esther's hand when I left the first time. A rabbi's son didn't shake hands with a girl when the family was present.

Years passed and I didn't hear from Esther. She wrote me only once, when her father, my uncle, died. Suddenly, she showed up in Warsaw, by now a grown woman of twenty-three. She had learned the milliner's trade. She had read many books in Polish and Yiddish, my stories as well. She had become "enlightened" and had given up religion. She had come to Warsaw seeking a job in her trade, but also with the intention of revealing to me what she had kept concealed for so many years. She had confided the truth to only one girl friend, Tsipele. Tsipele now lived in Warsaw too, and worked as a cashier in her uncle's stores. Esther and Tsipele shared a furnished room on Swietojerska Street, across from Krasinski's Gardens.

I presumed that Stefa would interrupt me and call me a liar,

as she so often did, but she heard me out and said, "This
sounds like a fairy tale out of a storybook, but it seems to be
true. What did you do with this Esther? Did you manage to seduce her yet?"

"Absolutely not."

"What is her hair doing on your lapel?"

"Truly, I don't know."

"You know, you know! Wait, I'll get you your letters."

Stefa went out, then came back with a stack of letters that she
flung on the table. I started to open them one after the other.
My hands were trembling. One letter was from my brother. I
could hardly believe my eyes. It contained a check from the
Forward in the amount of ninety dollars. I had sent my brother
one of my stories and he had sold it to the newspaper, of which
he was a staff member.

I opened a second letter from America. A known American
writer and critic had read my novella *Satan in Goray* and his
whole letter was a paean to this work.

The American consulate demanded one additional document
that would be required for the granting of a tourist visa.

The literary magazine for which I both published and served
as a proofreader for a time had forwarded a letter from a reader
who castigated me for writing too much about sex, saying it was
not in the tradition of Yiddish literature.

My brother informed me that as soon as I obtained my foreign passport he would send me the money for the fare.

I had momentarily mislaid the letter from Paris and I
searched for it among the others. Soon I discovered that I had
inadvertently stuck it into my breast pocket and I now opened
it. Inside lay the check for which I had been waiting so long. It
was for an amount in excess of a hundred dollars.

I grew frightened by the plethora of good fortune all at one
time. "You haven't earned it," someone within me exclaimed.
Stefa stood there and looked at me sidelong. She asked, "What
are you doing—praying?"

"Sheba Leah, you've brought me luck."

"Luck and I are not a pair."

4

Stefa accompanied me to the office of the Hebrew Immigrant Aid Society where they cashed my checks for American currency. The cashier opened a huge safe crammed from top to bottom with dollar bills. Afterward, we went to a bank where my check from Paris was cashed for nearly a thousand zlotys. I had exchanged my elegant and comfortable room at Mrs. Alpert's for a tiny cubicle on Nowolipki Street rented to me for thirty zlotys a month by a member (or a guest) of the Writers' Club, a principal of a Hebrew school and author of a grammar textbook. He and his family were away now on vacation and I actually had the entire apartment to myself, but he, M. G. Haggai, came back to Warsaw each week for a day or two and I could never know when he would show up.

It was certainly risky to bring Stefa to such a place, but the danger at her home was even greater. Although Leon Treitler pretended that he didn't even know the meaning of jealousy, one could never foresee how he would react if he caught us together.

Stefa wouldn't go to a hotel. Her mother had died, but her father, Isidore Janovsky, was still living and he had a room in a hotel on Milna Street, nearby. He liked to roam through the streets, to chat with other old people in Krasinski's Gardens, in the Saxony Gardens, or on a bench on Iron Gate Square. Even as Stefa walked with me she kept looking behind. She told me that if her father found out about her behavior, he would have a heart attack. She also had hordes of relatives in Warsaw who envied her good fortune, and who would have loved the chance to malign her. Stefa took my arm, then quickly dropped it. Each time she walked with me in the street she had some pretext ready in case we encountered her husband, her father, or someone from her or her husband's family.

We walked into the gate of the house of Mr. Haggai's apartment and climbed the two flights of stairs. Doors stood open.

Children cried, laughed, screamed. This was a respectable family building, not one for illicit loves. Before leaving Stefa's house, I had telephoned here to make sure M. G. Haggai wasn't at home. But what guarantee did I have that he hadn't come in in the interval? For renting me the room so cheaply, M. G. Haggai had stipulated that I behave decently. Tenants of the building enrolled their children in his school and I shouldn't dare do anything to damage his reputation.

I now rang the doorbell, but no one came. M. G. Haggai was surely lounging on a folding chair in Falenica reading the London Hebrew magazine *Haolam* and enjoying the fresh air. His apartment was decorated with pictures of Zionist leaders: Herzl, Max Nordau, Chlenov, Weizmann, Sokolov. There also hung here a portrait of the pedagogue Pestalozzi. Each time Stefa visited my little room she said the same thing: "This isn't a room but a hole."

This time I countered with: "Good enough for two mice."

"Speak for yourself."

I was in a hurry, since I still had to meet Esther. I had to stop by Bresler's Lending Library and select some books for Lena. I also intended to buy food, which was easier to obtain in Warsaw, as well as a small present for Lena. But Stefa had more than once said that she didn't equate lovemaking with speed. She had to begin with conversation and the subject was always the same: the reason she couldn't remain true to Treitler—he had always repelled her. He had won her in a moment of her deepest despair. One could truthfully say that he had bought her with money.

Stefa sat down on the only chair in my room and crossed her legs. Her knees had remained pointed although not as much as before. I had already had her many times, but I still felt a strong urge for her, since sooner or later we would have to part. She spoke and from time to time she took a drag on her cigarette.

I heard her say, "If someone had told me five years ago that I would be Mrs. Treitler and conducting an illicit affair with some jargon journalist, I would have considered him mad.

Sometimes it seems to me that I'm no longer me but someone
else—as if I were possessed by one of your dybbuks."

Abruptly, she began to study the walls.

"What do you see there?" I asked.

"I'm afraid there are bedbugs here."

"They sleep by day."

Stefa started to say something, but at that moment there was
a sound in the corridor. That which I had feared had occurred—M. G. Haggai had come home on his weekly visit.

Stefa tensed. Her face twisted momentarily. M. G. Haggai
coughed and mumbled to himself. I assumed that he would
immediately open the door to my room but apparently he went
into the living room. However, he was liable to peek into my
room at any moment. It was a miracle that he hadn't arrived a
half hour later.

Stefa put out her cigarette in a saucer to be used for an ashtray. "Let's get out of here! This very second!"

"Sheba Leah, it's not my fault."

"No, no, no! You are what you are, but I had no right to crawl into
such a slime. All the evil forces have turned against me. Come, let
us go!"

"Why are you so scared? We're both dressed. I've got a right
to have visitors."

"How close did we come to being caught without our
clothes? These Hebraists know everybody. Leon's daughter attended a Hebrew *Gymnasium*. He might have been her teacher
there."

The door to my room opened and M. G. Haggai stuck his
head inside. Outside, a heat wave raged, but he wore his overcoat, a derby (a "melon" as it was called in Warsaw), a high stiff
collar, and a black cravat. He had a round face and a gray goatee. A pair of horn-rimmed glasses with thick lenses sat upon
his broad nose. He hadn't even managed to put down the briefcase he was carrying under his arm. Seeing a woman, he re-
coiled, but soon after he crossed the threshold and said, "Excuse me. I didn't know you were here and that you had

company besides. My name is Haggai," he said, turning to
Stefa. "The name of a prophet among us Jews. But I'm no
prophet. I thought that our friend here was away on vacation,
not here in the hot city. I must come in every week since I am
the principal and owner of a private school and this is the
time when the students are being enrolled for the coming
term. What is your esteemed name, if one may ask?"

Stefa didn't respond. It was as if she had completely lost pos-
session of herself. It was I who replied. "This is Miss Anna Goldsober."

"Goldsober, eh? I know three Goldsober families in Warsaw,"
Haggai said. "One is Dr. Zygmunt Goldsober, a famous ophthal-
mologist. Someone told me he is even more distinguished than
Dr. Pinnes, or is it *Professor* Pinnes? The second Goldsober family has a wholesale dry-goods business on Gesia Street. Their
son attended my school. He is already a father himself. The
third Goldsober is a lawyer. To which of these Goldsobers do
you belong?"

"To neither—" Stefa said.

"So? You are not a Litvak?"

"A Litvak? No."

M. G. Haggai winked at me. "I have something to discuss with
you. If you'll excuse us, madam, I'd like a word with him
alone."

I followed him into the living room. He slowly removed his
hat and coat and put down the briefcase. His eyes, through the
thick lenses, appeared unnaturally big and stern. He said, "Your
visitor is no Goldsober as you have misrepresented her, and
she is surely no miss."

"How do you know what she is or isn't?"

"A miss doesn't wear a wedding ring. You gave me a promise
and you haven't kept it. I don't want to be your mentor, but you
can't receive such visitors at my house. You'll have to move out.
I'm sorry. When is your month up?"

"At the end of the coming week."

"You'll have to find another room."

"I've committed no sin, but if that's what you want, I'll do as you ask."

"I'm sorry."

I went back to my room and Stefa stood there already wearing her hat and holding her bag, ready to go. She asked, "Why did you pick Goldsober of all names? Oh, that one is a pest. The whole time he kept staring at my wedding ring. What did he say to you? Probably asked you to move. If a grave would open for me, I'd jump into it this minute."

She said this in Polish, but the expression was pure Yiddish.

5

We walked in the direction of Karmelicka Street and Stefa spoke, as if to herself: "This isn't for me. Warsaw isn't Paris but a small town. My father lives but a few blocks from here. He is liable to come upon us at any moment. He claims to be half blind, but the things he shouldn't see, he sees well enough. You know what? Let's head in the opposite direction. Where does this street lead to?"

"To Karolkowa, to Mlinarska, to the Jewish cemetery."

"Come, let us go there. I don't want to disappoint my father. He feels that I've enjoyed a stroke of great fortune. It's no trifle to be Mrs. Treitler. The very title makes me nauseous. I envy my mother. She knows nothing anymore. If people knew how happy the dead are, they wouldn't struggle so hard to hold on to life. The first thing my mother did after my sister died was to use her last few zlotys and buy a plot next to hers. Now they lie side by side. People still go to visit the graves of their parents. They really believe that the dead lie there waiting to be told all the troubles that have befallen those close to them. Here is a droshky. . . . Hey!"

"Where do you want to go?" I asked.

"What's the difference? Let's go someplace. You said yourself that your cousin, or whoever she may be, won't be home until seven. Today belongs to me."

"Where do the lady and gentleman wish to go?" the cab driver asked.

Stefa hesitated for a moment. "To Niecala Street. But don't turn around. Go by way of Iron Street and from there through Chlodna, Electoralna—"

"That's the long way around."

"You'll get double your fare."

"Giddy up!"

"We should have stayed there in the first place," I said.

"You had to cash your checks. For me, nothing comes easy. But since you're going away to America, what difference does it make? To have a maid is to have a spy in the house. I had enough of my parents' maid spying on me and reporting everything to my mother. If a young man phoned me occasionally, she ran to tell her. She herself was a widow. Her husband died four weeks after their wedding. Strange, she never spied on my sister. Now, I've got Jadwiga on my back. She worked for Leon years before he married me. She remembers his first wife and she looks at me as if I had murdered her. His daughters feel that way about me too, as do the neighbors. I'm nothing but an intruder. What will I do after you're gone? Start an affair with a new liar? Three liars in a lifetime is enough for me. In the morning when I look in the mirror, especially after a good night's sleep, I see a young person. But when I look at myself in the evenings, I see a broken woman ready for the scrap pile. Mark deserted me physically and shattered me spiritually—that's the truth. Going to live with Leon Treitler was for me a catastrophe. Then my foul luck directed me to start up with you . . . You don't forge promissory notes, but you're made of the same stuff as he—a timid adventurer."

"Thanks for the compliment."

The droshky entered Chlodna, passed the fire station with its huge brass bell, the Seventh Police Precinct, then turned into

Electoralna Street, where the Hospital of the Holy Ghost was located. Flocks of pigeons soared over the roofs and perched on the heads, shoulders, and arms of the holy statues. Below, some of them ate from the hands of an old woman. Every street we passed, every building, evoked within me memories of my childhood. The Poles still considered us aliens, but the Jews had helped build this city and had assumed an enormous participation in its commerce, finances, and industry. Even the statues in this church represented images of Jews.

Just as if Stefa could read my mind, she remarked, "We Jews are damned. Why?"

"Because we love life too much."

The droshky came to Niecala Street. Stefa's maid, Jadwiga, had left a note in the kitchen saying that Mr. Treitler would be detained at his work and would have dinner with his partner at a restaurant. Stefa had told Jadwiga that she would be eating dinner out, and Jadwiga had gone to visit a friend who had given birth to an illegitimate child and had to stay with it.

Stefa said, "I'm beginning to believe that there is a God."

"Since He obliges us, then He exists."

"Don't be so sarcastic. If He is truly our father and we are His children as the Bible states, He *should* oblige us from time to time."

"He is your husband's father too."

"That which I'm doing benefits him too. He wants it subconsciously. Where are my cigarettes?"

Stefa had become momentarily cheerful. We hadn't eaten lunch and she went to the kitchen to fix us a quick bite. She put on a short apron that lent her a particularly feminine allure. I sat down at the kitchen table and reread the letters I had received that morning. I also recounted the money. I told myself that this was one of the happiest days of my life. To avoid it being ruined, I offered up a silent prayer to the God whose commandments I was breaking. Actually, this was what thieves, murderers, and rapists did. Even Hitler mentioned the Almighty in his speeches.

6

Night had already fallen by the time I said good-bye to Stefa.
My wristwatch indicated a quarter to ten. Our mutual desire and
our powers had never been as strong as during those long
hours. Usually, gratification is contingent upon ennui as Schopenhauer contends, but my satiety that day brought no tedium.
Only the worries returned. I had committed a folly in cashing
both checks. I was afraid now of being robbed or of springing
a hole in my breast pocket and losing my fortune. I no longer
had time to visit Bresler's Lending Library, which was closed by
now anyhow. The stores were all closed too and I wouldn't
even be able to buy Lena the delicacies she preferred. There
was barely any time left to visit my cousin. What's more, I had
promised Lena to come back early, but I wasn't sure now
whether I could even catch the last train to Otwock, which left
at midnight and arrived around 1 A.M.

Thank God, an empty taxi came by. I was only afraid lest the
driver should—through some mysterious power—ascertain that
I was carrying a sum amounting to over two hundred dollars
and try to rob me. The taxi made the trip to Swietojerska Street
in five minutes. I climbed the stairs, which were illuminated by
a tiny gaslight. On the second floor I bumped into Esther's
roommate, Tsipele. She was going out, probably in order to
leave us alone. She wore a straw hat that Esther had made for
her. Tsipele had once been my pupil in an evening course in
Hebrew I had taught in Bilgorai. She had learned no Hebrew
from me, but just the same, she still called me "moreh"—
teacher.

I had never done this before, but I kissed her. Her face lay
completely in shadow. She exclaimed, "Oh, Moreh, what are
you doing?"

Tsipele was blond, taller than Esther, and younger by a year.
Esther had told me that Tsipele's uncle, for whom she worked
as an assistant bookkeeper, was in love with her. He gave her

money, sent her flowers, brought her candy, and took her to
the theater, the opera, and to restaurants. Tsipele's aunt was
suspicious that she was trying to steal her husband away, but
Esther assured me that Tsipele remained a virgin. The whole
world is either crazy with love or crazy with hate, I said to myself. I knocked and Esther opened the door. Her hair was a dark
red, her face densely freckled. We had both inherited our col-
oring from our Grandmother Hannah, the rebbetzin.

From the day of her wedding at barely twelve years of age,
no one, not even Grandfather, had seen her hair, for she
shaved her skull. Only her eyebrows were red. Our grandfather, Jacob Mordecai, was a year older than she. As a child he
had acquired the reputation of a prodigy. When he was nine
he gave a sermon in the house of study and scholars came to
debate with him on Talmudic subjects. Grandmother's father,
Isaac, after whom I am named, was a merchant and a man of
wealth, who had arranged for Jacob Mordecai to marry his
only daughter, Hannah. Grandmother Hannah had a fiery tem-
per and, although her husband became known as a sage and
she couldn't write a Yiddish letter without errors, whenever
they quarreled she called him a Litvak pig. This was undeserved,
as he had been born in Miedzyrzec, which was in Poland, not
in Lithuania.

Our grandparents were no longer living, but their blood
flowed in our veins. When Esther spoke I could hear in her
words, and even more so in her intonation, generations of
scholars, pious women, as well as something that seemed non-
Jewish, even typically goyish. Within our genetic cells, the sub-
jugators and the subjugated were forced to co-exist. I had
warned myself not to become involved with Esther. I was honest enough to tell her that I had no intention of getting married.
I told her about Stefa and Lena as well as of my efforts to settle
in America. But Esther had been influenced by the new concepts. She wasn't engaged to any man. There was no purpose
in saving her virginity for someone she didn't know or who
might never turn up. Her female coworkers at the millinery

shop all had lovers. Most young men no longer required that their prospective wives be virgins. The situation in the world was desperate, and that of the Jews in Poland especially. So why wait?

Esther and I now lay on the bed and from time to time I glanced at my watch. I didn't dare miss my train to Otwock! I felt guilty, but I had the consolation that I wasn't deceiving Esther. We both tried to steal something which belonged to us only. Esther's face was flushed nevertheless. She told me that she would never forget me and that if she was spared she would come to me in America. I had noticed that Esther too glanced at her wristwatch. Tsipele would be returning shortly.

We said good-bye, kissed at length, and arranged a rendez-vous for the coming week when I would absolutely, positively have more time for her. When we were at the door, Esther mumbled, "I hope you were careful."

"Yes, a hundred percent!"

The gaslight illuminating the stairs was out, which meant that the gate was already closed. I had descended half a flight when I heard Esther's voice. She called to me to come back. It turned out that in my excitement the roll of bills—all the money I had collected today at the bank and at the HIAS office—had fallen out of my breast pocket.

I seized it and stuck it back in my pocket. "I'm crazy, crazy as a loon!"

I started racing down the stairs in the dark. I had lost some two to three minutes. I would have to wait until the janitor opened the gate for me. I began to search for the bell with which to rouse him. I couldn't find it. I tapped around like a blind man. Luckily, someone rang the bell on the outside. The janitor was in no hurry to open up, and only after a long wait did he come out of his cubicle, grumbling, as did all janitors I have ever met. I groped in my pocket for a coin with which to tip him, but I couldn't find one. I was almost sure that I had had coins in both pockets of my jacket. I must have dropped them at Esther's. The janitor paused and stretched out a hand for my coin, and when I began to apologize, he spat and cursed. I heard him say *"Psia krew"*—dog's blood. He opened the gate with a large key and by the light of the streetlamp I saw Tsipele.

"Moreh!"

She made a move as if to embrace me, but I only managed to say "Good night!" I hadn't a moment to lose now. I ran in the direction of Nalewki Street. I had to catch either a streetcar, a droshky, or a taxi—whichever came first. One taxi passed after another—they were all heading away from the depot, not toward it. The streetcars also ran in the opposite direction. All I could do was run. It was eight minutes to twelve by the time I got to the Gdansk Station. Thank God there was no line in front of the ticket seller's cage and I quickly bought my ticket. This wasn't a local train running only between Warsaw and Otwock, but one that ran as far as Lvov. The cars were crowded with passengers, mostly Jewish salesmen and storekeepers from the provinces. Almost every one carried sacks, bundles, or crates of goods. Several coaches were full of soldiers. No civilian passengers were allowed in there. The soliders stood by the open windows and mocked the harassed Jews racing from car to car and dragging their bundles. The second-class cars were occupied mainly by officers.

I squeezed myself into one of the third-class cars as best I could. All the seats were taken. Some passengers read Yiddish newspapers, some chewed unfinished suppers from paper bags, others leaned their heads against the walls trying to catch some sleep. All the faces reflected the fatigue of the Diaspora, the fear of tomorrow. The train was scheduled to depart at midnight, but the clock showed a quarter past twelve and we still hadn't moved. The car smelled of cigarette smoke, garlic, onions, sweat, and the latrine. Facing me stood a girl with a gold, or gold-plated, Star of David hanging around her neck. She was trying to read a novel by the Polish sex novelist Gabriela Zapolska in the murky light of the gas lamp. Just as I, she had accepted the kind of secular Jewishness that defies all definitions.

This time, the trip from Warsaw to Otwock took not an hour but only half that time. The train stopped there for just a minute and discharged a few passengers. I started off across the sandy path leading to the broken-down villa where Lena waited for me. I had brought her neither food nor travel books, but I had resolved that first thing in the morning I would go to Slavin's Bookstore and buy her a book and take her to a restaurant.

Otwock, with all its consumptives, was asleep. Inside the sanatoriums' morgues lay those who earlier that day had breathed their last. I climbed the dark stairs of the house we lived in and every board squeaked beneath my heavy shoes. I opened the door to our room. Our bed stood empty. I called, "Lena! Lena!" and an echo answered. I opened the door to the balcony even though I could see through the glass door that no one was there. I began searching for matches, but I didn't find them. It was Lena who smoked, not I, and she had probably taken them with her. After a while my eyes had grown accustomed to the dark and I began to see by the light of the stars and that of a distant streetlight. Lena had taken her coat and her satchel. She hadn't left a note.

I went out onto the balcony and stood there for a long time contemplating the heavenly bodies. I asked them mutely, "What do you say to all this?" And I imagined that they replied, "We have seen it all before."

Two

1

EVERYTHING CAME HARD TO ME—
the passport, the visa. Even a naïve Yankee like the American
consul didn't believe that I was being invited to America to
speak about literature. I looked like a frightened boy, not a
lecturer. He posed many questions to me through his interpreter, a Jewish girl with a big head of bleached curly hair.
The consul had received information from someone that I was
having an affair with a leftist woman and he asked, "How is it
you come to be involved with such individuals?"

I was overcome by a silly sense of frankness and I countered
his question with another: "Where else can you get free love?"

The interpreter laughed, and after she had translated my response, laughter broke out among the other officials.

This answer, like all my others, was not true. Many of the so-
called bourgeois girls were already far from being chaste. The
only difference lay in that the bourgeois girls weren't interested
in some Yiddish scribbler who was a pauper besides. They sought
doctors, lawyers, or wealthy merchants. They demanded to be
taken to the theater, to cafes. Neither was I interested in their
banalities. With Lena at least I could have discussions, dash her
hopes for a better world. To her I was a cynic, not a *schlemiel.*

After a long interrogation, and shaking his head dolefully, the
consul affixed the stamp designating a tourist visa in my passport. He shrugged his shoulders and wished me a happy journey. Oddly, all the lies I told the consul that day came true years

later. How does Spinoza put it in his *Ethics*: There are no lies, only crippled truths. I might add, The truer a truth is, the more crippled it appears to us.

Of course I felt exalted that I had been granted, one might say, the privilege of life, a reprieve from Hitler's executioners. Yet, at the same time, I thought, This is man. His life and death depend on a piece of paper, a signature, the whim of another, be he consul, *starosta,* judge, or commissar. When I left the consul's office, I passed a hallway where many others like me were waiting. Their eyes seemed to ask, Did he get his visa or was he refused it? And what will be *my* fate? On that pre-spring day I felt more than ever the dependence of man, his helplessness. I envied the cobblestones in the streets, which needed no passports, no visas, no novels, no favors. It wasn't I that was alive and they that were dead, I told myself. Quite the contrary. The stones lived and I was dead.

From time to time I fingered the passport in my breast pocket. Had all this really happened? And what had I done to deserve this? Again and again I stopped at shop windows and leafed through the passport. It was valid for a period of six months, as was the visa. After that I would have to apply for an extension at the Polish consulate in New York and to the Immigration Service in Washington. Even if it became possible to obtain a permanent visa outside of the quota, I couldn't obtain it in America. According to law, I'd have to go outside the country to apply for this visa—to Canada or Cuba, for instance. But to do that required another visa. . . .

Several years before, when I had been exempted from military service, it was Gina who had been waiting for me to hear the news. But Gina no longer lived. Lena had vanished. As for Stefa, my visa to America was hardly good news. She told me this at every opportunity. Nor would my cousin Esther be pleased that I'd be leaving.

Although M. G. Haggai had asked me to move out that summer day, I still lived there. He had changed his mind. I had convinced him that I had committed no sin in his house. He enjoyed chatting with me about literature and about the fact that most Hebrew writers didn't know their grammar. They made errors in their texts and the critics knew even less than they did. Haggai often told me that in order to know Hebrew properly one had to devote one's whole life to it, and sometimes it appeared that even one life wasn't enough.

I telephoned Stefa now. She wasn't home. Esther had a job at a milliners with a store and workshop on Zabia Street and she wasn't due home till evening. I went to have lunch at the Writers' Club and possibly to try to telephone Stefa again. The Writers' Club wasn't yet twenty years old but I had the feeling that it had existed forever. A number of the writers had grown old; many had died; a few had grown senile. Everyone who belonged to the club had endless complaints against the world, against God, against other writers, editors, reviewers, even against the readers and their bad taste.

I had the urge to show off my visa to somebody, but I decided against it. The telephone rang and the woman at the hatcheck counter came to fetch me. It was Stefa. I told her the news and she exclaimed, "Come right over!"

I went out into the street and raced toward Niecala Street. Warsaw suddenly appeared to me a foreign city. I barely recognized the stores, the buildings, the tramways. I recalled something out of the Gemara: "That which is about to be burned is like already burned." I paraphrased it in my mind: That which one is preparing to abandon is like already abandoned.

As usual before spring, cold winds blended with warm breezes. One tree in the Saxony Gardens bloomed all by itself amidst the other bare trees and bushes. A few days before I had seen a blossom fall along with snow while a butterfly fluttered amidst it all. I wanted to leave the city, yet at the same time I already longed for this city where I hadn't properly settled but had merely sampled a meager portion of its allures. I now compared Warsaw to a book one must lay aside just as the story is approaching its climax. I rang Stefa's doorbell and she came to answer. While still in the doorway, she said, "I should congratulate you, but it's all happening faster than I can digest it."

"Why did you happen to phone to the club today?" I asked.

"Oh, my cursed intuition. Last night, Leon said, 'You'll see.
Your lover will go away and not even write to you.'"

"Is that what he called me?"

"Yes, he knows everything. Sometimes he speaks of you as if
he knows nothing, then suddenly he sounds as if he knows it all.
Actually I wanted to ring you at Haggai's, only I made a mistake
and dialed the Writers' Club instead. Come, show me the visa.
We'll have to make a party, or whatever. Before you even began
talking about America I knew that you would do the same as
Mark—leave me. In New York someone already waits who
doesn't even know of your existence. But she'll take you in her
arms and you'll be hers. That's how destiny works. One thing I
want to assure you, I'll never depend upon anyone again."

"Stefa, you promised to tell me the truth." I heard my lips form
the words. I knew that Stefa knew what I meant. That day when
she phoned me at Mrs. Alpert's and I asked if she had had a boy
or a girl, she told me that she had had nothing, and her answer
remained the same thereafter. I could never determine from her
if she had had the child or a late abortion, or possibly had given
birth to a stillborn infant. Each time I returned to this subject,
Stefa offered the same response with the resolution of one who
has determined to take a secret along to the grave. I wasn't all that
concerned. The child, if it existed at all, was Mark's, not mine.
One of the womanizers at the Writers' Club had once given me a
list of symptoms by which to determine if a woman had ever
given birth. Later, a gynecologist I had met on vacation told me
that all these alleged signs were pure nonsense.

I was ashamed of my curiosity and tried somehow to justify
it, but Stefa gave me no opportunity to do so. She seized my
wrist, cast a solemn look at me, and said, "I have a daughter!"

I had the feeling that the words had been torn from her
mouth.

"Where is she?"

"In Gdansk."

Stefa didn't let go of my hand but squeezed it forcefully, as if
waiting for me to ask more.

"Leon knows?"

"Yes, he knows. He pays for her. He even wanted to bring her to Warsaw, but I didn't want our families to have something to gossip about forever. My father is alive and I don't want to cause him grief. He will never know that he has a grandchild. Mark's mother died without this satisfaction. Nor does Mark know that he's a father. I've wanted to speak to you about this on many occasions, but somehow I always postponed it. The Nazis are on the verge of seizing Gdansk and the whole Corridor. I don't want my child to fall into the hands of those murderers."

"If they seize Gdansk, they can seize Warsaw too," I said, not sure whether I should say this and for what purpose.

"Yes, true, but Leon is an optimist—so deeply involved in his business that he is blind to all other matters. He keeps predicting that it will never come to war. In his own fashion, Leon is a good person. If only I could love him—but something about him repels me. The worst of it is that I absolutely cannot understand him. His whole way of thinking and all his emotions are those of someone who has come down from another planet. His whole being is focused on money, yet he gets little pleasure from all his earnings. He loves me, but in a way as if I were a bargain he had caught at some bazaar."

"If he loves you, convince him to get your daughter and take you both to America."

"That he wouldn't do. He's even afraid to go to the country for the summer. When he took that trip around the world with me, he claimed to have lost half of his fortune because of it. He remains in the city during the worst heat waves. It's gotten so I myself don't want to go anywhere anymore. Not with him. When he's away from Warsaw and his business, he becomes completely mad."

"Why don't you have a child together?"

"Oh, I don't want his child. I don't want any more children. What for? I shouldn't say this, but the older Franka gets—I named my daughter after my dead aunt—the more she resembles Mark. The German woman who is bringing her up keeps sending photographs, and her resemblance to him is uncanny.

If I were raising her myself perhaps I might not notice this so clearly, but when I receive the photos I see things a mother shouldn't see. I still hope to God that she won't have his character. Oh, you shouldn't have asked me about it, then I wouldn't have had to say these bitter words. My love for Mark has changed into revulsion. Once I found a photograph of him among my papers and when I looked at it I literally threw up."

"Where is he?"

"I don't know and I don't want to know. You are, in a sense, the witness to my fiasco—to all my fiascoes. Because he was so passionately assimilated, I grew closer to Jewishness, but I can't stand the Jews either. The whole species of man is revolting to me. I ask no favor of God, but I would like my father to die in his sleep. That's an easy death. Then I would put an end to the whole rottenness."

Three

1

I HAD PACKED MY CLOTHES AND MY
manuscripts into the two valises that I took with me to America.
I said good-bye to Aaron Zeitlin, to J. J. Trunk, and to a few
others. The Jewish section of the PEN Club was issuing my first
book in Yiddish, *Satan in Goray,* but copies weren't yet ready
for me to take along.

Stefa, Leon Treitler, and my cousin Esther came to see me off
at the railroad station. They had wanted to make a farewell party
for me at the Writers' Club, but I demurred. I had observed
many such parties. The writers ate, drank tea, and made long
and often inane speeches about the guest of honor. The wags
made quiet fun of the speakers and of their silly praises. I had
occasionally been one of those wags and more than once I had
heard some hack being praised in superlatives. The speakers
often justified this by claiming that they had done it out of compassion for a neglected writer, a foreign visitor, or whoever he
might have been. I wasn't anxious to be a part of this sort of
literary philanthropy. I was already close to thirty and all I had
accomplished in Yiddish literature was one novella and several
short stories that I had published in magazines and anthologies
no one read. I had seen writers, actors, and other creative people literally arrange banquets and jubilees in their own behalf.
Long before they reached the age of fifty, they began mention-
ing the date of their birth, or the date of their first publication,
or appearing on the stage, hinting and grumbling about the lack

of public appreciation. Invariably, a group of friends evolved
who did recognize and did remember. Sometimes a "surprise"
banquet was then arranged for the forgotten hero, who wrote
the invitations himself. I recall one time when they tried to en-
list J. J. Trunk in such a masquerade, but he had enough sense
to decline. "It's not that I dislike honor," he told me, "but I
refuse shame."

In a way, the last few weeks prior to my departure were to
me like a long holiday. People were friendlier to me than ever,
often sentimental, as if sensing that we would never see each
other again. Women with whom I had conducted semi-, quarter-,
or might-have-been affairs suddenly determined that this was
the time for us to go further or all the way.

In those days, a trip to America was still considered an adventure. True, Lindbergh had already flown the Atlantic, but passenger service to America was still by sea. My biggest concern was
that as a single passenger I would have to share a cabin with
another man. My need for privacy was so strong that I was ready
to spend my last groschen for a private cabin. The fact is that
even my last groschen wouldn't have helped. I confided my pre-
dicament to my travel agent and he was astounded that I should
be perturbed about such a trifle.

At that time the famed French ship the *Normandie* was
scheduled to make her maiden voyage to New York. All the
snobs of Europe strove to be aboard. My agent himself was
booked to make this voyage. He had become so friendly with
me that he suggested that I wait two weeks and share his
cabin on the *Normandie*. But I declined the privilege. First of
all, I feared an imminent Hitler invasion; but mainly I still
hoped to get a private cabin aboard some other vessel. After
a lengthy search, the agent located what I had been seeking—a cabin for one, without portholes and also without air,
on a French ship.

Everything was over—the frantic words, the kisses, the em-
braces, the fervent promises to bring over almost everyone I
knew to America even though all I held was a six-month tourist
visa. It was the month of April, 1935. The following day was the

birthday of one of the most cruel murderers in world history, Hitler. I had to travel by train through Nazi Germany because it would have been too expensive to take a different route. I had heard that Jewish passengers were forced to get off the train and they were searched and subjected to other indignities. I would be proceeding directly into the hands of the evildoers. They could easily take away my passport and visa and send me to a concentration camp. I fully grasped the danger, but somehow fear within me had gone into a kind of hibernation, to be replaced by a sense of fatalism.

I stood by the window of the coach looking out at the lights of Warsaw, and what I saw appeared as strange to me as if I were seeing it for the first time. Soon the lights of the city faded and in the semidarkness emerged factories, and structures that were hard to identify. Only the glowing sky gave evidence that we weren't far from a large city.

This international train had sleeping cars and a diner. I traveled tourist-class, which was better lit than the usual third-class car and had more comfortable seats. Three Chinese men sat facing me and conversed in their language. Or maybe they were Koreans? This was the first time I had been that close to people of another race. I had seen several Orientals in Warsaw, and once a black man, but always from afar, perhaps through a streetcar window.

Although we were still close to Warsaw and the train ran past little depots of familiar towns, I felt as if I were already abroad. I knew that I would never come this way again and that Warsaw, Poland, the Writers' Club, my mother, my brother Moishe, and the women who were near to me had all passed over into the sphere of memory. The fact is that they had been ghosts even while I was still with them. Long before I ever heard of Berkeley and Kant, I felt that what we call reality had no substance other than that formed in our minds. I was, one might say, a solipsist long before I ever heard of the word; actually, from the day I commenced pondering the so-called eternal questions.

There had been moments when I had assumed that once I got the visa to America I would be happy. But I felt no happiness now, not even a trace. I was glad somehow that the passengers on the other bench didn't know my language so that I wouldn't have to converse with them.

I sat by the window looking out at the dense darkness, and from time to time, glanced up at the stars. I wasn't leaving *them*. The universe rode along with me. I recognized the shapes of the constellations. Perhaps the universe accompanied us on our journey into eternity when we concluded the little incident we call life?

I stretched out on the seat and from time to time I fingered the passport inside my breast pocket. "Up there, there are no borders, no passports," the babbler within me babbled. "There are no Nazis. Could a star be a Nazi? Up there, there is no lack of living space. Up there—let us hope—you don't have to fight for your existence if you exist."

I toyed with my thoughts like a child playing with knucklebones. By dawn, we had reached the border. There was a change of conductors. I saw a man wearing a swastika. He took my passport and turned its pages. He asked how much money I was carrying and I told him and showed him the bank notes. He said, "Not necessary," and returned the passport. Another individual wearing a swastika came in and the two exchanged a salutation: "Heil Hitler!" Then they left.

I saw through a window Jews being herded inside a building to be searched. I later heard that some had been stripped naked. We had entered the land of the Inquisition.

As in all other inquisitions, the sun remained neutral. It rose and its light illuminated balconies decorated with Nazi banners. It was the Führer's forty-seventh birthday. I forgot to mention that all this occurred during the intermediary days of Passover. Leon Treitler had invited me to the seder. Stefa had prepared matzohs, the bitter herbs, as well as fish, meat, and matzohballs. Leon Treitler had donned a white robe and recited the Haggada. I had asked the Four Questions. None of us took the ceremony too seriously. None of us believed the miracle of the Exodus from Egypt and the parting of the Red Sea. Stefa's father had declined to attend the seder at his daughter's home. He

didn't trust her *kashruth*. He probably didn't want to see me
either.

I don't recall if we rode the same train the whole way or if
we changed trains at the border. In Berlin a young man came
into the car and called my name. I became frightened. Had they
come to arrest me? It turned out that the young man worked
for (or was associated with) my travel agent and he brought me
some matzohs and a Passover delicacy. At that time the perse-
cutions of the Jews in Germany had just commenced. The other
passengers looked on in amazement as I sat chewing the matzoh. The day was sunny and balmy, and outside of the flags with
the swastikas, one couldn't tell that the country was in the hands
of a savage dictator. German families sat out on balconies eating
lunch. Their faces appeared genial. The streets in the cities and
towns that we rode through were clean and almost empty.
Someone had left a German newspaper on the seat and I read
an enthusiastic article about Hitler; about what he had already
accomplished and what he would do for Germany in the future.

Late at night the train stopped at the Belgian border and I
had to show my passport again. This was my second sleepless
night and I no longer had any curiosity about the country
through which we were passing. I lay on the hard bench and
stopped trying to straighten my limbs. My half-muffled ears
heard conversations in French and Flemish.

I had resolved not to become too excited over Paris, like all
the others. Someone at the Writers' Club had given me the address of a cheap hotel in a section called Belleville. I was scheduled to spend two or three days in Paris, then take the train to
Cherbourg, where my ship was docked. In the thirty-six hours I
had been traveling, I had accustomed myself to the enforced
sleeplessness, to eating meals from a paper bag, to not exchang-
ing a word with anyone, and not changing my clothes. I didn't
even glance at the stamps that the border officials affixed to my
passport. I made no effort to study those who got on and off in
the various countries. I had grown indifferent to the notion of
traveling abroad, which had once been my dream.

Day started breaking and rain was falling. We were already in

France and the train was approaching Paris. I thought about the travelers of earlier days who had to endure long journeys in stagecoaches, carriages, even on horseback. Where did they gather the strength and the patience for so many hardships? Why hadn't they chosen to stay home?

I had dozed and yawned. The conductor prodded my shoulder. We had arrived in Paris. I felt my breast pocket, where I kept my passport and the ship's ticket, and the trouser back pocket, where I kept my money, some fifty dollars in American and French bank notes. Then I seized the two valises, which seemed to have grown heavier. The taxi driver didn't understand me and I handed him the slip of paper with the address written on it. He glanced at it and shook his head. Although I had told him that I understood no French, he began speaking the unfamiliar language, perhaps to himself. It seemed to me that he was saying, "Of all the respectable passengers, I had to catch such a piker as you."

He whistled and began driving the car recklessly fast. It was still raining and the people out in the streets were of the type that cruise cities at dawn simply to prove that they can overcome all hardships. They crossed the streets oblivious to all signs and warnings. They seemed to say mutely, "If you want to run me over, go to it." The taxi driver blared his horn and abused them with what sounded like foul language in French. From time to time he turned to look back at me as if to make sure that I hadn't jumped out during the ride.

Despite all this, I was overcome with a strong affection for this city. It exuded a serenity I had never experienced before. I felt the mute presence of generations of inhabitants who were both dead and alive, remote and near, unearthly sad and also gay, full of ghostly wisdom and divine resignation. I sensed the very danger I had resolved to avoid—falling in love with Paris at first sight, as so many enthusiasts had done before me. Every street, every house had its individual allure—not one artificial or planned, but that originality that evolves by itself out of genuine talent, a harmony that no one can imitate. Every roof, chimney, balcony, window, shutter, door, and lamppost suited the complete image. Even the shabby pedestrians seemed oddly appropriate to the scene. The deceased who had left this rich inheritance were watching.

We drove into a street and the taxi stopped. I took out the French bank notes and the driver peeled off the amount coming to him, or perhaps more. At the same time he mumbled to himself and winked, mocking my helplessness.

A female concierge led me up five flights of stairs to a garret room with a wide brass bed and a sink. The rain had stopped and the sun had come out. Across the narrow street a girl stood and beat a worn rug with a stick. On the pavement nearby a pigeon hopped on its red feet, pecking at what looked to me like a pebble. The fact that the creature didn't flee from someone waving a stick and making noise struck me as strange. Windows were thrown open by half-naked women and radios chattered, droned, whistled, played music, sang. I had never heard such sweet tones, such lighthearted melodies. Two prostitutes conversed from window to window and called down to men in the streets. I fell back onto the brass bed and sank into a deep sleep.

Unbelievably, someone knew of my arrival in Paris and came to take me to breakfast and show me the city. Paris had its own Yiddish Writers' Club. Someone at the Warsaw Writers' Club had apparently alerted the local club members to my arrival. I couldn't believe my sleepy eyes. No one had ever granted me such an honor. The small, dark youth addressed me in a tone one would employ toward an older writer. He had read my stories in *The Literary Weekly* and in *Globus*, he said. He knew that the PEN Club was issuing my book. He was five years younger than I, and he had already published several poems in the Yiddish newspapers in Paris. For a moment I thought he was confusing me with my brother, but it turned out he knew about both my brother and about myself. He proposed an interview with me for a Paris Yiddish newspaper.

The weather had turned warm and my guide told me that I wouldn't be needing my overcoat. We walked down the five flights of stairs and went outside. The street was crowded with people and they all spoke Yiddish. Many carried the local Communist Yiddish newspaper, others the paper of the Labor Zionist Party. I recognized several of the Communists who used to visit the Writers' Club in Warsaw. The Yiddishist world was a small town. They came up to me and greeted me coldly. They asked, "What's the fascist Pilsudski up to? Is he still alive?" They gathered in little cliques here just as they had in the Writers' Club in Warsaw. Their eyes flowed with sly triumph. Mussolini had just attacked or seized Ethiopia. The worse conditions became, the better grew the chances for the world revolution. Each one of them was grooming himself to be not less than a commissar. I asked my guide how these Warsaw Communists survived in France, and he told me that there were wealthy Jews in Paris who supported them. They reckoned that this would save them when the day of revenge came.

He took me to a restaurant and it smelled just the same as the Jewish restaurants in Warsaw, Cracow, Vilna, and Gdansk. Patrons ate chicken soup with noodles and conversed across the tables. A small man with a huge head scribbled figures on a tablecloth. A man in black-rimmed glasses went from table to table issuing cards attesting to the fact that he became crippled in a Polish prison and was in need of financial aid. After a while he came back to collect the cards and any coins the guest might have donated. At almost every table they discussed the peace conference that the Communists were planning to convene, as well as the merits of a united front. A Yiddish writer from America, Zachariah Kammermacher, came up to me and asked, "What are *you* doing here?"

I recognized him from the photograph that the editor of *The Literary Weekly* had published. He had been both for the Communists and against them. He agreed with them on certain points and disagreed on others. As he spoke to me he gestured with his thumb. One eye looked up, the other down. He had written a poem in which he compared Rosa Luxemburg to Mother Rachel. He considered himself a Zionist, but he was also against Zionism and sought a territory in Australia or South America where the Jews could settle. Essentially, he had con-

fided to me, he was a religious anarchist. He had come to Paris
now to arrange the peace conference and, at the same time, to
organize a commission to study the Jewish question the world
over. He was awaiting a meeting with Leon Blum. Some words
he enunciated clearly, others he snorted through his nose. My
guide remarked to me later, "One thing you can be sure—he
didn't come here at his own expense."

"Who pays for him then?"

"Someone pays. He is so immersed in politics that he's no
longer a writer. I tried to read him once and I couldn't make
head or tail of a single sentence."

2

I settled back in the train taking me from Paris to Cherbourg.
The day was a sunny one, but my spirit was blighted by my own
broodings and by everything I had seen and heard around me.
My pious forebears called this world the world of lies, and the
graveyard they called the world of truth. I was preparing to be
a writer in that world of lies, eager to add my own portion of
falsehood. But the trees bloomed, the birds sang, each with its
own tune. Cool breezes wafted in from somewhere, carrying
scents that intoxicated me. I had an urge (actually, a fantasy) to
spring down from the train and lose myself in the green vegetation where every leaf, every blade of grass and fly and worm
was a divine masterpiece. Even the peasant huts nearby appeared to be the product of some unique artistic instinct. I slept
over in Cherbourg in a hotel arranged for me by the shipping
line. That night is totally erased from my memory. All I can
remember of this hotel is that it contained a sink with hot and
cold running water; I had never before seen anything like this
in Poland except in a public bath.

The next day, I boarded the ship, they took my ticket, and my
pockets felt empty. All I had there now was my passport. I had

been left practically penniless. Thank God, I didn't have to share
my cabin with anyone. My two valises stood in the dark cabin,
silent witnesses that I had lived nearly thirty years in Poland,
which that day seemed to me more remote than it does now,
forty years later. I was what the cabala calls a naked soul—a
soul which has departed one body and awaits another. This trip
made me forget so many facts and faces that I began to suspect
that I was becoming senile. Or was it a temporary attack of am-
nesia? Was this what happened to the soul directly following
death? Was Purah, the Angel of Forgetfulness, also the Angel of
Death? I wanted to make a notation of this thought in my notebook but I had forgotten to take it along.

The ship remained in the harbor for many hours, but I stayed
in my windowless cabin, which was illuminated by a small electric lamp. I heard running in the passageway, talk. The other
passengers had friends seeing them off. They drank, snapped
pictures. People quickly struck up friendships. I heard foreign
languages. I had dozed off, and when I opened my eyes, I
sensed a vibration under the mattress upon which I was lying. I
went out on the deck. Evening had fallen and the sun had gone
down. Cherbourg faded in the distance. Those on deck gazed at
me with a kind of surprise, as if asking themselves, "What's *he*
doing here?" A tall individual in a checkered suit, knickers, and
a white cyclist's cap, and with a camera hanging from his shoulder, paced to and fro, taking long strides. He greeted the ladies,
addressing them in English and French. Men of such height
were rarely seen in Poland, and certainly not among the Jews.
His square-jawed face seemed to say, This is my world, my ship,
my women. Suddenly it occurred to me that I had forgotten the
number of my cabin. I was supposed to have taken the key to
my cabin with me but I had apparently left it inside. I had lost
the stub of my ticket, too. I tried to locate my cabin without the
help of others (who could have helped me?) but I only strayed
through the passageways and climbed up and down countless
stairs. I tried to seek someone's assistance and I stopped a
member of the crew, but he knew only French. I traveled in
circles, like a jackass around a millstone. Every few minutes I

saw the same faces. The passengers apparently divined my confusion, since they smiled and winked at each other. My demons had not abandoned me. They were accompanying me to America.

I climbed a staircase to where a long line of passengers stood before a window where an official marked something down on cards for them. I heard a woman in the line speaking German and after some hesitation I asked her what the people were waiting for. She explained to me that this concerned seating arrangements. I told the woman that I had forgotten my cabin number and she said, "It's easy enough to find out. Ask the purser." I wanted to ask her where the "purser" could be located but at that moment a man came up and began talking to her. Was it possible that I would spend the entire eight days of the journey searching for my cabin? It's but a single step from neurosis to insanity, I admonished myself. The woman had mentioned something about a first or second sitting but I didn't understand what this meant. Still, I took a place in the line. If you won't have a place to sleep, I said to myself, at least assure yourself of food. One could spend the night on the stairs. I knew full well that my nerves required suspense and I had to create it. Whenever I became overly excited, irritated, lonesome, the anxieties of my childhood returned to me with all their daydreams, false assumptions, ridiculous suspicions, superstitions. I lost my sense of direction completely. I stopped recognizing people, I made flagrant mistakes in speaking. Some mocking demon began to play games with me and even though I realized it was all sham and nonsense I had to cooperate.

I had reached the official issuing the cards and informed him that I understood only German. He began speaking German to me, but in such an accent that I couldn't figure out what he was saying. How is this possible? I had translated a half-dozen books from German. Was he speaking in slang? Or had I lost my mind? He considered a moment, then handed me a card: "second sitting." He might have been a Nazi who had signed on this ship to spy on the passengers and, possibly, to torment Jews. This card might be a signal to the waiter to poison my food. Sud-

denly, I recalled the number of my cabin. I went to look for it
and located it immediately. The door was not locked. I had left
the key on the table. My two valises stood where I had left them.
I grasped what was meant by the term "sittings"—the time at
which breakfast, lunch, and dinner were served. It was good
that he gave me the second sitting. Otherwise, I would have
been forced to get up at 7 A.M.

I changed my clothes—I had only one other suit—then went
out on deck. Cherbourg had vanished from sight. To the best of
my recollection, the moon wasn't out that evening, but the sky
was thickly sprinkled with stars. They appeared to me lower
than on land and somehow bigger. They didn't remain fixed,
but bobbed and swayed with the ship. Somewhere a lighthouse
cast beams of light.

Here, heaven and earth weren't separate and distant from
each other but merged into a single cosmic entity, endowed
with an otherworldly light. I stood in the center of the universe,
the ferment that hadn't abated since Genesis and perhaps even
long before that, because according to the Bible the abyss and
the divine breath had preceded Creation. A solemnity hovered
over it all, blue, prediurnal. The sound of the waves fused into
a monotonous roar, a seething, a foaming, a splashing that
didn't weary the ear or the brain. God spoke a single word,
awesome and eternal.

The waves assaulted the ship in an arc, locked it in a watery
dance, ready to suck it in within their vortex, but at the last
moment they retreated like maneuvering armies, prepared to
commence their war games again. Creation played with the sea,
the stars, the ship, with the little human beings bustling about
within its innards. My despair had begun to fade gradually.
There was no room for suffering in the midst of this celestial
frolic. All my worries were insignificant and groundless to begin
with. Who did it concern whether I managed to accomplish anything or nothing? Nothing itself became an essence. I stood
there until my watch showed that it was time for the second
sitting.

I went down to my cabin and headed for the dining hall. The

people in the first sitting hadn't yet finished eating, but a crowd
already stood by the door, ready to rush inside and grab their
places the moment the first sitting was concluded. Were all
these people really so hungry? And which of them would turn
out to be my dinner partners? How would I communicate with
them? I was the last to enter. The headwaiter, or whatever his
title may have been, glanced at my card and his face expressed
something akin to astonishment. He flipped the card over and
looked at its other side as if expecting to find there the solution
to the puzzle. He arched his brows and shrugged. Then everything appeared to have become clear to him and he said in a
clear German, "There is only one single table in the whole dining room and it's been assigned to you. If you're reluctant to sit
alone, we can ignore the card and seat you with those close to
you. Maybe you'd prefer the kosher table? You'd surely find
agreeable companions there."

"I thank you very much," I replied, "but a table for one is
actually what I'd like."

"You prefer isolation, eh? Your table is in a corner. We occasionally have passengers who choose to eat alone. On the last
trip, there was a priest, a missionary, or God knows what he
was. He demanded his own table and we accommodated him.
Come."

He led the way through the crowded hall and I noticed
that hardly anyone here was alone. English was spoken,
French, Italian, German. How long ago was it that they had
waged war? How long ago did they drop bombs on each
other? But all that was forgotten. Some passengers were already seated, with that air of assurance of those who always
belong where they are. I didn't see one shy face. Women
laughed that world-affirming laughter that has no connection
with humor but rather with something bosomy, fleshy, ab-
dominal. The men seemed as earthy and as anxious to strike
up friendships as the women. Finally, we reached my table.
It stood in a corner and somehow off balance, crooked, between two walls and two tables, the diners of which stared at
me in a kind of amazement that seemed to ask, "Why was *he*

picked as the victim?" My chair was a narrow one and I barely managed to squeeze myself into it. From where I sat I could see practically the entire hall, but my eyes had grown so bedazzled that I saw everything as if through a dense mist. After a long while a waiter came over and said, "Your order, please?"

Oddly, I had for years contemplated becoming a vegetarian. I had actually gone through periods during which I had eaten no animal flesh. But I often had to eat on credit at the Writers' Club, and I lacked the courage to demand special dishes. I had put it all aside for the time when I could act according to my convictions. Abruptly now, I blurted, "I am very sorry, but I'm a vegetarian."

The waiter shook his head. "We don't have a special vegetarian kitchen. You were told that you could eat at the kosher table, but you refused."

"Those who are kosher aren't vegetarians," I told him. My voice had grown so weak that he had to bring his ear close to my lips to hear me.

"Eh? But there is some kind of connection there." His tone grew more genial. "I understand all your motives, but our kitchen simply isn't geared for such exceptions."

"You needn't make any exceptions. Be so good as to bring me whatever you want and I'll eat only those things I'm allowed."

"Do you eat eggs? Milk?"

"Yes."

"Well, in the eight days you're aboard the ship, you won't starve. We have bread, butter, many good cheeses and egg dishes."

"I'll be satisfied with whatever you bring me."

Immediately, questions came at me from the tables among which I was squeezed. Some people addressed me in French, some in English, some in German. What was the reason for my vegetarianism? Was it on account of my health? On doctors' orders? Did it have to do with my religion? The men appeared insulted that I had introduced a sort of controversy into their presence. They had come here to enjoy themselves, not to phi-

losophize about the anguish of animals and fish. I tried in my
mangled German to explain to them that my vegetarianism was
based on no religion but simply on the feeling that one creature
lacked the right to rob another creature of its life and devour
it. I turned momentarily and against my will, propagandist.

"What right have we to curtail a life that God has granted?
The animal in the forest and the fish in the water have done us
no harm."

A man with a stern face said to me, "If you allowed the animals and birds to multiply, they'd eat up all the grain in our
fields. I myself live in a region where deer roam. It's forbidden
to hunt them out of season and it's happened not once but ten
times that they ate all the plants in my garden. You're allowed
to hunt them a few months in the year only, but no matter how
many are shot, it isn't enough. Well, and what would you do
about the hares and rabbits and birds? The Department of Ag-
riculture has just now advised that the hunters should shoot at
least thirty crows a day. Otherwise, America would become a
land not of plenty but of famine. Do you know all this? Did you
ever read a book about such matters?"

"No, I don't know. But at least we should leave the fish alone.
They stay in the water in their own element. They don't come
out on land to devour our crops."

"They don't, eh? In certain lakes in America, the fish have
multiplied to such a degree that they allow themselves to be
caught with bare hands. Creatures have instinct and they know
that when they overmultiply they must perish. . . . Here is our
waiter."

One waiter brought a magnum of champagne and another a
tray that he balanced overhead. They seemed as excited as the
people they served. One opened the champagne with a pop, let
a man taste it before pouring for the ladies. The other served
the plates of appetizers. For a while it appeared that the waiter
would ignore me completely. He didn't even glance into the
corner where I sat. But soon he seemed to have reminded himself and he remarked, "There will be something for you too."

And he ran off with his tray.

Four

1

IN PAST YEARS I HAD GROWN AC-
customed to meeting strangers. Once in a while readers ap-
proached to pay me compliments for an article or a story. I had
girl friends and a few other friends among the writers. I had
established the minimum contact necessary for existence. But
aboard this ship my sense of solitude came flooding back in all
its magnitude. My neighbors in the dining hall had apparently
resolved to leave me to myself. I greeted them but they didn't
respond. I don't know to this day if it was my vegetarianism that
put them into a hostile mood or the fact that I chose to sit
alone. The waiter did bring me food but it seemed to be made
up of leftovers he had collected: mostly stale bread, an occasional chunk of cheese, an onion, a carrot. I had committed the
sin of isolating myself from others, and I had been excommunicated. Each diner was served a carafe of wine daily, but I got no
wine. Much as I brooded about this treatment, I could never
come to accept it. One thing I knew for certain, I was at fault,
not they. Eating in the dining hall became so annoying to me
that I proposed to the waiter that he serve me in my cabin. He
grew angry, glared, then told me to go to a certain office with a
name I couldn't pronounce. This must have been on the third
day of my trip, but I felt as if I had been already swaying on this
ship for weeks.

After lengthy questioning and straying, I made my way to the
office where a small man sat scratching away at a sheet of paper

with a pen that reminded me of my days in cheder. It consisted of a wooden holder, a ferrule, and the steel pen itself. The point looked old, rusty, broken. Every few seconds the writer dipped the pen in an inkwell that seemed nearly empty. The ink appeared dense and it kept spotting. Even in Warsaw such a pen would have been an anachronism. The sheet of paper was unlined and the writing emerged so crooked that each line rode piggyback upon the next. I cleared my throat and spoke some of the French words I knew—*"Monsieur, s'il vous plaît"*—but the other didn't react at all. Had my voice grown so quiet or was he deaf? This, I told myself, was a French Akaki Akakevich, a throwback to Gogol's times. I forced myself to wait patiently, but a good half hour went by and he still didn't give the slightest indication that someone was waiting for him. I noticed that he was coming close to the bottom of the long sheet and this gave some hope. And that's how it was. The moment he had written the last crooked line and blotted it with an ancient blotter, he raised his head and looked at me with eyes that could have belonged to a fish, totally devoid of expression. They were spaced far apart. He had a short, broad nose and a wide mouth. He appeared to have just wakened from a deep sleep or a trance. I started explaining to him in German, in Yiddish, and with my few words of French, the nature of my request, but his pale eyes gazed at me without any comprehension.

I said several times, *"Je manger en cabine,* no restaurant."

He gathered my meaning finally, for after protracted searching he handed me a card and asked me to sign it. Then he gave me another card. The ship had agreed to provide me board in my own cabin. I asked him in sign language what to do with this card and as far as I could determine the answer was, "Hold on to it."

From that day on I was going to America as if on a prison ship—a windowless cabin with little air—and with food brought by a man who could be a prison guard. He never knocked but barged right in, kicking the door open with his foot. He slammed down the tray without a word. If a book or a manuscript was lying on the little table, he inevitably drenched it. I tried several times to speak to him, at least to learn his name, but he never responded. He looked to me to be a native of the French colonies.

The food he brought me was always the same. In the morning—bread with black coffee. For lunch—some groats with no wine or dessert. For dinner—he threw me a piece of stale bread, some cheese, and a kind of white sausage I had never before seen in Poland. My order for vegetarian food was ignored. He never even glanced at me. I tried to give him a tip but he wouldn't touch the bank note.

I knew already how impossible it was to explain the human character and its whims. Still, as I lay nights on the hard mattress, which was apparently located directly over the ship's engine, I tried to deduce the reason for his surly behavior. Did he despise the white man and his civilization? Was the act of bringing me food three times a day too strenuous for him? Did he resent those who demanded special privileges? Because I threw away the meat he brought me, I actually subsisted on stale bread and cheese. The black coffee was never more than a half cup, cold and bitter. I knew that I would arrive in America (assuming they let me in, considering my appearance) looking wasted.

I had a number of choices of how to improve my lot. First, I didn't have to spend all my time inside my dark cell. The steward on deck rented folding chairs and I could sit all day sunning myself in the fresh air. Second, the ship had a library. True, most of the books were in French, but there were several in German. But some force kept me from doing what was best for me. Somehow, I had acquired a fear of the sun and its light. The deck was too crowded with people. There was a place to play badminton, and young men ran, shouted, often put their arms around the women. I had taken from the ship's library a German translation of Ilya Ehrenburg, but somehow I couldn't take the impudent style of one who assumed that only he was clever while the rest of the world was made up of idiots.

It was the fifth day of the journey. In three days I would be

landing in New York. I had finally dared to rent a chair on the
deck and I had another book from the ship's library that I was
anxious to read. It was a German translation of Bergson's *Creative Evolution*. I also carried with me a Yiddish magazine in
which I had published my latest story before I left Poland. I
was so engrossed in Bergson's work that for a while I forgot
about my spiritual crisis. One didn't have to be a professional
philosopher to realize that Bergson was a talented writer, a
Schöngeist, not a philosopher. This was an elegant book, interestingly written, but lacking any new concepts. *"Élan vital"* is a
pretty phrase, but Bergson didn't even try to explain how it
came to be a creative power. I had already grown accustomed
to works that evoke a sensation of originality at the beginning
only to find that when the reader reaches the last page he is
just as wise as he had been at the first. There had been many
vitalists among biologists prior to Bergson, even prior to Lamarck.

As I sat there reading, a steward came up escorting a young
woman. There was an empty chair next to mine and he seated
her in it. He carefully covered her legs with a blanket, then
brought her a cup of bouillon. He offered me the same but I
declined. It was hard to determine my neighbor's age. She
might have been in her late twenties or early thirties. She also
held a book—Baudelaire's *Fleurs du Mal* bound in velvet. She
wore a white blouse and a gray skirt. Her dark complexion was
pitted from acne. I read on for a long time. I didn't have the
slightest urge to talk to her. She probably spoke only French. I
still tried to grasp how the *élan vital* could have created or
formed the sky, the stars, the sea, and Bergson himself and his
beautiful phrases and illusions. For a long time we each read
our books. Then she turned toward me and said in a halting
Warsaw Yiddish, "You're reading a book I always wanted to
read but somehow I never did. Is it really as interesting as it
seems?"

I was so surprised that I forgot to be embarrassed. "You
speak Yiddish!"

"I see that you read Yiddish." And she pointed at my magazine.

"Yiddish is my mother language."

"Mine, too," she said in Polish. "Until I was seven I knew no
other language but Yiddish."

"You undoubtedly come from an Orthodox home."

"Yes, but . . ."

I sat quietly and waited for her to go on. For the first time in
five days, someone was speaking to me. I said, "You speak Polish without a trace of a Jewish accent."

"Do you really think so? My feeling is that my Polish sounds
foreign."

"At least your parents had the wisdom to send you to a secular school," I said. "My father sent me to cheder and that was
the only source of my education."

"What was he—a Chassid?"

"A rabbi, a *moreh horoah,* if you know what that means."

"I know. I was brought up in the same kind of household as
you, but something happened that turned everything upside
down for us."

"May I ask what happened?"

She didn't answer immediately and seemed to hesitate. I was
about to tell her that she need not reply when she said, "My
father was a pious Jew. He wore a beard, earlocks, and a long
gaberdine like all the others. He was a Talmud teacher. My
mother wore a wig. I often demanded of my father that he send
me to a Polish school, but he always postponed this with all
sorts of pretexts. But something was going on in our house. I
was an only child. My two brothers and one sister died before
I was born. At night I often heard my father screaming and my
mother crying. I began to suspect that my parents wanted to
divorce. One evening when I came home and asked Mother
where Father was, she told me that he had left for England. I
had often heard that men on our street—we lived in the very
midst of poverty, on Smocza Street—went off to America. But
England seemed to me even farther away than America. On

Smocza Street if you wanted to say that someone was acting
strange, you said he was acting 'English.' I'll make it short—my
father converted, became a member of the Church of England
and a missionary. Strange, isn't it?"

"Yes, strange. What was his name?"

"Nathan Fishelzohn. He didn't change his name."

"I knew Nathan Fishelzohn," I said.

"You knew him?"

"I visited him once in his chapel on Krolewska Street."

"Oh, my God. When I saw you with that Yiddish magazine, I
thought that—many young men used to visit him. Did you even
intend to . . . ?"

"No. I went to see him just out of curiosity, not alone but
with a friend of his who is also my friend, a Yiddish writer, Dr.
Gliksman."

"I know Dr. Gliksman. What a small world! Are you a Yiddish
writer?"

"I try to be."

"May I ask your name?"

I told her my name.

"My name is Zofia now, or Zosia. It used to be Reitze Gitl.
Did you write *Yoshe Kalb?*"

"No, my older brother did."

"This book just came out in Polish translation. I read it. So
did my father. Really, the big world is a small village!"

And for a long while we both looked at one another in silence. Then she continued, "Smocza Street, as you know, is
full of Jews. The only Gentiles around were the janitors in
every courtyard. Ours would come around every Friday for his
ten groschen. To hear that my father had become a *goy* was
such a shock that I really have no words for it. When they
learned on Smocza Street that our family had converted, the
boys threw stones at me. Girls spat at me. They smashed our
windows. Then the mission bought a house on Krolewska
Street and we all moved in there. Some rich lady in England
had left a fortune to have Jesus brought to the Polish Jews.

There I started attending a school where all lessons were
taught in English except for the Polish language and Polish history. But my parents continued to converse in Yiddish. . . .
Why am I telling you all this? I noticed you from the very first
day you boarded the ship. You seemed strangely lost. Each
time I saw you, you weren't walking but running, as if you
were being chased."

"May I ask what you intend to do in America?"

"A good question. I don't know. I don't know myself. Ever
since the rise of Hitlerism, our school in Warsaw began to become strongly anti-Semitic. Later I was attending the Warsaw
university, but somehow I lost interest. You mustn't laugh at
what I'm about to tell you, but I write too. I have a letter of
recommendation to a lady professor at Radcliffe, however, I'm
not sure I want to continue my studies in general. I made two
visits to England. I hoped to study there, even settle there, but
I soon realized that to them I would always be a Jewess from
Poland. There if you don't speak with an Oxford accent and you
don't have an earl for a grandfather, you don't belong. I guess
you aren't a religious Jew in the accepted sense of the word
either."

"Far from it."

"They assigned me a cabin with two Englishwomen and
they're making me crazy with their silly talk. For whom do you
write? For Jews who read Yiddish?"

"Yes, those are my readers."

"I tried reading a translation from Peretz, but it didn't capture
my interest. I liked Bialik better, but he is kind of primitive too.
My father reads all the Yiddish books. As soon as a Yiddish book
comes out, he reads it. I'm certain that he has read you. Where
does your brother live? In Warsaw?"

"He is now in America. It's to him that I'm going."

"Does he have a family?"

"Yes, a wife and child."

"Well, it's a small world, and particularly so, the Jewish world.
One time in my life I had one ambition—to tear myself away

from this world as firmly as possible. I dreamed of discovering a planet where the word 'Jew' had never been heard. What evil did the Jews commit that one must be so ashamed of them? It was they who were burned by the Inquisition—they didn't burn others. Now that Nazism has evolved, Christians of Jewish descent face the same danger as do the Jews on Smocza Street. Really, at times it seems to me that I'm living in one great insane asylum."

"That's what it is."

"What do you write about? Where do you eat? I seldom see you in the dining room."

I had to tell Zosia about my dark cabin and the man who threw me my bread and cheese with such resentment thrice daily, and she said:

"Come eat with me. My table is half empty. There is only one elderly couple there. He is a retired captain of a freighter owned by a fruit company. He and his wife are both quiet people but they are alcoholics. When they come down for breakfast mornings, they are both already drunk. They're so drunk that they can't speak properly. They stutter and mumble. They hardly eat a thing. The waiter would be pleased to have you at his table."

"I don't have a number for this table."

"No one asks for any numbers. Many of the passengers are seasick and they don't show up at the dining room."

"I'm a vegetarian."

"What? You'll get whatever you ask for. There's no reason for you to lock yourself up in a self-imposed prison."

That evening I joined Zosia at her table. I got a rich vegetarian meal. I even drank two glasses of wine. The elderly couple gave me a friendly reception. The husband, the ex-captain, muttered something inarticulately to me. I told him that I didn't know English but this didn't stop him from rambling on.

I asked Zosia what he was saying and she replied in Polish, "I don't understand him myself."

His wife seemed somewhat less drunk. After a while, the couple left the table. The old woman was suffering from seasickness. She suddenly grew nauseous. The husband tried to keep her from falling but his own legs were wobbly.

Zosia observed to me in Yiddish, "Now you can speak to me in the mother tongue."

"I don't believe in miracles," I said, "but our meeting today is a miracle to me."

"To me, too. I haven't spoken to anyone in five days."

2

Night had fallen. The stewards had cleared away the folding chairs and the deck loomed long, wide, and deserted. A concert was scheduled for that evening in the salon. Several well-known musicians were aboard ship and the passengers scurried to secure seats. Zosia and I strolled to and fro for a long time in silence. She had already jotted down her address in Boston in my notebook. And I had given her my brother's address in Seagate, Brooklyn. We stopped by the rail and gazed out to sea. Far away, at the horizon, a ship sailed in the opposite direction—from America to Europe. Our ship's horn grunted a greeting. Zosia said, "What an eerie sound these horns produce. It's a good thing fish are mute and probably deaf as well. Otherwise, think of the uproar there'd ensue in the ocean. I myself grow terrified by these deep roars, especially when I am reading. I've resolved on many occasions to read no more Baudelaire. It's true that he's great—in my opinion, the greatest poet of all time. He may be the only one with the courage to tell the human species the unadorned truth. But what good is the truth if you can't live with it? Have you ever read Baudelaire?"

"I don't know French. I've read several of his poems in Yiddish translation. A dreadful translation by someone who was inadequate in both languages. Still, he couldn't manage to destroy Baudelaire altogether."

"I literally learned my French from him. From the day I began reading him I was no longer able nor cared to read any other poetry."

"The same happens to me," I said. "I fall in love with a writer and I remain faithful to him for a long time. In that sense I'm totally monogamous, so to say. My great love was Knut Hamsun. I even translated into Yiddish some of his books."

"You know Norwegian?"

"No, how could I? I did it from German and Polish. A Hebrew translation of *Pan* exists as well."

"Well, this has been a day—or a night—of surprises. Several passengers had tried talking to me, but I have no patience for all this chatter about the weather and whether the food aboard ship is good or bad. Usually when I encounter someone carrying a book, I become interested, but the few people who did were all reading trash. I don't know if you've noticed, but there is a large group of German Jews on board and they all carry cameras and teach-yourself English textbooks. Their pockets bulge with maps of America or New York. I know no German, but if you know Yiddish, you can understand what they're saying. All they talk about is business. It's somehow hard for me to grasp how people escaping from Hitler can be so practical, so well informed, so resolute. I often tell myself that Jews are my brothers and sisters. The fact that my father has a job with the missionaries hasn't altered my genetic cells. I've resolved that in America I will be to myself and to others that which I really am—a Jewish daughter. But somehow I cannot understand these sisters and brothers of mine. They are terribly alien to me. You will probably think that I sound like some self-hating Jew, and you'd be right too."

"No. I won't think that."

"What will you think?"

"I'll think that since you love Baudelaire, you cannot love such optimists as Jews are."

"True, true. But one must love them."

"They don't seek our love. They have wives, children, friends. Baudelaire's every line is an ode to death, but these Jews want to live, to bring forth new generations. If one decides to live, one cannot spit at life all the time as Baudelaire did."

"Oh, you are right. I wander about this ship and I ask myself, 'Where am I going? To whom? To what?' I am neither a Christian nor a Jew. And why should I suddenly become an American? I tell myself that my goal is to rescue my parents from the Nazis, yet how will I ever manage this? My parents have one desire—that I should marry. In this aspect, they are totally Jewish. They want to enjoy some satisfaction from me. But somehow I'm in no mood to grant them this satisfaction. We've only just met and here I am telling you things I've never told another soul. You'll surely think I'm a total extrovert when in fact I'm just the opposite."

"I know that too."

"How? I've been close-mouthed from childhood. All those who tried to get close to me in my later years complained that I closed up like a mimosa. I had a friend, a young professor, and that's what he called me. But enough about myself. Why should you be so dejected? You're going to your brother and he undoubtedly has connections in all the Yiddish circles. You didn't cut yourself off from your roots. I'm convinced that you have talent. Don't ask me how I know this. You'll be happy in America, as much as a person of your kind can be."

"Happy? I surely lack this kind of aptitude."

"Come, let's see what's happening with the concert."

We went below. The salon where the concert was being held was jammed. Many passengers stood alongside the walls. A crowd had gathered around the open door. Those who occupied seats at tables all had drinks before them. The performance consisted of an excerpt from some opera. From time to time, a flashbulb flared. There had been a time when I envied those who took part in such recreations. I regretted the fact that I couldn't dance. But this urge had evaporated within me. There reposed within me an ascetic who reminded me constantly of death and that others suffered in hospitals, in prisons, or were tortured by various political sadists. Only a few years ago millions of Russian peasants had starved to death just because Sta-

lin decided to establish collectives. I could never forget the
cruelties perpetrated upon God's creatures in slaughterhouses,
on hunts, and in various scientific laboratories.

Zosia asked, "Do you want to stay here? I don't have the patience for it."

"No, no. Definitely not."

"May I ask what you would like to do?"

"I've told you about my dark cabin. I'd like to go there. Do
me a favor and come with me. That waiter has surely brought
my supper and I can't just let it sit there. I must also alert them
to stop bringing me any more meals tomorrow. I don't know to
whom I should speak about it. I don't know a word of French."

"Oh, all you need do is inform the steward in the dining
room that you're eating at my table. I'll do it tomorrow at breakfast. Come, let's see what the waiter has brought you. I must tell
you that Frenchmen don't understand vegetarianism. If you told
them you were a cannibal, they'd be less mystified."

Zosia smiled, revealing a mouthful of irregular teeth. It struck
me that she didn't look Jewish. She might have been taken for
a Frenchwoman or possibly a Spaniard or a Greek. The ship
rolled and Zosia occasionally stumbled. Odd, but once again I
had forgotten the way to my cabin. We came to a passageway
and I was sure that my cabin lay within it, but the numbers on
the doors didn't match mine. Had we gone too far below? Or
should we go even lower? Zosia asked, "What happened—are
you lost?"

"So it would seem."

"Well, the absentminded writer! What's the number of your
cabin?"

I told her the number, but I was no longer sure that I wasn't
making an error. We now climbed up and down staircases. We
turned right here, left there, but my cabin had vanished. There
was no one to stop and ask directions since everyone was at the
concert.

Zosia said, "Are you sure that's your cabin number? It seems
that such a number doesn't exist at all."

"What number did I tell you?"

She repeated the number. No, that wasn't the right one. On the first night of the journey I had resolved to take the cabin key along with me wherever I went, but the key was too big and heavy to carry around and I had not locked the door. Why hadn't I at least written the number down?

Zosia asked, "Are you not by chance a stowaway?"

"Figuratively, yes."

"Well, don't be so perturbed. My father is just like you. Ten times a day he loses his glasses. He comes in and starts to yell, 'Where are my glasses? Where is my fountain pen? Where is my wallet?' Quite often the glasses are sitting right on his nose."

At that moment the correct number came to my mind. Within a minute we were standing before my cabin door. I opened it, lit the lamp, and encountered a fresh surprise. On my table stood a huge fruit salad and a bottle of wine. Either the surly waiter had repented or someone had realized that I was being done a disservice. Or could it be that my resentment toward the waiter was a result of a whole series of hallucinations? Everything was possible. I had compromised myself before Zosia in every sense.

She winked and said, "Quite a nice meal. I would be glad to have such a cabin instead of sharing one with those two ninnies. They stay up till 2 A.M. babbling about some church in the small town to which they belong. Sometimes they both talk at the same time and both say exactly the same things, as if they were identical twins."

I showed Zosia to the chair while I sat down on the bunk. After some hesitation, she sat down on the edge of the chair.

"Is it totally dark here during the day?"

"As dark as a hundred miles beneath the earth. Sometimes I lie here during the day and imagine that I have already departed this world and that this is my grave. But I have neighbors who shatter the illusion—a French couple. I don't understand what they're saying, but they quarrel constantly. One time it even seemed to me that they were hitting one another. She threw something at him. He threw something back. She cried.

Strange, but every nationality cries in a different fashion. Did
you ever notice that?"

"No, but I've never had the opportunity. I've been to England
twice, and I never heard anyone crying there. I can't even picture an Englishwoman crying. When my father decided that we
must become Christians, Mother cried for days and nights at a
time. One time Mother came to my bed in the middle of the
night and exclaimed, 'You'll soon be a *shiksa!*' I began to wail
and wasn't able to stop."

We sat there until 1 A.M. We drank the wine and ate the fruit
salad. We had grown so close that I told Zosia about my affairs
with Gina, Stefa, Lena, and with my cousin. After a while, I began questioning her and she confessed that she was still a virgin. She hadn't found the opportunity to alter that condition
either in Warsaw or in England. There had been many close
calls, but nothing had come of any of them. She suffered from
a phobia regarding sex, she said. So great was her fear of it that
she transferred it to the men too. Her one true great love had
been that professor or instructor who had called her Mimosa.
He even wanted to marry her but his family demanded she convert to Catholicism.

Zosia said, "To convert twice would have been too much
even for such an unbeliever as I."

"Was that the reason you broke up?"

"That and other things. He introduced me to his mother and
the disregard was mutual. He himself, Zbygniew, could not
make up his mind. We went so far as to spend a whole night in
bed, but it never went beyond that."

"So you're a pure virgin?"

"A virgin yes, pure no."

"Someone will do you the favor."

"No, I'll go to my grave this way."

Five

1

THANK GOD, NONE OF MY FEARS AND premonitions came true. I wasn't detained on Ellis Island. The Immigration officers didn't make any trouble for me. My brother Joshua and a fellow writer of his, Zygmunt Salkin, a member of the Anglo-Jewish press in America, came to meet me at the ship. After a few formalities I was seated in Salkin's car.

I wanted to carry my valises but Zygmunt Salkin snatched them out of my hands. I had heard of him back in Warsaw. When my brother visited America following the publication in the *Forward* of his novel *Yoshe Kalb*, Zygmunt Salkin escorted him around New York, presented him to a number of American writers, theater people, editors, publishers, and translators. Salkin himself had translated several works from Yiddish into English.

He and Joshua were the same age, nearly forty, but Salkin appeared much younger. In the nearly two years we had been apart, my brother seemed to have aged. The hair surrounding his bald skull had grown nearly gray. Zygmunt Salkin had a head of curly brown hair. He wore a blue suit with red stripes, a shirt of a similar pattern, and a gaudy tie. He spoke an old-home Yiddish without the English words employed by the American tourists I had encountered in Warsaw. Still, I could determine from his speech that he had already spent many years in the land of Columbus.

He had heard about me through my brother. He had read in the magazine *Globus* the serialization of my novel, as well as several of my stories in the *Forward,* and he began to call me by my first name.

Before driving my brother and me to Seagate, where Joshua was now living, he wanted to show me New York. In the two hours that he drove us around I saw much—the avenues with the metal bridges, the "els," looming overhead and the electric trains racing, as well as Fifth and Madison avenues, Radio City, Riverside Drive, and later, Wall Street, the streets and markets around the Lower East Side, and finally the ten-story *Forward* building where my brother worked as a staff member. I had forgotten that it was the first of May, but the columns of the *Forward* building were completely draped in red and a large throng stood before the building listening to a speaker.

We crossed the bridge to Brooklyn and a new area of New York revealed itself to me. It was less crowded, had almost no skyscrapers, and resembled more a European city than Manhattan, which impressed me as a giant exhibition of Cubist paintings and theater props. Without realizing it, I registered whatever uniqueness I could see in the houses, the stores, the shops. The people here walked, they did not rush and run. They all wore new and light clothes. Within kosher butcher shops, bones were sawed rather than chopped with cleavers. The stores featured potatoes alongside oranges, radishes next to pineapples. In drugstores, food was served to men and women seated on high stools. Boys holding sticks resembling rolling pins and wearing huge gloves on one hand played ball in the middle of the streets. They bellowed in adult voices. Among shoe, lamp, rug stores and flower shops stood a mortuary. Pallbearers dressed in black carried out a coffin decorated in wreaths and loaded it into a car draped with curtains. The family or whoever came to the funeral did not show on their faces any sign of mourning. They conversed and behaved as if death was an everyday occurrence to them.

We came to Coney Island. To the left, the ocean flashed and flared with a blend of water and fire. To the right, carrousels whirled, youths shot at tin ducks. On rails emerging from a tunnel, then looming straight up into the pale blue sky, boys rode metal horses while girls sitting behind them shrieked. Jazz music throbbed, whistled, screeched. A mechanical man, a robot, laughed hollowly. Before a kind of museum, a black giant cavorted with a midget on each arm. I could feel that some mental catastrophe was taking place here, some mutation for which there was no name in my vocabulary, not even a beginning of a notion. We drove through a gate with a barrier and guarded by a policeman, and it suddenly grew quiet and pastoral. We pulled up before a house with turrets and a long porch where elderly people sat and warmed themselves in the sun. My brother said, "This is the bastion of Yiddishism. Here, it's decided who is mortal or immortal, who is progressive or reactionary."

I heard someone ask, "So you've brought your brother?"

"Yes, here he is."

"Greetings!"

I got out of the car and a soft and moist hand clasped mine. A tiny man wearing a pair of large sunglasses said, "You don't know me. How could you? But I know you. I read *Globus* faithfully. Thanks is due you for writing the naked truth. The scribblers here try to persuade the reader that the *shtetl* was a paradise full of saints. So comes along someone from the very place and he says 'stuff and nonsense!' They'll excommunicate you here, but don't be alarmed."

"He's just arrived and already he's getting compliments," remarked another individual with a head of milk-white hair and a freshly sunburned round face. "I had to wait twenty years before I heard a kind word in America. The fact is that I'm still waiting . . . cheh, cheh, cheh. . . ."

My brother and Zygmunt Salkin exchanged a few more words with a girl who served someone a cup of tea, then we got in the car and drove for a few seconds and stopped before another house. My brother said, "This is where we live."

I looked up and saw my sister-in-law, Genia, and their son, Yosele. Genia seemed the same but Yosele had grown. Out of habit I started to address him in Polish but it turned out that he had completely forgotten that language. He spoke English now and also knew a little Yiddish.

My brother lived in a house built as a summer residence. It consisted of a bedroom and a huge room which served as a combination living and dining room. There was no kitchen here, only a kitchenette, which opened like a closet. Joshua told me that he planned to spend only the summer here. The furniture belonged to the landlord, who was the brother of a well-known Yiddish critic. The bathroom was shared with another tenant, a writer too. Genia reminded me to latch the door to the other apartment when I used the bathroom, and to unlatch it when I was through. Fortunately, the neighbor was an elderly bachelor who was away most of the day, she observed.

My brother had rented a room in the same house for me. The death of Yasha, the older boy, had driven the family into a depression and I saw that the passage of time hadn't diminished it. My sister-in-law tried to cheer up in my presence. She asked me for all kinds of details about Warsaw, the literary crowd there, and about me personally, but her eyes reflected that blend of grief and fear I had seen there back in Warsaw. She barely restrained herself from crying. My brother paced to and fro and praised America. He told me that he had grown enamored of this country, its freedom, its tolerance, its treatment of Jews and other minorities. Here in the United States he had written a new novel, *The Brothers Ashkenazi,* which had appeared in Yiddish and which was now being translated into English.

Zygmunt Salkin had said good-bye to us and had gone back to Manhattan. Before leaving, he told me that he had plans for me. He mentioned casually that I was dressed too warmly for an American summer. Here, there was practically no spring. The moment winter was over, the heat waves began. No one here wore a stiff collar, such a heavy suit as mine, or a black hat. The vest had gone out of style too. America aspired to lightness in every aspect of behavior. I watched him get into his car. He turned the steering wheel and, in a second, he was gone.

My sister-in-law confirmed Salkin's words. Here, the climate was different and so the life-style—eating, dressing, the attitude toward people. Only the Yiddish writers remained the same as in the old country, but their children all spoke English and were full-fledged Americans.

After a while, my brother took me to my room. It was small, with a sofa that could be transformed into a bed at night, a table, two chairs, and a glass-doored cabinet which my brother had stacked with a number of Yiddish books for me. On a rod running the length of a wall hung hangers for clothes. I wasn't used to removing my jacket during the day but my brother insisted I do so, along with my vest, collar, and tie. He critically considered my wide suspenders and jokingly remarked that I resembled a Western sheriff. He said, "Well, you're in America and one way or another you'll stay here. Your tourist visa will be extended for a year or two and I'll do everything possible to keep you from going back. All hell will break out over there. Should you meet a girl who was born here, and should she appeal to you enough to marry, you'll get a permanent visa on the spot."

I blushed. In the presence of my brother, I had remained a shy little boy.

2

My sister-in-law didn't prepare dinner that night. We ate with our landlord and his family. Although he was the brother of a well-known critic and fervent Yiddishist, his children knew no Yiddish. They sat at the table in silence. When they did speak, it was in a murmur. Our presence at the table apparently disturbed them. They might have been leftists and heard that my brother was an anti-Communist. My brother remarked that Jewish youths in Poland had already grown disenchanted with communism, or at least with Stalinism, but here in America the young were communistically inclined. What did they know of the evils perpetrated in Stalin's paradise? True, if one of them did go to Russia to help build socialism, he was never heard from again, but this was interpreted by those remaining as meaning that he no longer wished any contact with the capitalist society, not even with his old comrades.

My brother said, "They are all hypnotized. I never knew that a few pamphlets and magazines filled with banalities could possess such a strength. On the other hand, if such a scoundrel as Hitler could hypnotize Germany, why shouldn't Stalin be able to fool the world?"

We finished our meal quickly. My brother told me that he still had some work to do on his novel that day. Yosele attended school and he had homework to do. My brother confided to me that Yosele suffered from nervous anxiety. He was afraid to remain alone in the house, even by day. He hadn't forgotten his elder brother. My sister-in-law wasn't able to sleep nights.

I said good night and went to my room. I didn't have to use my brother's bathroom since there was a bathroom with a shower and a tub in the hall. In my room I lit the ceiling lamp, took a Yiddish book out of the cabinet, and tried to read, but I quickly became bored. I glanced into my notebook, where I had jotted down various themes for short stories. None of them appealed to me at the moment. A deep gloom came over me, the likes of which I had never before experienced, or at least I thought so. I gazed out the window. Seagate lay in suburban darkness. It had grown cool toward evening. The roar of the ocean sounded like wheels rolling over stone. A bell tolled slowly and monotonously. Whirls of fog spun in the air. For all my difficulties in Warsaw, I had been self-sufficient there, an adult, connected with women. I could always drop in at the Writers' Club if I had nothing better to do. I knew that this sort of club didn't exist here. I had heard of the Cafe Royal, which was frequented by Yiddish literati, but my sister-in-law had informed me that to get there I had to first take a bus to Surf Avenue, a streetcar to Stillwell Avenue, then travel for an hour on the subway, and after getting off in Manhattan, still have to walk a good distance to Second Avenue. Besides, I knew no one there. And what of the trip back? I lay down on the sofa, not knowing what to do with myself. I didn't have the slightest desire to write. I had read accounts of the difficulties encountered by immigrants to America, but these hadn't been lone individuals. Whatever they went through they shared with fellow countrymen, relatives, co-workers in sweatshops, boarders with whom they shared a corner of a room or even a bed. Some arrived with wives and children at their sides. But I had managed it so that I would arrive all alone in a dark cabin, and stay with a family of strict individualists who were as isolated and withdrawn as I myself. And what would I do here? Since the urge to write had deserted me, I had to find some other occupation. However, as a tourist, I lacked the right to work. How was it I hadn't foreseen all this? What had happened to my logic, my imagination?

I had opened the window. The air here was damp, oppressive. I wanted to go for a walk, but how would I find the house again? As far as I could see, it had no street number. I didn't know a word of English. I would get lost and be forced to stay out all night. I was liable to be arrested and charged with being a vagrant (I had read in translation Jack London's stories about tramps). Still, I couldn't just sit here. To cover any contingency, I took along my Polish passport with the American visa. True, I could have stopped by my brother's apartment and obtained such information as the address of the house, but I knew that he was working on his novel. Genia might have gone to sleep.

After a long hesitation I decided to take a walk. Outside, I made a mental note—there were two white columns at the front of the porch. No other house on the street had them. I walked slowly and each time glanced back at the house with the two columns. I had read accounts of spies, revolutionaries, of such explorers as Sven Hedin, Amundsen, and Captain Scott who wandered over deserts, ice fields, and jungles. They were able to determine their locations under the most bewildering conditions, and here I trembled about getting lost in such a tiny community as Seagate. I had walked, not knowing where, and had come to the beach. This wasn't the open sea, since I could see lights flashing on some faraway shore. A lighthouse cast its beams. The foamy waves mounted and crashed against a stony breakwater. The beach wasn't sandy but overgrown with weeds. Chunks of driftwood and vegetation spewed forth by the sea lay scattered about. It smelled here of dead fish and something else marinelike and unfamiliar. I trod on seashells. I picked one up and studied it—the armor of a creature that had been born in the sea and apparently had died there as well, or had been eaten despite its protection.

I looked for a star in the sky but the glow of New York City, or maybe Coney Island, made the sky opaque and reddish. Not far from the shore, a small boat tugged three dark barges. I had just come from eight days at sea, yet the ocean seemed as alien as if I were seeing it for the first time. I inhaled the cool air. Maybe simply walk into the sea and put an end to the whole mess? After long brooding, I headed back. It was my impression that I had been following a straight path, but I had already walked quite a distance back and the house with the white columns was nowhere in sight. I reached the fence that separated Seagate from Coney Island and spotted the policeman guarding the gate.

I turned around to go back. Someone had once advised me to always carry a compass. I'm the worst fumbler and clod under the sun, I scolded myself. A compass wouldn't have helped me. It would only have confused me further. Possibly Freud might have unraveled my mystery. I suffered from a kind of disorientation complex. Could this have anything to do with my repressed sexual urges? The fact is that it was inherited. My mother and father lived for years in Warsaw and they never knew the way to Nalewki Street. When Father journeyed to visit the Radzymin Rabbi on the holidays, Joshua had to escort him to the streetcar and later buy his ticket and seat him in the narrow-gauge railroad running to Radzymin. In our house there hovered the fear of the outside, of Gentile languages, of trains, cars, of the hustle and bustle of business, even of Jews who had dealings with lawyers, the police, could speak Russian or even Polish. I had gone away from God, but not from my heritage.

What now? I asked myself. I felt like laughing at my own helplessness. I turned back and saw the house with the two white columns. It had materialized as if from the ground. I came up to the house and spotted my brother outlined within the illuminated window. He sat at a narrow table with a pen in one hand, a manuscript in the other. I had never thought about my brother's appearance, but that evening I considered him for the first time with curiosity, as if I weren't his brother but some stranger. Everyone I had encountered in Seagate this day had been sunburned, but his long face was pale. He read not only with his eyes but mouthed the words as he went along. From time to time, he arched his brows with an expression that seemed to ask, How could I have written this? and promptly commenced to make long strokes with the pen and cross out. The beginning of a smile formed upon his thin lips. He raised the lids of his big blue eyes and cast a questioning glance outside, as if suspecting that someone in the street was observing him. I felt as if I could read his mind: It's all vanity, this whole business of writing, but since one does it, one must do it right.

A renewed surge of love for my brother coursed through me. He was not only my brother but my father and master as well. I could never address him first. I always had to wait for him to make the first overture. I went back to my room and lay down on the sofa. I did not put on the light. I lay there in the darkness. I was still young, not yet thirty, but I was overcome by a fatigue that most probably comes with old age. I had cut off whatever roots I had in Poland yet I knew that I would remain a stranger here to my last day. I tried to imagine myself in Hitler's Dachau, or in a labor camp in Siberia. Nothing was left for me in the future. All I could think about was the past. My mind returned to Warsaw, to Swider, to Stefa's apartment on Niecala Street, to Esther's furnished room on Swietojerska. I again had to tell myself that I was a corpse.

3

My brother apparently sensed my melancholy since he did things for me with a particular energy. He and Zygmunt Salkin took me to Manhattan and forced me to exchange my heavy black Warsaw suit for a light American summer outfit. I also had to discard my stiff collar for a soft-collared shirt. Without even consulting me, Joshua arranged for the *Forward* to provide me with work and possibly publish a novel of mine as well. He took me along to the Cafe Royal downtown on Second Avenue and introduced me to writers, to theater people. But my shyness returned with all its indignities. I blushed when he introduced me to women. I lost my tongue when men spoke to me and asked me questions. The actresses all claimed that my brother and I were as alike as two drops of water. They joked with me, tried flirting with me, made the comments of those who have long since shed every inhibition. The writers could hardly bring themselves to believe that I was the one who had written such a diabolical work as *Satan in Goray* and had published in *Globus* biting reviews of the works of famous Yiddish writers in Poland, Russia, and America. My brother fully realized what I was enduring and he tried to help me, but this only exacerbated my embarrassment. I sweated and my heart pounded. A waiter brought me food. I couldn't swallow a bite. A rage filled me against America, against my brother for bringing me here, and against myself and my accursed nature. The enemy reposing within me had scored a smashing victory. In my anxiety I resolved to book a return trip to Poland as quickly as possible and to jump overboard en route there.

I had reverted to boyhood, and those who came up to the table to greet me wondered and shrugged their shoulders. Zygmunt Salkin went off to make a phone call, someone called my brother to another phone, and I was left sitting there alone. The waiter came up and asked, "Why aren't you eating your blintzes? Don't they look good?"

"Thank you. Maybe later."

"When blintzes get cold they turn into knishes," the waiter joked.

Those at the nearby tables who had heard laughed and repeated the joke to others. They wagged their fingers at me. Outside, night had fallen. The lights went on on the marquee over the Yiddish theater across the street. The door to the cafe kept on swinging to and fro. Men and women who apparently weren't part of the literary establishment or the Yiddish theater came in to catch a glimpse of the writers and actors. They kept on entering and leaving. They pointed to those occupying the tables.

Some of the writers here peddled their own books. They wrote dedications on flyleaves and stuck the money uncounted into their breast pockets. A German-speaking tie salesman came in and tried to display his colorful wares and a waiter chased him. A heavyset woman entered. She was bedecked with jewelry, her cheeks thickly smeared with rouge, her eyes heavy with mascara. She teetered as if about to fall. The women applauded her and the men rose to assist her to her seat. I heard mention of a name that struck me as familiar and murmurs of "Just out of the hospital . . . A woman past eighty . . ."

My brother and Zygmunt Salkin returned simultaneously. Joshua glanced at me in reproof. "Why don't you eat? What's the matter with you?"

"Really, I can't."

Salkin said good-bye. He had an appointment. He promised to phone me. After he left, my brother observed, "He has countless appointments. He has a thousand schemes on how to elevate the so-called culture in America, but nothing ever comes of any of them. He has already divorced three wives and is playing around with a woman who will destroy whatever is left of him."

We left and walked up Second Avenue toward Fourteenth Street. Boys dashed about hawking the next day's newspapers in English and Yiddish. Before the Yiddish theaters, crowds had begun to gather. My brother said, "We came to America too late.

Even in the nearly two years I've been here, three or four Yiddish theaters have gone under. But there are still hundreds of
thousands of Jews who know no other language but Yiddish.
They are force-fed on *kitsch,* but that's what they're accustomed
to. It's not much better on Broadway. The same mentality prevails
there too. Hollywood is one chunk of nonsense, literally an insane
asylum. But one talent they all possess—to make money."

We had come to the subway station and my brother bought
a newspaper featuring a picture of Hitler. We rode to Grand
Central Station. From there we took a train to Times Square,
then transferred to a third train heading downtown to Coney
Island. Doors opened and closed on their own. The brick-red
linoleum floor of the car was littered with newspapers. All the
girls chewed gum. I knew it couldn't be true, but they all
looked alike. Little Negroes shined shoes. A blind man entered
on his own, waved a white cane, and collected alms in a paper
cup. The bare electric bulbs cast a yellowish glare. The fans
whirled and whistled over the heads of those clinging to the
leather straps. Past the windows raced black boulders, the
violated innards of the earth which bore the yoke of New York
City. My brother began reading the English newspaper and
read it until we came to Stillwell Avenue. Then we took the
Surf Avenue trolley. The lights of Coney Island made the sky
glow, darkened the sea, dazzled my eyes. The clang and
clamor deafened my ears. A drunk was making a speech praising Hitler, cursing the Jews. I heard my brother say, "Try to
describe this! There are hundreds of objects here for which
there are no words in Yiddish. They may not even have names
in English. All life in America keeps constantly changing. How
can such a nation create a real literature? Here, books grow out
of date overnight just like newspapers. The newspapers print
new editions every few hours. I get an occasional urge to write
about America, but how can you describe character when everything around is rootless? Among the immigrants the father
speaks one language and the son another. Often, the father himself has already half-forgotten his. There are a few Yiddish writ-

ers here who write about America, but they lack flavor. Later on in the summer they'll all come to Nesha's and you'll meet them."

"Who is Nesha?"

"Oh, hasn't Genia introduced you to her yet? She rents rooms to writers in her house. She is one of my most fervent admirers. Yours, too. I gave her *Globus* to read. Whatever happens, you stick to your work. I'll buy you a Yiddish typewriter."

"What for? I can't write on a typewriter."

"You'll learn. Abe Cahan is already an old man, and it's hard for him to read a handwritten text. The linotype operators make fewer errors when they work from typed material. You've got your own room and, for the present, you needn't worry about a thing. Find the right theme. Cahan loves description. He hates commentary. In that aspect, he is on the right path. I often envy scientists. They discover things and aren't completely dependent upon opinions. Well, but it's already too late for me to change and for you, too."

4

No, Genia had not introduced me to Nesha yet, but one day she did. Nesha's house was just a couple of steps from our house. The writers who were staying there presently would be on the beach after breakfast and no one would disturb us. I didn't have the slightest urge to go there but I couldn't go on thwarting Genia. I surmised that she had already promised Nesha to bring me over, and I couldn't make a liar out of her.

The month of May hadn't yet passed but the heat had already begun. We walked less than five minutes and came to the house with the turrets where we had paused on the first day of my arrival in America. On the lawn stood a woman watering flowers. I saw her from behind—a slim figure, her black hair done up into a chignon. Genia called her name and she turned to face us, holding the watering can. In a second I saw that hers was a classic beauty, but she was no longer young—in her late thirties or maybe already forty. Her eyes were black, her nose straight, her face narrow, with a delicately shaped mouth and a long neck. She wore a white dress and a black apron. I even managed to notice that her legs were straight and her toes showing through the open slippers weren't twisted and gnarled as were those of most of the women of her generation.

She too regarded me for a moment, and before my sister-in-law could manage to introduce me, she said, "I know, I know, your brother-in-law. I am a reader of yours. Your brother gave me that magazine—what's it called?—and I read your novel from beginning to end. My only regret was that it ended so soon."

"Oh, I thank you very much."

"Since she already knows you, there's no sense in introducing you," Genia said. After a while, she added, "This is Nesha."

For some reason, my bashfulness had left me and I asked, "Shortened from Nechama?"

The woman put down her watering can. "Yes, right. My parents lost a child before me and when I was born my father named me Nechama—consolation. It's truly an honor and a pleasure," she continued. "I was told Mr. Salkin brought you here straight from the ship but unfortunately I was in the city that day. Come in, come in."

She led us into a hallway which appeared far too elegant for a boardinghouse. The ceiling was high and carved; the walls were hung with old, gilt-framed paintings; an oriental rug covered the floor; the furniture was of the type occasionally seen in museums.

Nesha said, "You're probably wondering at how richly I live. It's not my house. This house was built by an American millionaire for his mistress some seventy years ago. He was already then an old man and she was still young. In those days, Jews didn't live here. Seagate was a summer resort for American aristocrats. After several years, the millionaire died and his mistress became a recluse. She isolated herself from everything and everybody and lived here for over fifty years. After her death, the house stood empty for a long time. Later, a wealthy doctor bought it but he didn't live long either and a bank took it over. From the bank it went over to the present owner, and soon after, his wife died. I was warned that the house was unlucky, that it was cursed, but I took it over not for myself but as a business venture. But it seems it's not lucky for business either."

Nesha smiled and her face grew momentarily girlish.

Genia said, "Since the Yiddish writers became your tenants, it can't be too lucky."

"Yes, true. My God, I am thrilled to know you. Let's go inside. The writers who are here will soon be coming back from the beach, and when they see you they'll snatch you away. I'll make coffee. I want the pleasure of spending some time with you. What do you say, Genia?"

"Yes, you entertain him. He's always alone. We wanted to take him to the beach and to the cafe but he refuses to go anywhere. He was like this in Warsaw too. Aloof and stubborn. I'd sit here with you for a while but I have an appointment at the dentist. You'll be better off having a chat without me."

"Why do you say that? No."

"We'll see each other later."

Genia cast a glance at me that seemed to say, "Don't be in such a hurry to rush away."

After a while she left and Nesha said, "A noble woman, your sister-in-law. A clever and refined lady. Unfortunately she can't forget the tragic loss of her child. They're here two years already and she still can't get back to herself. As for your brother, you know yourself—a man is stronger, after all. Come."

Nesha led me down a long corridor. It was half dark and she took my arm. She said, "It must have cost a fortune to build such a house even in those days. But it isn't at all practical. You can't live here in the winter. The heat comes up from the cellar through brass pipes and how that woman could have endured the cold is beyond me. It's a mile to the kitchen. The architect must have been an idiot or a sadist. Practical people won't move in here, even in the summers. They want their comforts, not art. For the writers, it's something of an attraction, but they come late in the summer and either can't pay or won't pay. They stay up till two A.M. with their discussions. If they were real writers, at least, I would forgive them, but . . . ."

We entered a room with an open entrance to the kitchen—a huge kitchen with an enormous stove. We sat down at a table and Nesha said, "When that millionaire's mistress died, she apparently left no will and those who took over the house got it along with the library, the paintings, and many other things which were later scattered and stolen. She apparently was interested in ghosts since a large portion of her books deal with this subject. To this day I feel that the house is haunted. Doors open and close by themselves. Sometimes, I hear the stairs creaking. It's always cold here even on the hottest days. Or maybe I only imagine this. Apparently no one was interested in the paintings that were left behind. Bad pictures, even though the frames should be worth something. I've heard that the owner is ready to tear down the house and build a hotel on the site. But why talk about the house? What about you? How do you feel in the new country?"

"Confused."

"That's how we all felt when we first came. Uprooted, as if we had dropped down here from some other planet. That feeling has remained with me to this day. I can't seem to become adjusted. I'm here over twenty years and I'm still torn between America and Russia. In the meantime, Russia has changed too and if I went back, I surely wouldn't recognize it. You hear such terrible stories. Absolutely unbelievable. And that's how the years fly by. As far as I know, you aren't married."

"No."

"I had a husband, but he is gone. I have a son of twelve. He is now in school. An exceptional child, a born scientist. He's won prizes at school and what not. My husband left us nothing. He was an artist, not a businessman, and I had to earn a living for myself and for my child. Someone recommended this house to me but the income from it decreases from season to season. This is my last summer here. I hope you brought some new work along with you. For me, literature isn't merely a way of passing the time but a necessity. If I don't have something good to read, I'm twice as miserable."

5

We drank coffee and nibbled on cake. Nesha questioned me about my life in Warsaw and I gradually told her everything—about Gina, Stefa, Lena, and Esther. I heard her say:

"If someone had told me something like this twenty years ago, I would have considered him promiscuous, but today, for a man of nearly thirty, and a writer besides, to have had four sweethearts is not considered excessive. My husband had six or seven before we got together. He was a highly talented portrait painter and he painted mostly women. American men have no time to sit for portraits. They have to make money so that their wives can have it to squander."

"Yes, true."

"You are a different case altogether. You have no idea where this Lena is? Her parents must know."

"I don't have their address. They wouldn't answer me in any case. Her father is a fervent Chassid. Outside of her, her whole family is fanatically pious."

"Have you heard from Stefa or from your cousin? Actually you couldn't have in such a short time."

"I haven't written them."

"Why not?"

"Somehow, I have a block about writing letters. It's even a burden for me to write to my mother. I make solemn vows to write the very next day, but when tomorrow comes, I forget all about it, or I make myself forget. As soon as I remind myself to write, I become as if paralyzed. This is a kind of madness, or the devil knows what."

"You remind me of my husband. He left parents behind in Europe and he didn't write them either. They would never have heard from him if I didn't write them an occasional letter to which he would add a few words. It was even hard for me to get him to write those few lines. At the same time he assured me that he loved his parents. How can that be explained?"

"Nothing can be explained."

"You speak like him too. Since you have shown me so much trust at our very first meeting—I don't know what I've done to deserve it—I can't hide the truth from you—my husband committed suicide."

"Why? How?"

"Oh, he was one of those people who can't bear life, who can't stand any responsibility. The smallest trifle was for him a burden. He wanted to paint his pictures, not portraits, but we had a child and no income. The truth is that he hadn't wanted the child either, but I forced him into it. He had one great desire—to be free—and he gradually arrived at the conclusion that life is nothing but slavery and death is freedom. This is true in a sense, but when freedom comes, the one who is free doesn't know that he is free."

"Maybe he does. If there is such a thing as a soul, it knows."

"If. There is no proof whatsoever that it exists. And what does the liberated soul do? Where does it fly around? Oh, I spent night after night begging Boris—that was my husband's name—to reveal himself to me or to give me some sign of his existence. But he had vanished forever. I still dream of him at times but I forget the dream the moment I waken and all that remains is renewed sorrow."

"How long is it that he is gone?"

"Nearly four years. There's a Yiddish writer here who believes in spiritualism and things of that sort. He recommended a medium to me and I went to her even though I knew beforehand that it was all a sham. She turned out to be the worst fake

I've ever come across. She demanded ten dollars in advance, and when she had the money in her hand, a greeting promptly arrived from my husband. How people can allow themselves to be deceived by such liars is beyond me."

"That's no proof that there is no soul," I said.

"No, but neither is there proof that there *is* a soul."

For a long while neither of us spoke. I looked at her and our eyes met. I heard myself say, "You're a beautiful woman. Men surely run after you."

"Thank you. No, they don't run after me. I'm thirty-eight years old and I have a son. Men don't want to take on responsibilities. Of those who did propose to me, no one appealed to me. After a woman has lived for years with an artist, with all his good and bad characteristics, she can no longer be content with some storekeeper, or insurance agent, or even a dentist. I'm not looking for a husband. Sometimes it seems to me that I'm one of those old-fashioned souls that can love only once. . . . Oh, the phone! Excuse me."

Nesha ran toward the room from which the sound of the telephone came—a muffled ringing. I drank the cold residue of my coffee. That Boris had had courage. He wasn't the coward I was. I won't try anything with her, I resolved. One Gina was enough. She needs someone who would support her and her child, not another potential suicide. . . .

I rose and studied a painting hanging there—mounted hunters and a pack of hounds. Was this an original? A lithograph? What a horrid form of amusement! First they go to church and sing hymns to Jesus, then they chase after some starving fox. Still, great poets wrote odes to hunting, even such a master as Mickiewicz. One could apparently be highly sensitive and utterly callous at the same time. There were undoubtedly poets among the cannibals.

Nesha came back.

"Forgive me. I advertised in the newspaper and people keep on calling me. They arrive in new cars, haggle for hours over every penny, then leave and never come back. They all complain that they lost a fortune in the Wall Street crash. Actually they bargained the very same way before they lost their fortunes. What is man?"

The telephone rang again. "Oh, these idiotic telephones! Please forgive me."

"Of course."

I looked at my wristwatch. A half hour had not yet passed since we were introduced. The writer in me has often pondered about how quickly things happen in stories and how slowly in life. But it isn't always so, I said to myself. Sometimes life is quicker than the quickest description.

Six

1

I SHOWED MY BROTHER THE FIRST chapter of my novel and his response was favorable. Abe Cahan, the editor of the *Forward,* had read it too and had published a friendly note about it. I was supposed to get fifty dollars a week as long as the installments were printed—a fantastic amount for someone like me.

The writers who rented rooms from Nesha were already jealous of me, but somehow I knew that there was something wrong with this work. I had marked down in my notebook three characteristics a work of fiction must possess in order to be successful:

1. It must have a precise and a suspenseful plot.
2. The author must feel a passionate urge to write it.
3. He must have the conviction, or at least the illusion, that he is the only one who can handle this particular theme.

But this novel lacked all three of these prerequisites, especially my urge to write it.

As a rule, almost everything I had written had come easy to me. Often, my pen couldn't keep up with what I had to say. But this time, every sentence was difficult. My style was usually clear and concise, but now the pen seemed, as if of its own volition, to compose long and involved sentences. I had always had an aversion for digressions and flashbacks, but I now resorted to them, amazed over what I was doing. A strange force within me, a literary dybbuk, was sabotaging my efforts. I tried to overcome my inner enemy, but he outwitted me with his tricks. The moment I began writing, a sleepiness would come over me. I even made errors in spelling. I had begun the novel on the Yiddish typewriter my brother had bought for me. However, I made so many mistakes that no one would be able to make out the mess. I had to go back to my fountain pen, which suddenly started to leak and leave ugly blots. There was an element of suicide in this self-sabotage, but what was the source of it? Did I yearn for Lena? Stefa? Did I miss the Writers' Club? My coming to America has demoted me in a way, thrown me back to the ordeal of a beginner in writing, in love, in my struggle for independence. I had a taste of what it would be for someone to be born old and to grow younger with the years instead of older, diminishing constantly in rank, in experience, in courage, in wisdom of maturity.

The *Forward* had not yet started to print my novel, although I had already sent along a number of pages to them, through my brother, and had received an advance. My picture had been shown in the rotogravure section. Almost everyone in Seagate was a *Forward* reader, and when I went out into the street, passers-by stopped me and congratulated me. Nearly everyone used the same cliché—that I had gotten off "on the right foot in America" while other writers had had to wait years to get their names and pictures in the paper. Some of those who envied me added that I owed it all to my brother. Without his intercession, the *Forward* wouldn't have opened its doors to me. I knew full well how true this was.

I was allegedly a success, but in a short while, following the appearance of the second or third chapter, my downfall would come. I couldn't delay publication of the novel because its date had already been announced. A number of columns had been set in type and I had proofread the galleys. In the works on mental hygiene I had read, it said there was no sin or error that couldn't be righted, but in my case, this was far from being true.

During the first weeks after my arrival in America, I used to stroll the streets of Seagate, but now when I wanted to take a walk I took a side street to the Neptune Avenue gate and walked along that avenue or on Mermaid Avenue. I avoided the board-walk since that was where the Yiddish writers took their walks. I would walk as far as Brighton Beach or even Sheepshead Bay. Here no one knew me. I already had money in my pocket and I tried eating at my brother's as infrequently as possible since they would never let me pay for anything. Sometimes I devoted long hours to these walks and when I came back after dark I sneaked into my room without seeing my brother and his family. My table was strewn with heaps of papers so high that I no longer knew where I stood with my pagination, which had grown as involved as my writing.

My sister-in-law would knock on my door and ask, "Where do you go off to for days at a time? Where do you eat? I prepare meals for you, they get cold, and I have to throw them out. You're causing us a lot of grief."

"Genia, I can't remain a burden to you and Joshua forever. Now that I am earning money, I want to be independent."

"What's the matter with you? What kind of burden are you? If I prepare something, there's enough for you too. The food in those cafeterias where you eat is junk. Really, you're not behav-ing right. Even Yosele is asking 'Where is Uncle Isaac? Has he gone back to Poland?' He never sees you."

I promised Genia to eat all my meals with them, but af-ter a few days I again started going to the cafeterias. I was afraid that my brother would ask me how I was progress-ing with my novel. I neither wanted to deceive him nor could I tell him the truth. He would demand to see what I had written and I knew that he would be shocked. I had but one urge—to hide myself from everyone.

One day as I sat in a cafeteria on Surf Avenue eating lunch, Nesha came in. I had the impulse to leave my plate and flee, but she had already spotted me and she came right over to my table. She wore a green dress and a wide-brimmed straw hat. I rose and greeted her. Her face expressed the joy of an unex-pected encounter with someone close. She said, "I stood in front of the cafeteria debating whether or not to go in for a cup of coffee. I drink too much coffee as it is. Well, I never expected to meet you here. You eat here rather than at your brother's?"

"I took a walk and I got hungry. Have a seat. I'll bring you coffee. Something to go with it?"

"No, thanks. Nothing at all. May I smoke?"

"Certainly. I didn't know you smoked."

"Oh, I had stopped already but I started again. Let me get my own coffee."

"No, I'll get it for you."

I went to the counter and brought back two cups of coffee and two pieces of cake. Nesha's eyes filled with laughter. "A true gentleman!" We drank coffee and Nesha tasted the cake. She said, "If I stop smoking, I begin putting on weight immediately. I had never smoked before but I began after what happened to Boris. I even began to drink. But the situation was such that I had to think about paying the rent and getting a piece of bread for my child and myself. That was how I got myself involved in that debacle of a house. All the writers are there now and they often ask about you. 'Why doesn't he show his face?' 'Where is he hiding?' You're probably occupied full-time with your novel. I'm already awaiting the day when it will appear in print. The newspapers are all so void of anything good."

"I'm not sure my novel will appeal to you," I said.

"You're modest. Everything of yours I read in the magazines was interesting."

"Oh, I thank you, but there are no guarantees. Good writers have written bad things."

"I'm sure that it will be good. You're looking somewhat pale. Are you working too hard? You're not at all sunburned. One never sees you on the beach."

"The sun is bad for my skin."

"Redheads have unusually white skin. They burn quickly. As long as you don't overdo it, a little is healthy. Really, you remind me of Boris. I could never persuade him to go to the seashore for the summer. He claimed to prefer the mountains. But when we went one time to the Adirondacks, he sat inside all day

drawing. He tried to reach the unreachable in his art. This was
his misfortune. Your brother does go bathing, but with no particular pleasure. He walks into the water and just stands there
and muses."

"We don't swim."

"The others don't either but they splash around and make
noise. They keep on discussing literature, quote this critic, that
critic, but what they write themselves seldom has any flavor.
Have you heard anything from your friends in Warsaw?"

"Yes, two letters came addressed to the *Forward.*"

"What's the situation in Warsaw?"

"It worsens from day to day."

2

We strolled down the boardwalk. Black and white men were
pushing rickshaw-like rolling chairs toward us and away from
us. I had seen this often before but somehow I could never get
used to seeing people harnessed like horses. The day was a hot
one and a large crowd overflowed the boardwalk, Surf Avenue,
and the beach from Seagate to Brighton Beach. The ocean
teemed with bathers and swimmers. A din rose up from the
throng, a roar that muffled the sound of the waves. I saw so
many faces that they all assumed the same appearance. Nesha
spoke to me but I could barely hear what she was saying. Airplanes flew low towing signs advertising suntan lotions, laxa-
tives, and seven-course meals both kosher and non-kosher. An
airplane wrote an advertisement in the sky for a beverage. The
mass of people flowed by chewing hot dogs with mustard, cot-
ton candy, ice cream that melted from the heat, hot corn, greasy
knishes, gulping down from the bottle all sorts of sodas and
lemonade. Foreheads were burned, noses peeling, eyes bedazzled by the sun and by the wonders displayed here—two-
headed freaks, Siamese twins, a girl with fins and scales. For a

dime one could see the guillotine that had beheaded Marie Antoinette, as well as Napoleon's sword, the gun with which President Lincoln was assassinated, a facsimile of the electric chair used by New York State, and models of the murderers who had died in it. A small black-bearded man broke chains and sold bottles of the tonic which had endowed him with the strength to do it. He interspersed broken Hebrew words into his English.

Nesha took my arm. "If we should bump into one of the Yiddish writers, they'll have something to gossip about."

"What can they do to you?"

"Nothing, but we're better off on Mermaid Avenue."

We headed toward Mermaid Avenue, where there was another cafeteria. I proposed to Nesha that we go in for some rice pudding. She smiled and said, "I won't get anything done at home today anyhow."

"What do you have to do?"

"A thousand things. But if you don't get them done, it's all right too. Inanimate objects can't complain."

We ate rice pudding and washed it down with iced coffee. We chatted for so long that I finally revealed to Nesha that I had reached a dead end with my novel. She asked me the reason I didn't seek my brother's assistance and I replied, "I'm ashamed before him. I also know that he's busy with his own work."

"Maybe you'd be better off dictating it?"

"I've never tried this."

"Try it. You can dictate to me. I can type on a Yiddish typewriter. I still have one. For a while, I supported myself this way. The writers gave me their manuscripts to type. That's the reason they know me, and when I took over the house they all rented rooms from me. You won't believe this, but some of them don't even know Yiddish well. English, certainly not. They don't have an inkling of syntax or punctuation. In this aspect, your brother is a rare exception."

"Have you typed for him too?"

"One short piece only. Try it. You won't have to pay me."

"Why would you do this for me?"

"Oh, I don't know. You seem like a lost soul in America. I idolize your brother but I somehow grow tongue-tied when he speaks to me. He is so smart and has such a rare sense of humor. At times it seems to me that he's laughing at the whole female gender, actually at the whole human species. He was once sitting with the writers on my porch and whatever he said evoked laughter. He can mimic people better than all the comedians. Since Boris's death, I've simply forgotten that there is such a thing as laughter. But I couldn't help but laugh that evening. If you like, you can begin dictating even today. The quicker a crisis is brought to a head, the better."

"When the writers see that I'm dictating to you, they will start—"

"They won't see. Half the house is empty. We'll keep it a secret. I myself would feel embarrassed, especially before your brother and your sister-in-law. The third floor is unoccupied so far and the typewriter won't be heard. I'll try to help you. We can go in through the kitchen. No one uses that entrance. I have typed manuscripts, but no one has ever dictated to me before. I've heard of writers doing this, especially here in America. They even use Dictaphones."

"May I ask if you've ever tried writing yourself?"

"Yes, and I know the feeling of beginning a work and not knowing how to continue. I also know how it feels to come to the realization that the main ingredient required is lacking—talent."

"Maybe we can arrange it that I'll dictate to you and you'll dictate yours to me?"

Nesha flushed. "You come up with such weird notions. You're a writer and I'm an amateur, maybe not even that. No, I've resolved to sooner be a good reader than a bad writer."

We sat without speaking for a while. I studied her and she regarded me in return. Her gaze displayed a mixture of female submissiveness and boldness, maybe even a touch of arrogance, or the self-assuredness of those who follow the dictates of their fate. I liked older women, and the forces that guided the world had sent her to me, I mused. Somewhere within the universe,

the destiny of every human being, perhaps even of every creature, is constantly being decided. According to the Gemara:
Every blade of grass has an angel that tells it, "Grow." Apparently the same angel also orders the blade of grass to wither or
be eaten by an ox.

"If we are to begin today," I said, "I must go home and get
my manuscript."

"Yes, do that. Then come to my kitchen entrance. You remember where that is? The door will be open. And if I'm not
there, go right upstairs to the third floor. The number of the
room is thirty-six. I'll bring up my typewriter and the paper.
You once told me of your romantic conspiracies. Well, this will
be a purely literary conspiracy."

And I imagined that she winked at me.

3

We parted not far from the Surf Avenue gate. It wouldn't be
good for Nesha or me if we were seen entering together. Most
of all, I was eager to avoid my brother. But the moment I
crossed the border separating Seagate from Coney Island, I saw
him. He stood for a moment contemplating me with a half-
mocking, half-reproachful gaze, then said, "Where do you vanish to for days at a time? You got a call from the *Forward*. The
proofreader has found a number of errors and contradictions
in your work and he demands that you come to the office and
straighten out the 'copy.' That's what they call a manuscript
here. There were some other calls, too. Some *landsman* of
yours called; actually he is my *landsman* also, although I don't
remember him. His name is Max Pulawer. He told me that he
is a close friend of yours. He left his phone number. Your book
also came. Not bad for a Warsaw edition but full of typographi-
cal errors. In Zeitlin's Introduction they printed 'occulist' for
'occultist.' I hope that you're proceeding with your work. You've

stopped eating with us altogether. If you're not hungry, let's
take a little walk. If you haven't eaten yet, we'll stop at some
restaurant."

"I've eaten."

"Where did you eat? Come, I must have a word with you.
Zygmunt Salkin has been looking for you. In about two months
you'll have to apply for an extension of your visa and he is an
expert in such things. If you don't extend your visa in time, that
makes you an illegal alien and you can be deported to Poland.
These days, it's a matter of life and death."

"Yes, I understand."

"No, you don't understand. What's happened to you? I read
the beginning of your novel and it reads well, but I want to see
what happens next. They seldom start to publish an unfinished
work, but they made an exception in your case. If the subsequent chapters don't come out right, it will be a disappointment
to us all. You know this yourself."

"Yes."

"What's the situation? Tell me the truth."

"The truth is that I can't remain here," I blurted out, astounded at my own words.

My brother stopped. "You want to go back to the Nazis?
They'll be in Poland any day now."

"Not to the Nazis, but I can't breathe here. I can't even die
here."

"One can die anywhere. What is it—did you leave someone
behind there? Even if so, make the effort to bring her here
rather than go back to perish together. Really, I didn't know you
were such a romantic. You always kept secrets from me and I
didn't mind, but to go back to Poland now, one would have to
be completely mad. What's with your novel?"

"I can't go on with it. It's a physical impossibility."

"Well, that is bad news. I'm the one who's at fault. I had no
right to let them begin printing it until you had the whole thing
finished. I did it because you told me that this was the way you
wrote the book for the *Globus.* Maybe it's not as bad as you
think? Perhaps I can help you? How much of it have you got

written? Let's go home and you'll give me the manuscript. Sometimes you can improve a thing by just eliminating what's bad."

"It's all bad."

"Let's go home. How many pages approximately have you got done?"

"It's all so tangled you won't be able to make sense out of it."

"I'll make sense out of it. Don't panic. Even if it's all as bad as you say, they'll print the first chapters as a part of a larger work. It's no calamity. It's happened to me too that I've hit a dry spell, but I always had material ready for at least three months in advance. You had enough time to do the same. Come, we'll see what you have there."

I wanted to tell my brother that I couldn't show him my work, but I didn't dare cross him. We walked silently and we soon entered my room. Seeing the pile of papers on my table, my brother gave me a disdainful look. He had switched on the ceiling light and, with brows arched, began to glance through the papers. He asked, "What kind of numbering is this?"

I didn't answer. He took a long time trying to put my manuscript in order, then gave up and stacked the pages in a pile. He said, "I may read this tonight, and if not, then tomorrow. All literature isn't worth a pinch of snuff anyway. Come in and Genia will give you something to eat. You don't look at all well."

"I'm not hungry."

"Well, it's up to you. God knows I'm only thinking of your well-being."

"I know, I know. But I've lost the bit of talent I had."

"You've lost nothing. It'll all return. And don't even think about going back to Poland. That would be sheer suicide. Good night."

He left. My brother seldom mentioned the word "God." He spoke to me like a father. After a while, I switched off the light and quietly went out. Did it make any sense now to go to Nesha's? I had left her waiting. I could no longer bring myself to dictate to her. I didn't even know where to begin now that my manuscript was taken away. Still, I went on until I came to her kitchen. No one was there. I began climbing the dark and winding staircase to the third floor. On the second floor, someone called my name. It was that quasi-writer and total politician I had met in Paris, the participant in Stalin's Peace Conference, Mr. Kammermacher. He confronted me and asked, "What are you doing here?"

I had stumbled upon the worst gossip in the Yiddish literary family. I heard myself say, "I live here," and I immediately regretted my words.

"Oh? So you have been hiding right here all this time?"

"I just moved in today."

"You don't live with your brother?"

"I took a room here to work in."

"Where is your room?"

"On the third floor."

"Really? Nesha said the third floor is unoccupied."

I didn't answer him and continued up to the third floor. It was dark and I couldn't find number thirty-six. I stood and waited for Nesha to show up. Meeting that fellow traveler here had complicated everything. He would assuredly inform the writers downstairs that I had moved in here and place Nesha in an embarrassing position. They would begin pestering her as to her reasons for keeping this a secret. They were even capable of coming upstairs to welcome me and encounter me standing here in the dark. I felt around for a light switch on the wall but I couldn't find one. I tried the doors to the rooms and none of them was locked. I walked inside one of them and tapped around for a light switch. Why hadn't she had the sense to leave a light on in the hallway or in room number thirty-six? I supplied my own answer: She had been waiting for me there, but after close to an hour had gone by, and I hadn't appeared, she had decided that I had changed my mind about the whole matter.

My eyes began to grow accustomed to the dark. From somewhere outside issued the reflection of a light and I saw a bed with only a sheet over the mattress, without pillow or cover. I left the door open and stretched out on the bed. If Nesha came, I would hear her footsteps. I needed a rest after all those mishaps.

I had dozed off and a dream of flying took over—I didn't fly like a bird but I glided in the air, floating in twilight and wondering why I didn't attempt this before. I knew that mountains, forests, rivers, oceans were stretching out under me, but I had no curiosity to look at them. There was peace in this dusk. Night was approaching like a cloud, lit up by an otherworldly sunset. Thank God, it's all over, I said to myself. Someone touched me and woke me. It took a while before I realized where I was and who it was rousing me.

Seven

1

A YEAR HAD GONE BY. THE NOVEL turned out badly but the editor let it run to its conclusion and I managed to save up a thousand dollars. I had ceased writing fiction and supported myself from a short column that appeared every Sunday under the title "It's Worthwhile Knowing"—"facts" culled from American Magazines: How long would a man's beard be if he lived to seventy and all the hairs he had shaved off during his lifetime were laid end to end? How much did the heaviest specimen of a whale weigh? How large was the vocabulary of a Zulu? I received sixteen dollars per column and this was more than enough for me to pay five dollars per week rent for a furnished room on East Nineteenth Street off Fourth Avenue, and to eat in cafeterias. I even had enough left over to take Nesha to the movies once a week.

My tourist visa had already been extended twice, but when I applied for a third time, it was extended for three more months with the stipulation that this was the last time this would be done. I had some ten weeks in which to obtain a permanent visa or go back to Poland, where Hitler was liable to march in at any time.

I was connected with a lawyer who was supposed to obtain this visa for me, but the last time I had seen him he had told me frankly that I had nothing to hope for. I was lacking vital documents that the American consul in Toronto would demand—in particular, a certificate of moral character from Poland. I had written Stefa several times and she had made efforts to obtain this for me, but the Polish officials posed difficulties and demanded other documents which I couldn't supply. I had lost my military status booklet and other official papers. I suspected that Stefa wanted me back in Poland. She wrote me long letters frequently, forgetting to mention the certificate that I asked for. My cousin Esther had gone back to her hometown. My former publisher, who had gone bankrupt, had left Warsaw. I wrote to some others, but they didn't answer. Who in Warsaw had the time or the strength to stand in lines and to deal with lazy bureaucrats who merely sought an opportunity to say "no," particularly when the petitioner was a Jew? There remained one solution for me—to marry Nesha. But I had taken a holy vow not to marry on account of a visa, not even if it meant my having to leave America. The reason for my obstinacy regarding this matter is something that isn't clear to me to this day. I knew a few writers who had done just this and I looked upon them as undignified creatures. Perhaps the incident with my certificate to Palestine, years ago, about the time I met Stefa, had left a bad taste in my mouth. I loved Nesha, but I knew that all the Yiddish writers would know that I had married her for the visa. I was most of all ashamed before my brother. Our parents had raised us to have an aversion toward any kind of sham or swindle. The fact was that this marriage wouldn't have benefited Nesha either. She might have gone through with it to save me from the Nazis, but it would have represented a sacrifice on her part. Besides, I had told her at the very onset of our affair that I didn't believe in the institution of marriage. Nor did she have any desire to give her son a stepfather such as I, a pauper, a bohemian who was ten years younger than she. I knew that she had lost faith in me and in my future as a writer.

It had all become routine. Twice a week she came to me in my room up on the fourth floor and although I forbade her to do this, she often brought me food. She warned me constantly that cafeteria food was liable to make me sick. That summer Nesha hadn't leased the house in Seagate. She had gotten a job as a draper in a woman's underwear factory in downtown New

York City and had rented a walk-up apartment in the Bronx. My room consisted of a bed, a small table that wobbled on the rare occasions when I tried to write on it, one lame chair, and a sink with a faucet that constantly dripped brown water. From beneath the cracked linoleum, cockroaches crawled. At night bedbugs emerged from the walls. Once a month the exterminator came, leaving a stench that lingered for a week afterward. The vermin seemed to have acquired immunity to the poison. But the sun shone here in the afternoons and there was a bathroom in the hall where I could take a bath or shower after ten in the morning when the other tenants had gone to work.

I had lost the urge to write but I still kept a notebook in which I jotted down themes for novels, stories, regimens of behavior which I never followed, as well as ideas about God, "the thing in itself," angels, ghosts, and beings on other planets thousands or millions of light-years from the earth. I still hadn't completely abandoned my hopes of uncovering—while awake or dreaming—the secrets of Creation, the purpose of life, the mission of man. I was wasting hours on all kinds of fantasies about megalomaniac achievements. I had a harem of beauties. I possessed a magnetism that no woman could resist. I found the means of freeing mankind from the Hitlers, the Stalins, from all sorts of exploiters and criminals, and gave the Land of Israel back to the Jews. I cured all the sick, extended the life of man and of beast for hundreds of years, and brought the dead back to life.

Going to bed with Nesha was a new experience each time. She would come to me one day a week directly from work, and another day, from her home in the Bronx. True, she often reproached me for having ceased writing, for being lazy and lacking in practical ambition. She often scolded me for neglecting to visit my brother, who had rented a large apartment on Riverside Drive, and for staying away from the Cafe Royal and the writers' gatherings and banquets. A young man my age had no right becoming a hermit. Such conduct could lead to madness. But following her lecture and after we had partaken of the sup-

per she had brought or we had eaten at the Steward Cafeteria
on Twenty-third Street, we would begin a session of lovemaking
which would last for hours, sometimes until midnight.

This woman evoked powers within me I had never imagined
I had before. Apparently I affected her in the same way. We fell
upon one another with a hunger that astounded us both. She
hadn't lost her husband, she assured me—his spirit had entered
my body. He spoke to her out of my mouth, he kissed her out
of my lips. I, on the other hand, recognized Gina within her.
While Nesha was with me I lost all my worries, all the fears. I
called her Gina and she called me Boris. We played with the
idea that by some cabalistic combinations of letters we were
able to resurrect Boris and Gina for the time of our love game
and all four of us indulged together in a mystic orgy where
bodies and souls copulated and where sex play and heavenly
knowledge became identical. We often vowed to each other to
flee to California, to Brazil, to the wilds of British Columbia, and
surrender ourselves completely to our passion. Nesha even
blurted out that she would leave her son with Boris's relatives.
But as our lust gradually subsided, Nesha told me that she
would sooner let her eyes be plucked out than part with her
Benny, who was named after her late father, Reb Benjamin, a
pious Jew, a scholar. I reminded myself that my weeks in America were numbered. If I wouldn't or couldn't marry Nesha, I
would be forced to go back to Poland, or try to remain in the
United States illegally. But how? And where? And for how long?

Since Nesha had come to me early that day, our love session
ended sooner than usual. By ten-thirty, we were already
dressed. We walked down in silence the four flights, ashamed
of our ridiculous dreams, exhausted from our repetitious rav-
ing. Nineteenth Street was dim and deserted. So was Fourth
Avenue. Only the cars raced to and fro. I had neglected to deliver my column, "It's Worthwhile Knowing," and I had to go to
East Broadway this very night and leave it to be set early the
following morning if it was to appear on Sunday. Following my
fiasco with the novel, I avoided showing my face to the *Forward*

writers and I always dropped off my copy late in the evenings
when all the staff members were gone. On the tenth floor,
where the typesetting was done, there was a metal box where
writers deposited copy that didn't have to first pass through the
hands of editors. For some reason the editor of the Sunday edition trusted my Yiddish.

I escorted Nesha to the subway station and on the way we
stopped at the Fourteenth Street Cafeteria for a bite to eat and
a cup of coffee. This cafeteria did its best business at night. It
had become a gathering place for all kinds of leftists—Stalinists,
Trotskyites, anarchists, various radicals and social rebels. Here,
they discussed the latest issues of *The Daily Worker* and the
Yiddish *Freiheit,* articles in *New Republic* and *The Nation.* By 11
P.M. one could already get items from the next day's breakfast:
oatmeal, farina, dry cereals, fried eggs with sausage and potatoes. Many of the patrons were Jews, but there were some Gentiles too—men with long hair and beards, elderly socialists, vegetarians, and those who preached their own versions of
Christianity or predicted the imminent return of Jesus, who
would judge the world prior to its end. Homosexual males and
lesbians also made this their meeting place. The harsh glare of
the ceiling lights blinded the eyes; the noise of the patrons and
the dishes deafened the ears. The air was thick with the smoke
of cigarettes. Girls with short hair and in leather jackets *à la*
Cheka smoked, sipped black coffee, shouted the latest slogans
from Moscow, cursed all the fascists, social democrats, Hearst,
Leon Blum, Macdonald, Trotsky, Norman Thomas, Abe Cahan,
even Roosevelt for allegedly supporting the liberals while he
actually served Hilter, Franco, and Mussolini.

I had found a table for two in a corner and I brought coffee
and cake from the counter for Nesha and cereal and milk for
myself. I had gone some thirty-five cents over my budget, but
since I was soon to go back to Poland and perish in the hands
of the Nazis, what need had I of money? Just as I had been
enthusiastic shortly before, so was I seized by depression now.
I heard Nesha say, "Don't be so despondent. Much can be done

in these weeks. Uncle Sam isn't a murderer, after all. You won't
be deported to Poland so quickly."

"It isn't Uncle Sam. It's a single official who decides and does
just as he pleases. Someone like that is liable to be a Nazi."

"I'm sure his decision can be appealed. People wander
around here illegally for years. They hide, and later they're
granted legal status."

"Where could I hide?"

"You're hiding anyhow. Before they decide to come looking
for you, and until they find you, war would break out and you'd
be granted legal status. Until then, you might meet an American
girl who would really please you."

"Don't say that, Nesha, I love you."

"The main thing is that you remain in America. Come, it's
getting late and I have to get up for work in the morning."

I went with Nesha to the subway, then took a bus to East
Broadway. The night elevator man at the *Forward* already knew
me. He always made the same joke—that I dropped off my column like an unmarried mother disposed of a bastard. A single
light burned in the composition room on the tenth floor. The
linotype machines that clacked away all day stood silent. I often
had the feeling that machines were resentful of man because he
compelled them to do things that were against their nature.
From the tenth floor I walked down a dark flight of steps to the
empty editorial office. There was a box for received mail here
with separate compartments for the various staff members. My
brother had his own box where letters addressed to me were
deposited as well.

I found two letters for me and I stuck them in my breast
pocket. By the time I went outside, it was half past twelve. I
waited for a bus, but after a half hour it still hadn't come. I
started walking in the direction of Nineteenth Street. I stopped
under a lamppost and tried to make out the source of the letters. I couldn't believe my own eyes—one letter was from Lena
in Warsaw and one from Zosia in Boston—one in Yiddish, the
other in Polish.

It was too dark on Avenue B to make out the writing, yet I managed to gather from Lena's letter that she had just gotten out of Pawiak Prison. She had given birth to a son while I was still in Warsaw. She had been arrested a few weeks later. Her comrades took care of the child. She demanded that I send an affidavit for her and the child. Her letter consisted of six densely filled pages. Zosia's letter was only one page but I couldn't make out her handwriting by the light of the lamppost. I didn't walk but ran. My legs had grown unusually light. What a joke! Here I was on the verge of being deported from America and Lena demanded an affidavit from *me!* And during the worst crisis of my life I had become, of all things, the father of a child born to a Communist, a grandson of my pious father and the fanatical Reb Solomon Simon. What a combination of events and genes!

I had gone as far as Union Square without finding one restaurant or cafeteria where I could read these letters from the beginning to the end. I reached Nineteenth Street and climbed the four flights to my room. I threw myself on my bed and read. For someone the likes of Lena, her letter sounded almost sentimental. She was now a mother and she loved her child. She had named him after a grandfather and had him circumcised even though she considered this an act of barbarity. She had had to somehow make up with her mother. Because Lena had turned Trotskyite and those who kept the child remained Stalinists, they refused to nurse the child of a traitor to the cause. She feared that they might even harm the baby. One could expect the most terrible things from fanatics of this kind. Lena's letter was full of abuse against Stalin and his henchmen. She praised her mother for having saved the child's life. Reb Solomon Simon would never have allowed such a child into his house and the grandmother was forced to board it with some indigent woman, a retired nursemaid who was already caring for two other children of political prisoners. Lena's mother sold her jewelry and bailed Lena out for the second time.

Zosia wrote that she had written to me at my brother's address in Seagate but the letter had come back. Someone who knew about me had given her the address of the *Forward*. She was coming to New York City from Boston now for an indefinite period of time and she gave me an address and telephone number where I could reach her—assuming I still remembered her.

My wristwatch already showed three o'clock but I still wasn't able to fall asleep. I had never wanted to have children, particularly at a time when a holocaust was threatening the Jews, and certainly not with someone like Lena. However, the forces that guide the world always manage to get their way. I tried to convince myself that I felt nothing whatever for this creature, but I pictured it lying in some decrepit room in dirty bed linen, undernourished, weighed down with a heritage from which it could never be free. Lena wrote that he had blue eyes and reddish hair. Thus, he favored my family, not his wild grandfather and uncles with their pitch-black beards and fiery black eyes. I said to myself that already somewhere in his brain were hiding my doubts, my feelings of protest against Creation and the Creator. And would he be a Jew or would Lena raise him to be an enemy of our people? Somewhere within me I begged his forgiveness for bringing him into this mess of a world.

2

I called the hotel and was connected with Zosia. I couldn't invite her to my wretched room and we agreed to meet at the Forty-second Street Cafeteria, near the public library.

She was a half hour late and I was already preparing to leave when, through the window, I saw her coming. She wore a summer suit and a straw hat. She seemed to me taller, fairer, and more elegant than the last time I had seen her aboard ship. She had apparently achieved some success in America. I went out to meet her and escorted her to my table, where I had left a book and a newspaper along with my crumpled hat. I brought coffee for her and for myself. Zosia began questioning me and, as is my nature, I told her everything: about my failed novel, my affair with Nesha, and the fact that I had only two months to stay in America. Zosia said, "Do anything, but don't dare to go back to Poland!"

"What's my alternative?"

"Marry this woman, since this is a mere formality."

"With her, it wouldn't be a mere formality. Let us better speak about you. What's been happening with you in all this time?"

"Oh, a lot and nothing. I received a grant to conclude my studies at Radcliffe. This isn't some minor achievement, mind you. They aren't so generous with grants. I never knew that my father could be so energetic. He established connections with missionaries in Boston as well as in New York. I have often told my father that once I was in New York I would revert to Judaism—if this is possible for an agnostic—but the missionaries in Boston sought me out and tried to block my road back to Jewishness. They invited me to their homes, they began seeking subsidies for me, jobs, even marriage partners. Jews remain forever Jews with their energy and their rage to mind everybody's business. One of them, an elderly man, fell in love with me, or so at least he said, and wanted nothing else but that I become his mistress. He couldn't marry me since he had a wife who suffered from multiple sclerosis and was bedridden or confined to a wheelchair. If we have the time and you'll have the patience, I have not one story for you but a great many. Here in the cafeteria is no place for this. The plain facts are that I have given up my studies. I simply lost my patience for all those exams, the professors, and the girls with whom I shared the house. I had seriously considered putting an end to the whole tragicomedy when I met an elderly woman, a retired professor who was forced to give up her position at the university because she had lost her sight. She isn't totally blind, but she no longer can read. She couldn't exist on what the university paid her. She has a wealthy brother.

"I'll cut it short. I have become her eyes. She taught psychology at the university and also gave a course in religion. After the trouble started with her eyes, she got involved in psychic research. Actually, she dabbled in psychic research even before. She reads—that is to say, I read to her—almost all the literature on this subject, and although I'm far, far from convinced about all those miracles these books and she talk about, this is much more interesting than the religion that I studied in Poland and here as well. At least it has to do with the present, not with wonders that occurred in Palestine two thousand years ago. Even if all those visions or revelations of theirs are inventions, they are at least interesting from a purely psychological standpoint. The professor herself is a strange blend of intelligence, a critical mind, plus fanaticism and credulity that border on madness. I must mention that I have witnessed things at her home and with herself that couldn't be explained. She literally reads my mind. I had never told her of my Jewish extraction, but one day she told me that I had been born a Jew and that I must return to my Jewish roots."

"She probably opened a letter from your parents."

"She doesn't open my letters and my parents have never written to me about my Jewishness. Besides, I just told you she's blind. Do me a favor and let's get out of this cafeteria. It's so noisy in here I can barely hear you. I noticed a park near the library."

We went outside and found an empty bench in the park. Zosia said, "Here, I can breathe. Yes, about my Jewishness. At that woman's house I had time to think things over. I ate there, slept there, I learned to cook, and for the first time in my life I seem to have enjoyed the taste of rest. The problem is—what is Jewishness? Of what would my Jewishness consist? I thought that you would be able to tell me, but you are here, not in Boston, and you have your work. Some two months ago I happened to read in the paper about a lecture in a synagogue. It was announced that a guest from New York would speak on the subject 'What Does the Jew Want?' and I decided to go hear what he had to say. It just so happened that it rained all that day and it poured in the evening. My professor had gone away to her brother's—he has a house in Lenox—and I took the bus to the synagogue. I got there soaking wet and found exactly five people. Who goes to hear a lecture in such a storm? After a while, they left too. My impression was that the speaker was a rabbi. Actually, he had only called himself by that title. I soon learned that he was a businessman and quite wealthy. The money from the admissions was supposed to go to the synagogue. He seemed to me younger, yet he turned out to be a man in his late fifties. I don't want to overburden you with my problems. It's because of this speaker that I am now in New York."

"What is it—a love affair?"

"Oh, I don't know myself what to call it. We were together until late that evening. He took me to a restaurant and he spoke to me for hours. I had come, so to speak, to pour my heart out to him, although it ended with him pouring his heart out to me. He told me his whole life story. I forgot the main thing—he knows your brother and he knows about you, too. He reads that newspaper for which you two write, and he had met you in Warsaw in that club for writers."

"What's his name?"

"Reuben Mecheles."

"I've never heard of him."

"He knows all the rabbis, all the writers. He even knew my father. He told me that he received your book in the mail. They send him all the works in Yiddish from Warsaw. He married a rich woman here in America, but he is separated from her. They were incompatible, she was too bourgeois for him. I was interested in him for a short while, but such is my nature apparently that I get over my infatuations quickly. I'm afraid that I wasn't created for love even though I'm always enamored of some ideal. The thing that I want to tell you is so complicated that it appears even to me a fantasy, but I've convinced myself that it's true. He is involved with some sect—or how shall I describe it? The leader of the sect is a young man from Egypt, a cabalist who presents himself as no less than having had God appear before him and dictate a new Bible to him, one that is four or five times longer than the Old Testament. It isn't exactly clear to me how that so-called prophet is also connected with some people in New York, not only among Jews but among some

Christians as well. They even write about him in the newspapers. Mr. Mecheles assured me that he, I mean Mr. Mecheles, is terribly in love with me and that the leader of his sect wrote him of me long before I ever came to hear his lecture! He says that I look exactly the way he described me. Mr. Mecheles wants me to marry him after he has divorced his wife, but she demands a large settlement and a huge alimony. It just so happened that my lady professor went to spend six weeks of this summer with her brother in Lenox and she granted me leave. Mr. Mecheles sent me a train ticket from Boston to New York and he settled me here in a hotel. The leader of his sect will be arriving in New York any day now. Mecheles wants us to marry according to the law in the new Bible. I tell you beforehand that I won't do it. First of all, I'm not anxious to marry him. And secondly, I don't want to do anything that's against the American law. The whole thing is crazy from beginning to end, but I've already met so many madmen that I'm beginning to think that lunatics are the majority and the so-called normal people a small minority. What do you say to this?"

"Yes, man is mad, and from the ten measures of madness that God sent down on earth, nine measures were received by the modern Jew."

"Yes, yes, right! Right! Why am I drawn to such people? I'm beginning to suspect that I'm crazier than they are."

"In your case it's circumstances."

"You're trying to be nice. I shouldn't say this, but I'll tell it to you anyway. I might not have come to New York, but I wanted to see you. Mr. Mecheles isn't my kind of person. He is an optimist and an extreme extrovert. He must constantly be with people, and in the brief time that we've know each other he has introduced me to so many so-called friends that I'm dizzy from them all. I don't think he really believes in that prophet from Egypt, but he constantly seeks ways to avoid being alone. Even if I did love him, I still couldn't be with him."

For a long while we were both silent. Over the din of New York I could hear the chirping of birds. From time to time, a cool breeze blew. I bowed my head and gazed down at a worm

crawling on a newspaper someone had discarded beside the
bench. The tiny creature crawled forward, backward, in zigzag
fashion. Then it stopped. Was it hungry? Thirsty? Did it want to
be free of the paper surface and go back to the grass where it
had been born? Or did it feel no desire, no need, no suffering,
no joy? I would have liked to do something for this lost particle
of life, but I knew that whatever I attempted in its behalf would
only kill it.

As if Zosia had read my mind, she asked, "Are you still a
vegetarian?"

"Of course."

I wanted to point out the speck of life to her, but it had vanished.

3

A few days had passed. Zosia had promised to call but I
hadn't heard from her. One night as I groped in the mail com-
partment on the ninth floor of the *Forward,* I found there a
letter from Warsaw and an unstamped envelope that someone
had left me. I went down with the elevator, and in the half
minute that it took to get from the ninth floor to the lobby, I
managed to note that Stefa had sent me the document I had
requested of her so many times and that the unstamped letter
was from the managing editor of the *Forward.* My brother had
told him that Washington had declined to extend my visa beyond three months, and this noble man had written to say that
he had found a lawyer for me who specialized in helping immigrants. He gave me the man's name, address, and phone
number. For all my heresy, I considered both these events acts
of Providence. The document confirmed that I had committed
no crimes in Poland. Stefa's letter was long and I read it carefully only after I had gotten home. One half of the eight-page

letter described in detail the troubles she had encountered in obtaining this document. The red tape and the laziness of the officials was worse than ever. The other half concerned the situation in Poland and her, Stefa's, plans for the future. Her husband, Leon Treitler, had finally decided to liquidate all his holdings and to go to England or maybe to America, if he could obtain a visa. Of course, Stefa would not leave without her little daughter, Franka. The German woman in Danzig who was raising the girl had grown old and sick and she no longer had the strength to devote herself to the child. Besides, if her neighbors ever learned that the child was Jewish and if Hitler invaded Danzig, she could be severely punished. The child was now with Stefa in Warsaw and learning Polish, although she wouldn't be in need of this language soon. Of course, she was taking lessons in English. There was a photograph of Leon Treitler with Stefa and the little girl and a few words from Leon in Yiddish with hints about our uncommon friendship.

The next day I went to see the lawyer, a Mr. Lemkin. I brought along all the documents that I possessed. The managing editor had already spoken to him about my problems on the telephone. Lemkin was tall, blond, and youthful. His entire presence exuded the competence and energy of those for whom life with all its troubles and miseries is nothing but the kind of a challenge one encounters in solving some easy crossword puzzle. He received me standing up, eating an apple. He took one glance at my documents and said, "It's not enough, but we'll proceed with what we have."

I witnessed something that astounded me, the frightened Polish Jew. He picked up the telephone and asked to be connected with the American consul in Toronto or perhaps with one of his aides. He called him by his first name and told him about me and my documents. I would never have believed speed like this possible. My previous lawyer, an immigrant himself, had delayed everything for weeks and months. He always began his conversation with the words "We're having a problem." But Mr. Lemkin accomplished everything in minutes. In

him I had found the very epitome of the American notion that
time is money.

The party in Toronto informed him right then and there that,
among other things, I required a bank book to show that I had
money in the bank and wouldn't become a public charge. After
Mr. Lemkin hung up, he asked a fee of fifteen hundred dollars
for obtaining my visa. This was more than I had managed to
save up from the novel, but I knew that my brother would help
me out. Mr. Lemkin asked for my brother's telephone number;
he called him and told him what I required. He demanded a
five-hundred-dollar advance and my brother's assurance of the
fee that would be coming to him when I returned with the visa.
Then he handed me the receiver and my brother told me that
he would deposit the money into my account the next day.
Then Mr. Lemkin said to me, "You are already as good as an
American. However, the Canadian bureaucrats won't grant you
permission to enter Canada. Even if such permission could be
obtained, it would take too long to get it and in the meantime
your right to remain here would expire and complications might
ensue."

"What can I do?"

"You'll have to smuggle yourself into Canada."

Although I had a theory that life in general, human life in
particular, and Jewish life especially, was one long attempt to
muddle through, smuggle oneself past the forces of destruction,
the word "smuggle" made my throat dry.

Mr. Lemkin continued, "Don't be so timid. It's all a matter of
a few bucks. You'll take the train to Detroit and meet a little
man in a hotel lobby. He'll lead you across the bridge into
Windsor, which belongs to Canada. Thousands of Americans
and Canadians cross this bridge daily and the officials haven't
the time for long formalities. The man who will take you across
has his connections and his fee is one hundred dollars. When
you get to Windsor, you'll take a bus to Toronto. You'll carry no
documents on you. You will forward your passport and the
other documents to the King Edward Hotel in Toronto by mail.
I'll make a reservation for you there for a couple of days be-

cause it takes a while to obtain the visa. In case the Canadians should catch you, you mustn't tell that you are a Polish citizen. You can rest easy, this hasn't happened till now to any of my clients. Everything goes smooth as glass."

My throat was now so dry that I could barely speak.

"What happens if I am caught?"

"Why speak of failure? It's entirely superfluous."

"I want to know."

"They'll surely not hang you. In such a case, they'll put you in jail, then try to deport you to wherever you come from. But if you won't say where you are from, they can't very well deport you. In the meantime, we would have learned what had happened to you and would have begun proceedings to free you. Don't think about this for even a minute. The chances of this happening are as slim as of having a meteor fall on your head. If the bureaucrats in Canada weren't what they are, they would grant you the transit visa in a hurry and you'd avoid having to smuggle yourself across. They make difficulties so that the poor immigrants have to break the law and they, the bloodsuckers, can take bribes. I once thought that things in Russia are better, but there you have to steal to keep from starving to death. An uncle of mine came over from there and he told us things that made my hair stand on end. Don't carry any luggage with you to avoid any confrontation with the customs people. Take nothing along, not even a toothbrush. In Toronto, you can buy pajamas or sleep naked, as I do. I'll give you all the addresses. The main thing is not to display any fear when you're crossing the bridge into Windsor. Behave with the assurance of the native. The consul won't keep you there for long. Two or three days. How is your health? A doctor will examine you."

"I hope I'm not sick."

"How about your eyes?"

"Not bad."

"Don't be such a pessimist. Sign this paper."

He handed me a sheet of paper, which I signed without bothering to read it.

4

Everything transpired in a hurry. My brother deposited money in the bank where I had already saved up my thousand dollars. He also gave me money for the fare to Canada and paid the lawyer his advance. But the fear of being arrested at the border didn't leave me. At night I dreamed of being captured, bound, dragged off to jail. Mr. Lemkin's advice to keep silent as to my place of origin went totally against my nature. I knew that if I were arrested I would make a confession complete with all the details.

When Nesha heard that I was on the verge of obtaining a permanent visa, she congratulated me, but I detected a note of disappointment in her voice. Somewhere within, she might have been hoping for a situation in which I would be forced to marry her in order to obtain American citizenship. When I told her of my fear of being arrested at the border, she said half in jest, "If worst comes to worst, I'll come to save you."

In the last few weeks there had evolved between us a coolness that we could neither admit nor deny. The urge we had felt toward one another had left us. Nesha began to mention the fact that she would have to make some sort of change—the work was growing too hard for her and she was neglecting her son. She still loved Boris, but sooner or later she would have to remarry—not in order to provide someone with a visa but to a man who would love her and whom she could possibly love as well. She complained that the late-night visits to my furnished room exhausted her so that all the following day she walked around sleepy and made mistakes in her work. At times during the height of our sexual fantasies she would emit a sigh that seemed to say, Where can all these dreams lead to? This is all fine and good for a thirty-year-old bohemian, but not for a woman of forty and poor to boot.

In the next few days I was supposed to go to Detroit, but when I phoned Mr. Lemkin he told me that my trip would have to be delayed by a week. I was expecting Nesha that evening, and she called to say that our meeting would have to be postponed, and that if I was leaving in the interim, she wished me a pleasant journey. Zosia was still in New York, and although I had resolved that meeting with her was a waste of time, I phoned her and caught her in. She said to me, "I thought you'd be in Toronto already."

These words were a clear indication to me that my stock had fallen with her as well. Nevertheless, she agreed to meet me at the Steward Cafeteria on Twenty-third Street. I could already read English and I bought an afternoon paper. Another paper, a morning edition, had been left on the table. In the works on mental hygiene that I had read in Warsaw, like Payot's *The Education of the Will* and a similar book by Forel, it was written that reading too many newspapers was poison for someone who aimed to achieve some intellectual goal. The authors compared the reading of newspapers to cardplaying, smoking, drinking, and other such habits that kill time and offer no benefit. But lately I had come to the conclusion that a writer can learn much from the newspapers, particularly from the so-called yellow press. They were a treasure trove of human idiosyncrasies and quirks. The day-by-day parade of news mocked all the philosophical theories, every effort to seek out a basis for ethics, all sociological and psychological hypotheses. I had not forgotten that, of all the modern philosophers, Schopenhauer was the only one to quote events gleaned from newspapers.

I drank coffee and read. A combination of a slaughterhouse, a bordello, and an insane asylum—that's what the world really was. From time to time I cast a glance at the revolving door. Would Zosia show up? What would I do that evening if she didn't?

She came late and even from a distance I could see that she was distressed. Her hair didn't look properly combed. In the brief time we hadn't seen each other, she had lost weight and her cheeks appeared sunken. I asked her what I could bring her from the counter and she replied, "Absolutely nothing!"

Her tone was stern and expressed the annoyance of one no

longer able to control her emotions. Abruptly, she said, "I'm going to be married!"

I didn't answer and we sat silent for a while. Then she said, "I can no longer go back to that woman professor of mine with her spirits and the whole mishmash. Those things, as long as they last, they last, but the moment you tear yourself away from them, they become sheer nonsense. She herself is still to be endured, but the guests who come to her with all their brazen lies are more than I can stand. The books that I read to her are complete fakes. Spirits do exist, but they don't appear to those fakers on command. I had occasion to read Houdini's book and in a sense it opened my eyes. I happened to come across it accidentally in a bookstore on Fourth Avenue that sells books from outdoor bins for a quarter each. Have you read it?"

"Yes, I got it out of the library and I think that he was more of a medium than those he opposed. This man demonstrated things that can't be explained in rational fashion."

"Odd, I have the very same feeling."

"Who are you marrying—Reuben Mecheles?"

"Yes, him."

"Well, congratulations."

"Don't congratulate me yet. I'm not sure that I'm going to go through with it. He suddenly decided to give his wife what she's been demanding and she went off to Reno, Nevada, to get the divorce. He is apparently filthy rich since he is giving her forty thousand dollars plus a three hundred dollar weekly alimony. How he made so much money isn't clear to me. From the way he speaks, you can never tell what he is doing. Apparently, back in 1929, in the Wall Street crash, he bought up stocks for pennies, and those stocks later rose and began paying dividends again. He also owns houses, and paintings by the greatest French masters. He has a huge apartment on Riverside Drive and all the walls are covered with masterpieces. I shouldn't say this, but I don't love him and I know that I never will. Actually, I have told him this, maybe not as directly, but he knows it himself. He is definitely not my type, but then again, who is? What he sees in me, I don't know. He showers me with compliments but somehow they don't ring true. If I were rich and offered him a huge dowry, I could understand his purposes. But since I am penniless, why would he deceive me? I resolved not to meet with you again. I'm simply ashamed of my lack of character. But when you phoned me, I had to come meet you. You are actually the closest person I have here in America. I could never talk to my father since he was forever shouting and preaching to me and I didn't believe in his religiousness. My mother, on the other hand, can do only one thing—cry. The moment she begins to speak, the tears come pouring out. Weren't you supposed to go to Toronto today or tomorrow?"

"It was postponed for a week."

"What's with your sweetheart? Is she really going to marry someone else?"

I told Zosia the whole situation. Nesha was poor. She had to support a child. She was ten years my senior. She had no strength to go on working. She had actually been the breadwinner even when her husband had been alive. I myself lived off the one weekly column, which the editor was liable to cancel at any time.

"Can't your brother help you?"

"He helps me enough. I can't take a wife and let my brother support her. What's with the prophet from Egypt?" I asked.

A smile formed on Zosia's lips. "The prophet is on Ellis Island. They won't let him into America. Funny, eh?"

Eight

1

THAT NIGHT AFTER ZOSIA HAD gone home, I was convinced that she would change her mind about the plan we worked out that evening at our table in the cafeteria. The entire matter struck me as nothing more than one of my fantasies with which I killed time instead of thinking about my work. But when I telephoned her the next morning, I detected in her voice that senseless inspiration I often evoked in those who had the misfortune to know me. Besides, the forces that favor adventurers had done me a service. Reuben Mecheles was due to leave for Reno within the next few days to see his wife, who was awaiting her divorce, and Zosia now had the time and the opportunity to accompany me to Canada.

Had Mrs. Mecheles gotten sick, or had the couple decided to enjoy a sort of last honeymoon before parting forever? Zosia did not know, but I knew that anything was possible between a man and a woman. I had observed the very strangest and most incredible occurrences even among those simple couples who had come to my father's courtroom to marry, to divorce, or to settle a dispute. Love turned to hate overnight. Hate flared up again into love. Powerful affection sometimes went hand in hand with shameless betrayal. I often heard critics employ such words as "implausible" and "unrealistic," but I learned that many things that some consider impossible occur daily.

The quiet, reticent Zosia had turned energetic overnight. She was ready to accompany me to Toronto and go on a trip with me to some other Canadian places—"just for the sake of doing something before I expire from boredom," she explained. I had proposed it to her without believing for a moment that she would agree. Only after she consented did I realize how many complications—financial, legal, psychological—this little venture would bring about.

Zosia told me that an immigrant who has first papers requires only permission to leave the country, and she went to a lawyer to help her obtain this permission. She hadn't brought along enough clothes to New York, she told me, and she went shopping for the garments she would need on her journey. The whole thing had to remain a secret not only from my brother but from my lawyer as well. According to his schedule, I was to come back to New York the day after obtaining my visa, but why couldn't I remain in Canada longer? Even if the Canadian police nabbed me for being an illegal entrant, they wouldn't deport me to Poland after my getting the visa, but would send me back to the States.

My urge for conspiracy was, it seemed, even stronger than my cowardice. I became a sudden daredevil. Was I hoping that I would overcome Zosia's fear of sex and transform my trek to Canada into an erotic triumph? Was I looking to take on a new mistress in case Nesha should decide to marry? It was all these things, but chiefly a hunger for suspense. I had made up my mind a long time ago that the creative powers of literature lie not in the forced originality produced by variations of style and word machinations but in the countless situations life keeps creating, especially in the queer complications between man and woman. For the writer, they are potential treasures that could never be exhausted, while all innovations in language soon become clichés.

We had planned everything down to the last detail. We would take the train to Detroit together. There I would meet the guide who would escort me across the bridge to Windsor. Zosia would cross this bridge legally at the same time. Since she had an immigration visa, she was as good as an American citizen. We would then meet at the bus station in Windsor and buy our tickets to Toronto. Zosia was supposed to telephone the King Edward Hotel, where I would be staying, and reserve a room for herself. After I had obtained the visa, we would go on to Montreal. Zosia would tell Reuben Mecheles that during the time he was in Reno, she had to go back to Boston for her clothes, books, and other possessions. The half-blind professor had had her telephone disconnected while she was visiting her brother in Lenox so that Reuben Mecheles couldn't try to contact Zosia. Zosia suspected that he had gone to Reno in an effort for a reconciliation with his wife. She said to me, "For all his slyness, he is a fool, and for all his daring, he is a slave."

Among other things, Zosia told me that Reuben Mecheles' sudden trip to Reno had evoked bitterness among the followers of the Egyptian messiah, for it had been he, Reuben, who had sent the affidavit to the prophet as well as the fare to America. Only such a scatterbrain as Reuben would have abandoned a second Moses on Ellis Island and flown off to a wife who had filed for a divorce from him.

On the night before Zosia and I were to leave for Detroit, I didn't sleep a wink. The day had been a hot one and my furnished room was like a sweatbox. Although the water from the tap wasn't clean, I kept drinking it. I lay in bed naked and the sweat poured from me. My stomach had grown inflated and I had to urinate every few minutes. The same voice within me that had predicted all my other troubles now warned me that my enterprise would end in a dismal failure—jail, deportation, even death. It argued, "It's not too late yet to shake loose of the entire madness." I knew somehow that Zosia was experiencing the very same turmoil. In my imagination, I could hear her toss in her bed, muttering, sighing, seeking some pretext for getting out of the situation. By the time I dozed off, dawn was breaking. I awoke late with an ache in my spine. My mattress was torn and its springs protruded. Zosia and I had agreed to share the expenses equally, but even so, the trip would eat up a huge portion of my little savings. I owed money to the lawyer. I wouldn't dare to dip into the money my brother had deposited into my bank merely for me to be able to show the counsel that I wouldn't become a public charge.

I couldn't take along any luggage, but since Zosia was traveling legally, she had agreed to carry the most necessary things for me.

The train was leaving in the evening but that morning I wanted to stop at Zosia's hotel with my shaving equipment, a sweater, some underwear, as well as my passport. Mr. Lemkin had advised me to mail my passport to the King Edward Hotel, but I considered this too risky. What if it got lost in the mail? Without a passport, one couldn't get a visa. It was much safer for Zosia to carry it for me.

Thank God, the bathroom in the hall was empty—all the neighbors on my floor had gone to work—and I could take a bath without fear of someone pounding on the door or trying to force his way in. I had taken a huge dose of a laxative but my nerves were so taut that even this didn't help. I had forgotten to bring soap to the bathroom, but I found a piece someone had left there. Sitting in the bathtub, I thought that my adventure could be a theme for a story or even a comedy. Who knows? Maybe Casanova and all those other boasters had been just as frightened and befuddled as I was. I dressed, packed the belongings I intended to turn over to Zosia, and went to her hotel on Fifty-seventh Street. What if she announced to me that she had changed her mind? I both wished for it and feared that this would happen. The day was hot and humid. I didn't take the subway but walked. We were supposed to have lunch together at the Fifty-seventh Street cafeteria and later meet at Grand Central Station to buy the train tickets to Detroit. We planned to be there two hours before the train left to allow sufficient time for any eventuality.

I knocked on Zosia's door and it was a long while before she opened it. My imagination promptly began to work. Maybe she had moved out? Maybe she had committed suicide? Maybe she was nothing but a phantom? She opened the door and I saw that her night had been as nerve-racking as mine. She looked pale, sleepy, drawn. Two huge valises stood in the center of the room in addition to a small satchel. I wanted to ask why she was taking along so much luggage but I decided it would be best to keep silent. I saw in her eyes the resentment of someone who has allowed herself to be snared in a trap from which there is no escape. She said, "I'm sorry, but I haven't the room for your things. The valises are filled to bursting."

"Why do you need so many things?"

"Eh? I'm a woman, not a man. I can't go somewhere without clothes. In such hot weather, you have to change your underwear, your dresses, your stockings. And since I am vacating the room at this hotel, I can't leave my things here. They don't want to be held responsible for them."

"Yes, I understand."

2

Everything appeared to go smoothly for the time being. I was anxious lest I run into someone who knew me at Grand Central Station or that it might occur to my brother to see me off, but neither of these events happened. I had been forced to leave my sweater and underwear behind, but Zosia had managed to pack my shaving things in the small satchel and my passport in her bag.

We spent the night sitting up in the coach car. We had rented pillows for a quarter apiece and, since I hadn't slept the night before, I dozed the entire night. The car was half empty and Zosia found a bench on which to stretch out. I slept and worried. In my sleep I heard the conductor announcing the stops. In the novels I had read in my young days, the lovers were one hundred percent monogamous, certain of their love. They suffered only from external obstacles—ambitious parents, a wife or a husband who refused to grant a divorce, social objections or superstitions. They were seldom as poor as I was, burdened with problems of passports, lawyers, precarious jobs, sick nerves. But I had never read about any person whose emotions kept on changing, literally every second. It occurred to me more than once to write about myself as I really was, but I was convinced that the readers, the publishers, and the critics (especially the Yiddish ones) would consider me a pornographer, a contriver, mad.

Mr. Lemkin had written down for me the name of the hotel in Detroit where I was to await a man whom I would address as Mr. Smith. Mr. Smith was to leave a message with the desk clerk giving the time of our meeting. I would not need to rent a room at the Detroit hotel since I would be spending the coming night on the bus from Windsor to Toronto. I was simply to sit in the hotel lobby until Mr. Smith contacted me. But the fact that Zosia was to come along with her two heavy valises and the satchel posed unforeseen difficulties. It would look suspicious to arrive at a hotel with a lady and baggage, then sit for who knows how many hours in the lobby with her and wait for a message from a Mr. Smith. On the other hand, I couldn't afford the luxury of renting a room for merely a few hours. And what about Zosia? Was I to take a double room for Mr. and Mrs. So-and-so? Would Zosia consent to it? And what if the clerk asked for our passports?

I had fallen into a deep sleep before we reached Detroit and Zosia was waking me. She looked sick, faded, disheveled. We got into a taxi and we were taken to a hotel that seemed to me fancy and expensive. Two porters fetched Zosia's luggage and we were led to the desk where new arrivals registered. When the clerk asked me if I wanted a room with a double or twin bed, I hear Zosia say, "We aren't married."

"In that case I'll give you two adjacent rooms," the clerk said gallantly. He gave me a sidelong look and handed another card to Zosia for her to fill out. I was too shocked to remember to ask for the price.

Mr. Lemkin had assured me that Mr. Smith would call me

not later than 11 A.M., but it was already 3 P.M. and he had not
called. Zosia had gone to sleep in her room and, although I
was overcome with fatigue, I could not doze off. These spacious hotel rooms, complete with rugs, tapestried walls, and
luxurious furniture, would eat up my budget like locusts. I was
afraid to leave the hotel to look for a cafeteria or a cheap coffee shop outside for fear that I would miss the call from Mr.
Smith, and the prices for our breakfast and lunch in the hotel
restaurant were terribly high. Why didn't Mr. Smith call? Every
minute or so I glanced at my wristwatch. Maybe the employees
of the hotel were in cahoots with this Mr. Smith and informed
him that I brought a female with me? Maybe Mr. Smith called
Mr. Lemkin to pass along this information and Mr. Lemkin in
turn had informed my brother? Someone like Mr. Smith was
even capable of denouncing me to the police.

Zosia and I had realized it would endanger our plan if we
were seen together by Mr. Smith and so we decided that she
would cross the bridge before Mr. Smith took me there, and
she would wait for me at the bus station in Windsor. I was about
to fall asleep when the telephone rang. It was Zosia. She was
ready to go down and take the cab to the bridge to Windsor. I
wanted to carry down her valises and wait with her until she
could get a taxi, but Mr. Smith was liable to telephone me any
minute. Besides, if both of us were seen carrying valises outside, the hotel employees were liable to suspect that we were
running out without paying our bill. It appeared also that she
wanted to avoid being seen with someone who was preparing
to cross the border illegally, and she had to call for a man to
take down her luggage. I stayed in my room and sat down to
wait for Mr. Smith. Six came and six-thirty and still he didn't
show up. What if he didn't come at all? Since he was a smuggler,
it was quite feasible that he had been arrested. A person could
also suddenly fall ill or be run over, God forbid. I realized now
that I had committed a folly in entrusting my passport to Zosia.
I should have followed Mr. Lemkin's instructions exactly, and
mailed the passport to the King Edward Hotel in Toronto. Why

had I gotten involved with this Zosia in the first place? Of all my lunacies, this was the most dangerous.

The telephone rang and it was Mr. Smith. He said, "Come right down. I am waiting for you in the lobby. I'm wearing a hat with a little brush in it and I'll be holding a copy of the *Saturday Evening Post*. Make it snappy."

I went right out into the corridor and began searching for the elevator, but it had vanished. I raced up and down the lengthy corridor; there was not a trace of an elevator. It's all my cursed nerves, I told myself. The writer within me observed, Literature hasn't even touched on the fantastic tricks that sick nerves can play on people.

From somewhere, a black maid appeared. I asked her where the elevator was and she shouted something I couldn't understand. I began searching for the stairs, but at that moment a door opened and someone stepped out of the elevator. I quickly raced inside it. How was this possible? Could nerves render someone blind? Did they possess such hypnotic power? And if they did, could this power perhaps be turned into a force that worked miracles?

For some reason, I had pictured Mr. Smith as being tall, but he turned out to be a runt. He winked at me to follow him; however, I hadn't yet checked out. The bill came to over forty dollars. I went outside with Mr. Smith and we walked along. During the whole time, he didn't speak a single word to me. The bridge was crowded with pedestrians. We passed two officials and it seemed to me that Mr. Smith nodded to one of them. They let me pass without a word.

I no longer recall whether the distance to the bus station was long or short. It seems to me that the station was right on the other side of the bridge. The moment we had crossed it, Mr. Smith vanished. I had the anxious premonition that when I got to the bus station Zosia wouldn't be there. And that's how it turned out.

The station was small. If she had gone to the ladies' room, her suitcases would be out here. But there were no suitcases in sight. A catastrophe had occurred. Zosia had my passport. I could no longer return to the States. Nor could I obtain a visa without a passport. According to my calculations, Zosia should have been here more than an hour ago. "Well, this is my finish," I told myself.

I sat down on a bench and everything within me was mute. To forget my troubles momentarily, I began to add up my remaining money. I counted the bills and even my small change several times and each time I came up with a different total.

Each time the door opened, I trembled. I tried to imagine what might have occurred. Had Zosia been detained at the border? Had she changed her mind at the last minute and ordered the driver to take her to the train going back to New York? Had something happened to the cab and she was in a hospital? After much brooding, I decided to take the bus to Toronto. If Zosia lived, it would be easier for her to phone or wire me at the King Edward Hotel than to reach me here at the bus station.

The door opened and several policemen (or maybe these were border guards) entered. Had they come to arrest me? I began to mumble a prayer to the Almighty, assuming He existed, "Father in heaven, help me! Don't let me perish!"

I decided to buy the ticket to Toronto. Even to kill oneself it was easier in a hotel than in a bus station. But would they give me a room there without a passport?

The armed men spoke to the ticket seller. It apparently had nothing to do with me. I walked over and asked for a ticket, but the seller gave me a questioning look and his lips formed something like a smile. The policeman stared at me too and also seemed to be holding back laughter. What had happened to me? Had I addressed the ticket seller in Yiddish instead of English?

I repeated my request for the third time and the ticket seller asked, "Where do you think you are?"

At that moment I realized my error. Instead of asking for a ticket to Toronto I had been asking for a ticket to Windsor. Two of the policemen burst out laughing, but one who was older

and apparently of a higher rank kept a solemn face and asked
me, "You're from the States, eh?"

"Yes."

"Just come over from Detroit?"

"Yes."

Although Mr. Lemkin had admonished me repeatedly not to
give my name in such an instance, I immediately revealed my
full name along with my address both in Warsaw and in New
York, even though the other hadn't asked for it. I did this, first,
because it isn't my way to deny my identity. Second, there was
a bit of logic behind this. It would be better for me to be arrested and deported to Poland than to remain in a strange country without papers and with just enough money to last me one
week at most. Apparently, I was far from ready for suicide.

The policemen exchanged brief glances, as if mutely consulting on their next move. The ticket seller asked, "Do you want a
one-way ticket or a round trip?"

"One-way," I said.

I assumed that the policeman would continue his interrogation and I even considered the fact that it would be a waste of
money to buy a ticket if I was to be arrested, but the officials
began to discuss other matters among themselves and seemed
to have forgotten about me. I paid the fare and was handed my
ticket. In a way, I was disappointed that I hadn't been detained
on the spot. I was convinced that they would do this later, before I boarded my bus. They surely had to understand that I
had crossed the border illegally. I didn't have a piece of luggage
with me.

I sat down again, and after a while the policemen left and the
station began to fill up with passengers who were apparently
bound for Toronto, too. Suddenly, I spotted Zosia. Someone
carried in her valises and she handed the man a tip. I stood up
and Zosia said to me, "They detained me at the frontier. They
suspected me of being a Communist agitator, those idiots."

Nine

1

It was all in the past—the examination by the American consul in Toronto (not unlike the examination by the American consul in Warsaw), Zosia's congratulations, her wishes and kisses. As always when something propitious happens to me, I asked my inner I, my ego, superego, id, or whatever it should be called if I was finally happy. But they kept diplomatically silent. It seemed that I had a great talent for suffering, but no positive achievement could ever satisfy me. What was there to rejoice about? The skeptic in me, the nihilist and protester, quoted the words of Ecclesiastes: "Of laughter I said it is madness and of mirth what doeth it?" I was still a Yiddish writer who hadn't made it, estranged from everything and everybody. I could live neither with God nor without Him. I had no faith in the institution of marriage, neither could I stand my bachelor's loneliness.

We had eaten a combination of lunch and supper in a noisy little restaurant and then walked all the way back to the King Edward Hotel. For some reason Zosia kept on stopping at shop windows. I asked her what she was searching for but she didn't give me a clear answer. Her feet must have been hurting because she lingered at windows displaying ladies' shoes. I offered to wait until she got herself a pair of shoes but she assured me that she had comfortable shoes in her luggage. Besides, the stores were closing.

Night had fallen when we finally returned to the hotel. In all the excitement of getting the visa I had almost forgotten that Zosia and I had come here with an unspoken agreement to deliver her from the disgrace of remaining a virgin at an age when other women had husbands or lovers or both. I was anxious to keep my silent promise both for her sake and my own male vanity, but from the very beginning of our journey I was aware that something like an antisexual dybbuk had taken hold of me. A spiteful spirit was telling me that agreements of this kind are not only morally wrong but physiologically precarious as well. Sex, like art, cannot be made to order—at least not in my case. The little desire I had for Zosia that evening when we planned our trip together had vanished almost immediately and I began to feel something akin to hostility for that old maid who was clinging to me like a parasite. What shame, I thought, to have to depend on the little blood and the few nerves that evoke the erection! Unlike the other limbs of the body, the penis has the autonomy to function or not to function according to its ethical and aesthetic likes and dislikes. The cabalists called this organ "the sign of the holy covenant." It bore the name *yesod,* the same as one of the ten spheres of the divine emanation. What I really felt now was a kind of negative erection, if one may use an expression like this. My penis tried to steal into hiding, to become shrunken, to sabotage and punish me for daring to make a decision without its consent, to become a benefactor on its account. The resolver in me had resolved that I owed Zosia nothing. I had to remain completely passive, not take the slightest initiative. Let me imagine, I said to myself, that they actually arrested me in Windsor that late afternoon and that I am in a Canadian prison now.

Both of us were tired from the long walk and we decided to take a rest. Zosia had gone to her room to lie down for half an hour, and I tried to do the same in my room but I could not even doze, let alone sleep. I closed my eyes but they too had become autonomous and opened by themselves. If there is such a thing as Nirvana, let me try it right now, I decided. Zosia must have read my mind. My phone rang and it was she, stuttering and asking, "What became of our plan?"

"What plan?" I asked with a choked voice.

"We were supposed to celebrate."

"Come in and we will celebrate."

"All right, I will dress." And she hung up.

What does she have to dress for? I murmured to myself. Or does she mean undress? I waited what seemed to me a long time and she still did not appear. What is she doing in there? Preparing like a bride? I was impatient for her to come in—not in order to fulfill my self-imposed obligation but to void it once and for all. I could neither lie nor sit and I began to pace back and forth. I stopped at the window and looked out at the street seven flights below. How dark the city was! All the stores were closed. A single man, seemingly drunk, passed by on the sidewalk. He swayed and gesticulated. I envied this tramp. No one expected anything of him; he was free to spend the night as he pleased. I heard a knocking on my door and I rushed to open it. On the other side of the threshold stood Zosia in a black nightgown (or was it a negligee?) and silver slippers. For the first time she wore a trace of makeup, discreetly applied, her nose powdered, and a redness in her cheeks which might have been rouge. She had even changed her hairdo. "Unconditional surrender," the phrase so often used at the end of World War II, went through my mind. She smiled, half-frightened, with that naïvete which sometimes shows up in even the most shrewd woman. They understand as little about men as men understand them, I thought. She had armed herself with that weapon which had never yet conquered anyone. I heard her say, "Today should be a holiday for us."

"How beautiful you look! Come in."

"A day like this happens once in a lifetime."

This was no longer the same Zosia who admired Baudelaire for being the only poet and thinker who could tell the world the full dismal truth, but an old maid who had decided to lose her virginity at any price. I sat down on my bed and I offered her the chair nearby. In one way or another I had to inflate her confidence in me and in my masculine prowess, and I said, "I don't think that you made such a fuss when *you* got your visa."

"What? I got mine at a time when I wasn't even sure if I wanted to go to America. I have told you already, I had someone who I thought I could love and who loved me. Leaving for America was actually more my father's plan than mine. What could I have expected to find in America besides extreme loneliness? But you are a writer, you have a brother here, a newspaper that publishes you, a milieu. You will grow."

"No, Zosia, I'm completely alone."

"Today I don't want to hear this. Wait, I have a surprise for you."

"What kind of surprise?"

"This morning I bought a bottle of champagne especially for this occasion. The chambermaid saw me come in with it, and she brought me a bucket with ice. It has already melted but the water is still cold."

"Really, you needn't have done this."

"Can I bring it in?"

"Yes, if you want."

She went out and did not close the door, but left it half open. She dallied longer than would have been necessary to bring the bottle from one room to another in the same corridor. After a long while she came back. I got up to take the bucket from her and my hands trembled so that I almost dropped it. She said, "Where do you get a corkscrew in a place like this?"

I took the bottle out of the bucket and let the water drip back in order not to wet the rug. I could see that it was not corked but sealed with a foil wrapper that could be easily removed. I had barely begun to unwrap the foil when I heard a pop. The stopper sprang off and the wine began to fizz over its neck and my hand. Zosia screamed and ran to the bathroom, coming back with two glasses, while the champagne kept on running over my hand and onto the rug. Perhaps the champagne would help me, flashed through my mind, as I poured one glass for Zosia and one for myself. I clinked my glass to hers and gulped it down like medicine. Usually when I drank an alcoholic beverage, even wine, I had to eat something with it—a cookie, a pretzel, a piece of bread. But this time I wanted to get drunk. It occurred to me that this might have been Zosia's aim in buying this gift—to make me drunk as the daughters did to Lot.

We had emptied the bottle. I was still sitting on the edge of the bed and Zosia on the chair opposite. She crossed her legs and for a split second I saw she was naked under her fancy garment. I was waiting for my drunkenness to ascend from the stomach to the brain, but I felt that the opposite was happening—it descended from my brain to my stomach. I remained tense, sober, attentive to the slightest variation in my moods. I heard Zosia say, "I've read nothing of yours, but for some reason I believe in your talent. The trouble is that what a human being is, no one will ever be able to describe. What is a human being, eh?"

I did not answer. I seemed to have missed the question. For one fraction of a moment my mind remained blank. Then I realized what she had said, and I answered, "A caricature of God, a parody of the spirit, the only entity in Creation which could be called a lie."

2

The master of spite, as I call the special adversary of lovemaking, had had his way. The first half of the night Zosia was willing but I was inhibited. After I gave up all hope and had an hour of sleep, my potency came back as strongly as ever but then Zosia became possessed by the same dybbuk. She pressed her legs together and my bony knees could not separate them. I reproached her contradictory behavior but she said to me, "I can't help it." She informed me that exactly the same thing happened to her on that night when she had tried to give herself to that professor in Warsaw. I had gotten so accustomed to the games of the adversary in me and in those near to me that I stopped being surprised. I had already learned that our genitals, which in the language of the vulgar are synonyms of stupidity and insensitivity, are actually the expression of the human soul, defiant of lechery, the most ardent defenders of true love.

Day was breaking when we both gave up and Zosia went back to her room. In the morning we had breakfast in the dining room of the hotel, trying to make conversation about Hitler, Mussolini, the civil war in Spain. We avoided looking into each other's eyes. It was clear to both of us that our planned journey together was over. Zosia had gotten information about her return to the U.S.A. at the desk. She intended to travel directly from Toronto to Boston and I was to take the train to New York. Both of our trains were leaving in the evening and we had the whole day to ourselves. We checked out from the hotel after lunch, leaving our luggage in the storage room—partners to a disenchantment we could never forget.

I was told that Spadina Avenue was the center of Yiddishism in Toronto, and there we went. I again strolled on Krochmalna Street—the same shabby buildings, the same pushcarts and vendors of half-rotten fruit, the familiar smells of the sewer, soup kitchens, freshly baked bagels, smoke from the chimneys. I imagined that I heard the singsong of cheder boys reciting the Pentateuch and the wailing of women at a funeral. A little rag dealer with a yellow face and a yellow beard was leading a cart harnessed to an emaciated horse with short legs and a long tail. A mixture of resignation and wisdom looked out of its dark eyes, as old and as humble as the never-ending Jewish Exile.

Zosia was saying to me, "Oh, I was determined, and I still am, to return to Jewishness, but of what shall my Jewishness consist? If there is no God and if the Bible is a lie, in what way is a Jew a Jew?"

"He is a Jew by virtue of the fact that he isn't a Gentile," I said, just to say something.

"Maybe I should leave everything and go to Palestine?" Zosia asked. She spoke to me, to herself, and mostly in order to show that her mind could be occupied with things other than with our common disgrace. I said, "Unless you were to shave your head, don a bonnet, and marry some yeshivah student from Mea Shearim, all your problems would remain unresolved even in Palestine."

"Oh, I am lost. You are lost, too, but at least you received a Jewish upbringing. You know the Talmud and all the rest. You belong to these Yiddishists whether you want to or not. I am a total stranger here. I'm psychotic to boot. Last night, after I had fallen asleep in my room, I heard my father's voice. He yelled at me so loud that I was afraid you would hear it next door. He seized me by the throat and tried to strangle me. I'm seriously afraid that I will soon be committed to an asylum."

"No, Zosia, our so-called nerves are not madness but a true realization of the many misfortunes which lurk before us and of all the barriers that stand between us and our notions of happiness."

"What? They may lead to insanity. My father had a sister who went insane in her later years. She convinced herself that her husband was trying to poison her. I suspect that my father's conversion was an act of lunacy, too. This thing with Reuben Mecheles is finished. I shouldn't have started up with him in the first place. I'll go back to Boston to my professor and maybe we'll get through the few years left to her and to me. You see already that love and sex aren't for me. Come, let's have a cup of coffee."

Although it was too late for lunch and too early for dinner, the restaurant we entered—a kind of Jewish Polish coffeehouse— was crowded with young men and women. They all conversed— or rather, shouted—in Yiddish. The tables were strewn with Yiddish newspapers and magazines. I heard the names of Jewish writers, poets, and politicians. This place was a Canadian version of the Warsaw Writers' Club. Its patrons engaged in the same kind of conversations one always hears among Yiddishists: Could literature ignore social problems? Could writers retreat to ivory towers and avoid the struggle for justice? I didn't have to listen to their talk—their faces, voices, and intonations told me what each of them was: a Communist, a Left Poalei Zionist, or a Bundist. Hardly anyone here spoke with a Litvak accent. These were boys and girls from Staszow, Lublin, Radom, each one hypnotized by some social cause. I could tell by the way they pronounced certain words from which bank of the Vistula the speaker came, the left or the right. I imagined that even their gestures had unique meanings. Zosia and I found a table and sat down. She said, "Here you are in your element."

"Not really."

It was odd that having crossed the Atlantic and smuggled myself over the border I found myself in a copy of Yiddish Poland. I told myself that there had been no need to consider suicide when Zosia vanished with my passport. All I would have had to do was come to Spadina Avenue. Here, I could have become a teacher, a writer for the local periodical, or at least a proofreader. The Yiddishists would have hidden me here, provided me with documents, and sooner or later obtained Canadian citizenship for me. One of the girls sitting at these tables and smoking cigarettes would probably have become my wife and, like Lena had long ago, would have tried to persuade me to harness my creative powers to the struggle for a better world.

A waiter came over and I let Zosia order the coffee and the rice pudding for both of us. Somehow, I couldn't bring myself to address this youth in English, nor could I speak to him in Yiddish, since he would start questioning me about who I was, where I came from, and what I was doing in Canada. Some of those sitting at the tables had already cast curious glances at me. My picture had been printed in the rotogravure section of the *Forward* and all the New York newspapers were read here. I had even noticed a Yiddish Warsaw paper on one of the tables. Nor did I care to draw Zosia into a conversation that would be boring to her.

Zosia asked now, "Is it possible to go directly to Boston from here?"

"I believe so. Why not? You have nothing more to do in New York?"

"No, my dear. Absolutely nothing."

"Is your lady professor back home yet?"

"No, but she left me a key."

We grew silent. I reminded myself of my passport, my visa,

and the paper affirming my right to return to America and to take out my first papers leading to full citizenship. I stuck my hand inside my breast pocket and tapped both the passport and this paper. I had an urge, for the countless time, to read it over, but I was ashamed before Zosia and of my own weakness. Though it seemed that all my immigration worries were over, some force warned me that a new crisis was looming over me, although I couldn't for the life of me figure out what it might entail.

"What are you searching for?" Zosia asked. "Have you lost something or what?"

I had forgotten to take my hand out of my bosom pocket and I quickly withdrew it as my mouth replied of its own volition, "I have lost a woman with whom I might have been happy."

3

I had persuaded Zosia to go to Boston via New York, telling her that in spite of our sexual defeat I had become attached to her and without her my trip would be lonely and dismal. After a while, she consented. We checked out of the hotel and went by taxi to the railroad station. Evening had fallen. We had already gone through customs, showing the officials our papers, and they had passed us through without any difficulties. I had sneaked like a thief into Canada but I left it like a free man. We had traveled some distance, but I was still not completely at ease. Suddenly, the train stopped and two men who might have been policemen, border guards, or customs men entered the car. All the passengers appeared startled by this unexpected stop, or at least it seemed so to me. Maybe they are looking for me? the coward within me asked. Immediately afterward, I heard my name called. I rose and all the passengers, perplexed and not without pity, gazed at me. I confirmed my identity and one of the officials said, "Come with us."

The frightened Zosia had risen too and she made a gesture as if to indicate that she wanted to accompany me, or perhaps to argue with those who were arresting me, but I shook my head at her to desist. For all of my distress, I enjoyed a measure of satisfaction—my intuition hadn't failed me.

The moment we stepped off, someone signaled the engineer, and the train pulled away. The night was a dark one and all I could see was one lighted house. It was there that I was led. I entered an office where a card hung on the wall. It contained rows of letters, each smaller than the ones above—the eye chart seen in an eye doctor's reception room and, occasionally, in an optical shop.

An elderly man said to me, "The doctor at the consulate expressed some doubt about your eyes. I'll test them again."

As he spoke these words, I began to see spots before my eyes. I glanced at the chart and I could barely distinguish the very top row of letters. Soon even they had grown misted over. The doctor showed me to a chair and asked what I could see on the chart. I strained in an effort to guess at the letters behind the whirls of diffusion, but I knew that I was failing.

Behind my back I heard the doctor's mumbling. From time to time he helped me with a letter. He shone a lighted instrument into my eyes. A lump had formed in my throat and my palate and lips grew dry. Still, I managed to say, "It's not my eyes. I'm nervous."

"Yes, yes, yes. You are a bit nervous."

He tested me again and this time I saw better. He called to someone and the two officers who had arrested me came in. Only now did I notice how tall they were—a pair of giants.

The doctor said, "When is the next train?"

They replied, but I didn't hear what they said. Not only my eyes but my ears too had ceased functioning.

The doctor gave me his hand. "Don't worry. Your eyes are better than mine."

"I thank you, Doctor, I thank you very much."

"Have a good trip."

The two officers led me outside toward the tracks. They

stayed with me for about three quarters of an hour and chatted about horse races, hunting, forest fires, and other things in which Gentiles are interested. From time to time they also addressed a few words to me. One of them asked, "How did you get into Canada?"

Somehow, I couldn't bring myself to tell the lie that I had had permission to enter that country. Had I said this, they might have asked to see this permission or ask who had issued it. Then again, I couldn't admit that I had crossed the border illegally. I, therefore, said, "I believe that I had permission."

I had already long since perceived that, when necessary, the brain could function remarkably fast. The officer apparently gathered my insinuation for he dropped the subject. After a while, a train came and the officials put me aboard it. Just like the doctor before them, they offered me their hands and wished me luck in America.

I was fully aware that these officers and the officers in the Windsor bus station could have easily detained me. The law was on their side, not on mine. How would Stalin's NKVD men have behaved in such an instance? Even the officials of democratic Poland didn't display too much consideration in such instances. I had been raised to believe that a man with brass buttons, a badge, an insignia on his cap knew little compassion, particularly when his victim was a Jew. But Americans and Canadians seemed different. Why were they different? Did it bear on the fact that Americans and Canadians were richer? Was it the upbringing? Were Anglo-Saxons by nature more inclined to be understanding of another person's dilemma than Slavs or Germans, for instance? I was by then mature enough not to seek reasons and explanations for the conduct of individuals or even of groups.

The forces worked in such fashion that my return, after I had overcome all dangers and driven off all demons and evil spirits, was completely joyless. The car that I had occupied with Zosia had been new, with plush seats, clean, bright, resembling a second-class coach in Poland or France. The passengers were young and well dressed. It was my impression that many of the couples there were going to the United States on their honeymoons. The coach in which I traveled now was old, and its passengers struck me as just as dowdy and shabby. The panes hadn't been washed in such a long time that I could barely see anything through them, not even the darkness outside. I was left with no choice but to lean my head against the dirty seat and force myself to doze off. I didn't believe in true sleep. I had always considered sleep a sort of make-believe, not only among people but even among animals.

I slept and even dreamed, yet at the same time I thought about Zosia and the troubles she had endured during her few days with me. She was probably ashamed before the other passengers that her companion was the kind of person who had been removed from the train by armed guards.

4

I was back in New York, back in my furnished room on Nineteenth Street. Once again I read my visa in my passport and the card I would present when I took out my first papers, then I put them away in the drawer of my wobbly table. The day was hot. The sun baked my face and I lowered the torn shade over the window. Through its vents and holes, the sunlight painted a mural on the opposite wall, a brilliant network against a background of shadow which shimmered and vibrated as if reflecting the waves of a river.

I had failed in many areas, yet I now found myself on a continent where neither Hitler nor Stalin could threaten me. I had eaten a satisfying meal at the Automat opposite Grand Central Station and I was ready to get some sleep after the restless nights on the train to Detroit, on the bus to Toronto, on the train back to New York, and with Zosia at the King Edward Hotel.

I had called Nesha at the factory from the Automat, and from the way she answered me—curtly, impatiently (she wouldn't

even try to arrange a meeting with me)—I gathered that everything between us was over. She congratulated me halfheartedly.
I had phoned my brother at his home and at the *Forward,* but
there was no one at his home and someone at the *Forward*
office shouted, "Not here!" and hung up. My attorney, Mr.
Lemkin, wasn't in his office either and his secretary advised me
to call the next day since he would be tied up in court all that
day. I had fallen asleep, and when I opened my eyes, the solar
hieroglyphics on the wall across the window had vanished. My
shirt and the pillow beneath my head were wet. Suddenly, I
became aware that someone was knocking on my door. It was
undoubtedly the exterminator because it couldn't have been
Nesha and no one else ever entered my room. Although I
needed him to spray since toward evening the roaches began
to crawl out from under the cracked linoleum, I decided not to
let him in. He always left behind a stench that lingered for days.
Nor did I want to begin my first day of American citizenship, or
precitizenship, by condoning the poisoning of innocent cockroaches. I called out, "Not today!"

At that moment the door opened and I saw the superinten-
dent of the house, Mr. Pinsky, as well as my brother, Zosia, and
a small man in a checkered suit and with a pointed potbelly. He
wore a Panama hat and a colorful tie with a pearl stickpin in-
serted into its broad knot. His shoes were yellow, and although
it was blazing hot outside, he wore spats over them. A long
cigar stuck out of his mouth. He reminded me of the caricatures
of capitalists in Socialist and Communist brochures and the labor union publications. For a while, the three of them stood
silent, staring at me, then Mr. Pinsky said, "What did I tell you?
I saw him pass with my own two eyes. I'm in this business thirty
years already and when I see a face once, I recognize it years
later. I can see through my little window everyone who comes
in or goes out. You can't hide from me. I hear the telephone
downstairs. Good-bye!"

"Thank you, thank you!" my brother and Zosia called out together.

So deep had been my sleep that it took moments for me to

orient myself as to what was happening. I had been convinced
that Zosia had gone straight to Boston after she returned by
herself to New York. Instead, she had notified my brother that I
had been detained at the border. The small man in the Panama
hat exclaimed, "So that's him, eh? Yep, that's him. I've seen his
picture in the *Forward* rotogravure. The caption read, 'Two
brothers and both writers.' My name is Reuben Mecheles. Very,
very nice to make your acquaintance!"

"Oh, my God, on account of you I had a wretched night!"
Zosia said to me. "Everyone in the car thought they had captured Al Capone and that I was his moll. I explained to them
that it had to do with immigration and formalities. I didn't want
to disturb your brother, but I decided that under the circumstances somebody had to be notified. I went back to the hotel
where I had stayed before. Luckily, my room was still vacant. All
I knew was that your brother works at the *Forward*. At first, they
wouldn't give me his phone number. But I told them that it was
a matter of life and death—"

"Why did they detain you?" my brother asked.

"The doctor at the consulate wanted my eyes retested."

"That's exactly what I thought," Reuben Mecheles piped up.
"I'm an old hand at such things. I've helped, and I still help,
Jews to come to America. I've brought over my whole family
and strangers as well. I'm known at the HIAS. A week doesn't
go by that I don't come to them on some matter. I have already
sent out perhaps a hundred affidavits. The things we Jews have
to do—rather than curse Hitler, which does as much good as
giving a corpse an enema—is to bring over all those we can.
Not everyone wants to come here. There are such fools who
still think Hitler is bluffing. They're afraid to abandon their
stores and their Polish zlotys. If Hitler should come to Poland,
the zlotys will be worth what the marks were in 1919—toilet
paper, if you'll forgive me."

"It's terribly hot in here. Where is the heat coming from?" my
brother asked. "Why is the window closed?"

"Let's go down, let's get out of here," Reuben Mecheles said.
"I came back from a trip yesterday. I flew back from Reno, Ne-

vada. I don't have the time or the patience for trains. I tried
being good to a person who is doing everything possible to
destroy me and herself. Suicides are terribly obstinate. I
shouldn't say it but I made the same mistake as our allies are
making with Hitler. I tried to appease a person who knows war
only and nothing else and who considers human goodness as
nothing but weakness. If I could write a book about this woman,
I would become a multimillionaire overnight. I came back from
the trip dead tired and I lay down for a nap. All of a sudden, the
phone rings. And who is it? Our good friend, Zosia, and she tells
me you've been arrested at the border and that you must be instantly rescued or else the world will come to an end. You don't
know me, but from reading, I know your brother and you too.
Someone sent me your book from Warsaw. I told myself that
something must be done. What's the sense in sleeping? A bear
sleeps all winter and he remains a bear. So that was how I got
the opportunity to meet your brother in person and now you
as well. I simply telephoned the big shots at the border. America isn't Russia. Here when you phone, you get information. Our
greenhorns are afraid to call an office, but a telephone doesn't
bite. Here in America, I've already spoken to governors, sena-
tors. Such calls cost money, but money was made to spend, not
be kept under a pillow. What I'm getting at is, now that you're
back in America and a free man, thank God, a celebration is in
order. There is a restaurant here with a roof garden. That's
America for you. They plant a garden on a roof and the garden
is a restaurant offering the finest food, entertainment. Our fathers and grandfathers wouldn't have eaten there, but as far as
I know, none of you is that pious. I propose that you accompany
me there as my guests. It would be a great honor and a pleasure
as well for me—"

The whole time Reuben Mecheles was talking, my brother
was casting questioning glances at me and at Zosia. From time
to time, he nodded to Reuben Mecheles. He said, "I thank you,
Mr. Mecheles, but I'm having company tonight at home. Maybe
some other time. I'll be glad to reimburse you for all the money
you spent on the calls—"

"No, no, no! I'm not dunning you for any money. Simply to meet you is worth everything in the world to me. When do we, common people, have the privilege to be with writers, and with talented writers at that? I truly hope we will meet again. I have things to tell you that, when you heard them, they would stand your hair on end, that is, if you had hair. Not fabricated things but facts that I myself have witnessed and experienced, in my own case and with other people—some as good as angels and others vicious devils. Allow me to present you with my visiting card. I'm no writer, but from what I would tell you, you could write the greatest works. Do our writers know what goes on in the world? They sit in the Cafe Royal and gossip and this to them is the world. Promise me that you'll call!"

Reuben Mecheles seized my brother's hand in his small hands. My brother promised to phone him. He nodded to Zosia but he ignored me completely. He left and the three of us remained momentarily silent. Zosia had revealed the secret that she went with me to Toronto and my brother probably assumed that I had conducted this adventure on the money he had deposited in the bank in my name. Until I managed to withdraw the money from the bank and return it to him, he would consider me a swindler.

5

Neither Zosia nor I wanted to go to the roof-garden restaurant. Zosia explained that she wasn't properly dressed and that she wasn't hungry besides. She hadn't slept all night and she wanted to retire early. I had slept a few hours and I was hungry, but I didn't have the slightest urge for amusement and roof gardens. I proposed that we go instead to the Steward Cafeteria, but at the very word "cafeteria," Reuben Mecheles grimaced and said that it couldn't be otherwise but that I was trying to insult him. After a while, he proposed that we go up to his

apartment on Riverside Drive. He didn't even wait for an answer. He took Zosia's arm and led her out into the corridor. I
closed the door and followed them down the narrow stairs. It
wasn't until I was downstairs that it struck me that I should have
taken along my passport with the visa and the card. I had read
in the *Forward* about thieves who specialized in stealing passports and other documents and using them to bring in illegal
aliens. But I didn't want to detain Reuben Mecheles, who had
lost sleep, time, and money on my account.

On Fourth Avenue he hailed a cab and we got in. Reuben
Mecheles lit a cigar and said, "Since my wife has left me and
I've reverted to being a bachelor, I've stopped eating at home.
Still, you'll get a better meal at my house than you would in
those cafeterias where you can ruin your stomach. I have a new
refrigerator and everything is fresh. I'm usually not hungry during the day, but in the middle of the night a hunger comes over
me and I always keep food ready. I have been an insomniac for
many years. I wake up exactly at two o'clock every morning and
rummage around like a sleepwalker. I take walks which are absolutely dangerous. I take taxis just to be able to see how New
York looks in the early hours. I like to talk to the taxi drivers
and to hear their strange stories. That's how God arranged it—
that those who know life can't write, while those blessed with
talent are dreamers who know only their own fantasies. Zosia
has undoubtedly told you something about me, but she is an
impractical person herself. I call her a yeshivah student in skirts.
You won't believe this, but I knew her father when he was still
the head of a yeshivah on Twarda Street, and also later when
he turned his coat, as the saying goes. What he did is incompre-
hensible, but where is it written that we have to understand
everything? A time has come when all people are searching for
something. The Torah is certainly a great book and the prophets
were divine men and even Jesus of Nazareth can't be lightly
dismissed. But all this isn't enough for modern man. There is a
hunger for something more. What is Stalin? And what is even
such a murderer as Hitler? False prophets. Since no one has
been in heaven and God doesn't come down to the earth and

remains silent from generation to generation, how can one know wherein lies the truth? I listen to everyone, even if he preaches that there is a horse fair on the moon."

"Oh, I forgot to ask you—what's new with your prophet? What's his name again? Is he still on Ellis Island?" Zosia asked.

"They've released him, but he got sick and he is in Lakewood recuperating," Reuben Mecheles replied after some hesitation. "Why do you call him *my* prophet? I didn't discover him and I don't consider him a prophet. He wrote a work that can't be considered anything else but religious. He speaks in the name of God, but in my estimation, this is nothing more than a means of expressing truths as one man sees them. The acknowledged prophets weren't in heaven and God didn't speak to them either. Someone in the Gemara says that Moses never rose higher than ten cubits from Mount Sinai. He sat there on a rock and carved out the Ten Commandments. Whether he fasted the forty days or not doesn't concern me. If this be the case, why can't someone of our generation do the same? In what way is a fountain pen worse than a chisel and hammer? I am, as you see, a realist—"

The taxi had pulled up before a tall building on Riverside Drive, just a few blocks from where my brother lived. But this was a fancier house, with a uniformed doorman, a richly furnished lobby, with oriental rugs, paintings, tropical plants. The elevator had an upholstered bench—something I was seeing for the first time. Reuben Mecheles' apartment looked like a museum. All the walls were covered with paintings almost to the carved ceilings. There were antiques everywhere. Old books peered out of glassed cabinets along with objects made of silver and ivory. There were spice boxes, crowns and fescues for Torah scrolls, Chanukah lamps, Passover platters.

Reuben Mecheles said, "I have every kind of luxury here outside of a maid. My wife—I can already call her my ex-wife—couldn't get along with any maid. She kicked up such a fuss about every trifle that the maids fled from her. Now a woman comes here twice a week but I've learned to fix my own meals. Come into the dining room and I'll be your waiter."

"I'll help you," Zosia proposed.

"No, I won't allow it. By me, a guest is a guest, especially such honored guests. Here in America, there are no aristocrats. Here, a millionaire rolls up his sleeves and washes his car. Here, things are easy. I phone and they send everything up. It's summer outside but inside my refrigerator it's winter. I'll bring you whatever I have and you'll choose what you like. My kitchen is like a grocery. I'll show it all to you later."

Reuben Mecheles went to the kitchen. Zosia asked, "Why did his wife leave him? She had a paradise here."

"Now it can be yours," I said.

"No, it's not for me. He has established for himself a palace here, but he is always off to somewhere. He can't sit home a minute. He has told me things about himself that have revolted me. It's clear now that he went to Reno to plead with his shrew to come back to him. After what has happened between us, I'll never start up with anyone again."

I rose and began to study the paintings. Each picture was interesting individually, but collectively they exuded an air of tedium that astonished me. How could this be? Hundreds of talents had worked on these paintings and drawings. I felt often similar reactions in a library. I stood among the masterworks of world literature and yet I knew in advance that not one of those books could dissipate my misery. I actually felt better in my empty room. There, at least, no one tried to amuse me or to point the way to the truth.

Reuben Mecheles came in with a huge tray of food—bread, rolls, cake, milk, cream, cheese, sausage, fruit. He said, "If you're still hungry after all this, call me what my ex-wife called me—a phony."

6

Following the meal, Reuben Mecheles opened a drawer and handed me a huge mimeographed manuscript, so heavy that I

could barely lift it. The title page proclaimed that this was the
Third Testament, a Torah that God had revealed to the Prophet
Moses ben Ephraim. The manuscript contained both the Hebrew text and its English translation for a total of nearly two
thousand pages.

We went into the living room and I began to leaf through the
pages and scan a line here and there. The first chapters re-
corded that Moses ben Ephraim was a Sephardi, from his father's side a tenth-generation Sabra. His mother was from Jerusalem but her parents came from Egypt. The revelation had
come to Moses ben Ephraim in a cave not far from Safad. He
had run away from home to study the cabala with a blind cabalist. One night when the blind master had gone off to spend the
night on Rachel's grave, the cave had grown brilliant as if from
a thousand suns and Moses had heard a voice. . . .

I flipped through the pages at random—a scriptural style. The
Almighty bade all the nations should become a single people
and study the Torah of Moses ben Ephraim. God had revealed
that Hitler was a descendant of Amelek and that the English who
had come to America on the *Mayflower* were all descendants of
the Lost Tribes of Israel. God had labeled Roosevelt "my messen-
ger." He had praised Wilson and had predicted that following
Hitler's defeat the League of Nations would shift to Mount Zion
in the land of Israel and Moses ben Ephraim would use the
League as an instrument by which to teach the nations justice and
bring about peace and unity. All people would speak a common
tongue—Hebrew. The children would also be taught Aramaic
and English in the schools. Lord Balfour and Herzl would be
among the saints who would be resurrected and belong to the
Sanhedrin of seventy-one elders headed by Moses ben Ephraim.

I skimmed some hundred or so pages and learned that Jesus
of Nazareth and his apostles had been true prophets. Judas Is-
cariot had not been a traitor but had remained loyal to Jesus.
The tale of the thirty pieces of silver had been fabricated by
idolators in Rome. In subsequent chapters, God revealed that
Stalin was a product of Haman and Vashti, who had betrayed
King Ahasuerus and had been a secret mistress of Haman's.

Reuben Mecheles said, "You're smiling, eh? The world needs a new creed. The concept of a chosen people has done the Jews lots of harm. You're only scanning the book but I took the trouble to read it from beginning to end. Mankind must be united, not torn apart into races and cliques. The first Moses was a person, not an angel. He ordered the murder of the Canaanites, the Hittites, and the Amorites, but Moses ben Ephraim calls all Gentiles brothers. He wants peace between Isaac and Ishmael, between Jacob and Esau, between the whites and the Negroes. I don't believe in his miracles, but he wants unity, not a splintered humanity."

"I'm sorry to say that Moses ben Ephraim won't unite mankind," I said.

"Who then will unite it?"

"No one will."

"You mean to say that people will always hate each other and wage wars and that there will never be peace?"

"It's entirely possible."

"And you can come to terms with that notion?"

"Do I have a choice?"

"Well, I can't. I must believe that the human species is growing better, not worse."

"On what do you base your belief?"

"I don't know myself on what. After all, we were once apes and now we're humans. It's a long distance between a gorilla and Mahatma Gandhi or our Chafetz Chayim. You mustn't think that I don't know what goes on in the world. I've seen all kinds of villains—among Russians, among Poles, even among us Jews. I lived for years with the most wicked woman. No matter what I gave her it wasn't enough. No matter how good I was to her, she kept demanding more and more and cursed, and abused, and threatened suicide and even murder. She spent a fortune on doodads, clothes that she never had the opportunity to wear, jewelry that was stolen or robbed from her, fake art. When she fell into a rage, she tore, trampled, burned costly things, threw them in the garbage. She cheated on me with every brute she met and even had the gall to bring them to my house. They slept in my bed, wore my pajamas. When the time came when I could stand no more and wanted to put an end to it, she found lawyers as vicious as herself—Jewish lawyers—and they took everything I had. The American courts of law, which are supposed to concern themselves with justice, promptly took her side because not the victims but the evildoers and the criminals support the lawyers and the judges.

"I saw all this and much more, but I still couldn't completely lose my faith in man or my hopes for a better world. My mother, may she rest in peace, didn't behave like my wife. She bore my father eleven children and she buried seven out of the eleven. She worked at home and in the store sixteen hours a day, if not more, while Father sat in the study house or went to his rabbi's where he dallied for weeks on end. As poor as we were, Father, may he rest in peace, brought a pauper for dinner on the Sabbath and Mother took the food out of her own children's mouths to carry food to the poorhouse. . . ."

It grew silent for a while. Reuben Mecheles took a handkerchief from his pocket and wiped the sweat off his brow.

Zosia said, "May I ask you something? If you can't answer me, it doesn't matter."

"What do you want to ask?"

"How was it you flew to Reno to make up with such a wife?"

Something akin to a tearful smile came over Reuben Mecheles' face. "I'm crazy, that's what I am. I once read of a professor who predicted that all mankind would come to an end because of madness. Everyone would go berserk. It's not far from this now. If Russia lets itself be ruled by a maniac like Stalin, and Germany by a Hitler, how far is it from the time when the whole world will turn mad? My madness consists of the fact that I was cursed with an overdose of compassion. I try to put myself in another's place, to learn what led him or her to do what they did. There is a book out by a professor who maintains that criminals are not responsible for their acts. If a murderer kills someone the killer should be taken to a sanitarium and kept there until he is cured. Naturally, the cost for this would be borne by those who work to support themselves and their families. The truth is that the human species is already crazy and I am a part of it."

I had an urge to ask Reuben Mecheles how he could afford to pay rent for such a large apartment and how he had managed to accumulate so many paintings and antiques when his wife took everything away from him, but I decided against it.

Zosia said, "It's late. I must go."

"Where are you staying? Back in the same hotel?"

"Yes, there."

"You can sleep here if you like. I mean the both of you. I have not one bedroom but three, and I'm not going to spy on you through the keyhole."

"I thank you, but I must go," Zosia replied.

"I hope you'll be staying in New York for a while yet," Reuben Mecheles said.

"No, I'm going back to Boston tomorrow."

Ten

1

THAT SUMMER WAS A HOT ONE. THE air in New York was stifling. My brother had invited me repeatedly to come stay with him at the seashore, but I remained in the city. In my mind, Seagate was connected with Nesha and Nesha had married that would-be writer and genuine fellow traveler Zachariah Kammermacher, whom I had encountered in Paris and later in her house that evening when I had been delayed in coming to see her.

I had had a long chat with her on the phone. Nesha had told me that she didn't love Zachariah and she knew that she never would, but she lacked the strength to go on working. She had reached a stage in which she had been seriously considering suicide. She hadn't deceived him. She had told him frankly that she couldn't love him, but Zachariah Kammermacher had told her that he didn't believe in love. He had been widowed and he needed someone to run his household. He had a married daughter and a son who had been educated in England. The Communists provided Zachariah with all kinds of ways to earn money—articles in their magazines, lectures. He had a job on their Yiddish newspaper. He had a spacious apartment on West End Avenue and a summer house near Poughkeepsie. He had offered to adopt Nesha's son. Nesha said the usual things women say in such instances: She would never forget me, we would remain friends. At the same time, she hinted that she was sick and that she didn't expect to live much longer.

I asked her the nature of her illness and she replied, "Everything."

Two years passed by but I had been left alone. I heard nothing more from Stefa or from Lena. Only my cousin wrote to me. She had married an electrician from Galicia. Her friend, Tsipele, had gone to live with her uncle who had left his wife. I had read in a Yiddish newspaper that "the well-known philanthropist and art collector Reuben Mecheles had married Miss Zosia Fishelsohn," a convert to Christianity who reconverted to Judaism, and the pair went to live in Jerusalem.

My state of mind had robbed me of the appetite to write to such an extent that I had to make an effort each week to complete my brief column, "It's Worthwhile Knowing." My fountain pen invariably leaked and made blots. My hand cramped. My eyes took part in the sabotage, too. I had heard of hay fever while still in Poland, but I had never suffered from it there. All of a sudden, I started sneezing in August of that year. My nose became stuffed up, my throat grew scratchy, my ears filled with water and developed a ringing and a whistling. I took a daily bath and kept myself clean, but I suffered from an itch and had constantly to scratch. No pills helped my constipation. I spent whole days in bed being baked by the sun that shone in through my window from noon to twilight. I didn't even bother to lower the shade. My sexual fantasies grew even more bizarre. By day I dozed, at night I stayed awake. I still brooded on the mysteries of the universe. Maybe it was possible to find a way to penetrate the enigmas of time and space, the categories of pure reason, the secret of life and consciousness? I had read somewhere that Einstein had for years been searching for a kind of super-Newtonian formula that would include gravity, magnetism, and the electromagnetic forces. Maybe there existed somewhere a formula that could combine—along with what Einstein was seeking—life, thought, and emotion as well? Maybe there existed such a combination of words and numbers that would encompass the whole riddle of Creation?

Neither God nor nature could hide forever. Sooner or later

must come the revelation. Maybe it was I who was destined to
receive it. I mentally tabulated everything that I had read of the
philosophers, the mystics, the modern physicists. Einstein was
right, I told myself, God didn't play dice. Somewhere there was
a truth that explained Chmielnitzki's outrages, Hitler's madness,
Stalin's megalomania, the exaltation of a Baal Shem, every vibration of light, every tremor of the nerves. There were nights
when I awoke with the feeling that I saw the formula in my
dream, or at least some part of it and I stayed awake for hours
trying to recollect what I saw.

Each week when I delivered my column late at night I groped
in the mail box, but no one wrote to me. I had broken away
from people and they had abandoned me. An indolence settled
over me. I even lacked the energy to eat at the cafeteria and I
missed meals. I had fallen into a crisis that could last to the end
of my life.

One day in mid-July, someone knocked on my door. I
opened it and saw a man and a young woman. Both their faces
seemed familiar but I had forgotten their names as well as
where and when I had met them. I stood there for a moment
looking at them, perplexed. The man said, "I swear he doesn't
recognize me. It's me, Zygmunt Salkin."

"Oh, yes, yes, yes! Come in! Welcome!"

"We met on your first day in America. This young lady is Anita
Komarov. She tells me that she gave you your first English les-
son."

"Yes, I remember! What a pleasant surprise. Such guests!"

I wanted to extend my hand to my visitors but my palm was
wet. I was wet all over. Anita said, "What a heat in here! Like a
steel plant in Pittsburgh."

"Please, sit down."

As I said these words, it struck me that I had only one
chair in my room and it was broken and strewn with papers, shirts, socks, underwear. The bed was unmade and the
sheet showed traces of bedbugs. Across the cracked linoleum lay newspapers, magazines, and books I had taken out
of the public library along with those I had bought on

Fourth Avenue for a nickel each. Both Salkin and Anita had
changed. Salkin's hair had grayed around the temples. He
wore a light suit and white shoes. Anita was the daughter of
a Yiddish poet, Zalman Komarov. Anita had attended a
drama school. I had made her acquaintance when still in
Seagate. She was petite, thin to the point of emaciation, with
black hair that she kept as short as a boy's. She had a
pointed Adam's apple also like a boy's. Her face was narrow,
her cheeks sunken, her nose snub. She suffered from acne.

I heard Zygmunt Salkin say, "We didn't come here to sit. I've
been looking for you for weeks. Where have you been hiding?
Anita and I had a talk and it turned out that she knows you. We
decided to find you at any price and here you are. Such heat as
is in this room is rare even in Africa."

"I'm not shaved, and besides—"

"Come, come. You can melt here, and then it'll be too late.
You may be aware that I've founded a group for young actors,
and for old ones as well, if they have the talent. Something has
to be done for the theater in America. There was a time when I
dreamed about reviving the Yiddish theater, but I've convinced
myself that this was a waste of time. If something can be done
for the English theater, this may help the theater in other languages. The theater is like a body. If you help one part, it influ-
ences the other parts. Besides, this gives me an opportunity to
meet young and pretty girls. Isn't that so, Anita?"

Zgymunt Salkin smiled and winked, and Anita winked back
and said, "All men, without exception, are egotists."

Anita had told me her life story. At the age of seventeen, she
had been involved in an affair with a Morris Katzenstein, a philosophy student at City College, son of the Yiddish actor Shamai
Katzenstein. Anita (her parents called her Hannele) moved in
with Morris and became pregnant. The parents on both sides
demanded that the couple marry and they arranged a quick
wedding, but during the honeymoon in Bermuda, Anita miscar-
ried. Morris later became a Communist and gave up his studies.
He also left Anita and went to live with a female activist among
the Reds who was ten years older than he. Anita, an only daugh-

ter, moved back in with her parents. I had met her at Nesha's house.

I had forgotten that Salkin had his own car; it was now parked outside of the decrepit building in which I lived. Actually, it was the same car in which he picked me up the day I arrived in America. My brother told me that Salkin lived with a mistress in the area called Greenwich Village.

I had assumed that he would take Anita and me to a restaurant, but he let me know that he was taking us to his place where there would be a party. Had he told me this sooner, I would have changed my suit and shaved as well. Now, he had presented me with a *fait accompli*.

I was far from in the mood for meeting strangers. I had an urge to tell Salkin sharply that I wasn't some kind of rare animal to be put on exhibit at will, and to demand that he leave me alone, yet at the same time I knew that Salkin was out to help me, not humiliate me. He seemed to be in a cheerful mood. He was humming some song and he joked with Anita. He had turned into Fifth Avenue and he pointed out to me buildings, a hotel, a restaurant—all of which were connected with famous American writers or painters of whom I had never heard.

Soon we entered the narrow streets of Greenwich Village. Both the men here and the women appeared to me half naked. I saw youths with beards and long hair, in sandals on bare feet, in yellow, green, red trousers. One smoked a long pipe, another carried a monkey in a cage, a third had a placard draped over his back and as he walked he drank some liquid from a bottle and shouted slogans. The women displayed their independence in their own fashion. One walked about barefoot, a second led a huge dog on a leash and pushed a carriage containing a Siamese cat, a third wore a straw hat the size of an umbrella. Artists exhibited paintings on the narrow sidewalks. A poet sold his mimeographed poems. The neighborhood reminded me of Paris and of Purim.

The car stopped before a house with a dark, narrow entrance. We climbed up four flights and Salkin opened a door into a large, dim room filled with men and women. Apparently the

party had already started. On a long table covered with a red
tablecloth red candles burned in holders. It smelled here of
whiskey, wine, meat, perspiration and of the lotions women use
to subdue the odors of the flesh. The people were all talking,
laughing, expressing interest in some bit of news that seemed
to raise everyone's spirits. Out of the crowd pushed Salkin's
mistress—blond, blue-eyed, wearing a white blouse and a long
skirt embroidered in gold and silver. Her red fingernails were
long and pointed. A cigarette in a long holder extended from
between her red lips. On one of her fingers was a ring resembling a spider. Salkin introduced her as Lotte. For a moment
she appeared to be young, a girl of perhaps eighteen or nineteen, but then I saw the wrinkles at the corners of her eyes and
the slackness in her neck that no makeup could hide. When
Salkin announced my name and added whose brother I was,
over her face came that sweet smile and glow of confidence that
worldly women can evoke at any time and under any circum-
stance. She tried to speak to me in Yiddish and soon switched
over into English: "Your brother talks of you whenever we
meet. Salkin, too. He's read your book—what's its name?—and
he was enchanted. Unfortunately, I can't read Yiddish, but my
grandmother used to read the Yiddish newspaper every day.
Zygmunt tells me that you hide from everyone. But today he
vowed that he would nab you. What are you drinking?"

"Oh, nothing. Maybe some soda."

"That's all? At a party you have to drink. Wait a minute, the
phone is ringing."

How odd, but I had forgotten all about my bashfulness. It was
almost dark in here and no one would be able to tell whether
my suit was pressed or wrinkled, whether I was shaved or not.
After a while, Salkin and Anita drifted away and I was left alone.
I walked over to a table on which bottles of liquor were standing. I noticed that the guests poured drinks for themselves. I
knew what I had to do—get drunk. I picked up one of the bottles and poured myself a half glassful. It was cognac. I took one
large gulp and drained the glass. A burning blazed up in my
throat and soon after in my stomach. A bowl of rolls stood on

the table and I quickly bit into one. I felt the fumes of the alcohol rushing to my brain. My head began to spin and my legs wobbled. Since everyone was drinking, I mused, they probably weren't so sure of themselves either. Apparently, they too suffered from inferiority complexes. I wasn't drunk, nor was I sober. I poured myself a little more of the liquor. I noted that the guests were walking around with the drinks in their hands and I did the same. A black maid carrying a tray came up and spoke to me but I didn't hear what it was. After a while, I caught on that she was offering me something to eat from the tray. I wanted to pick up a half of hard-boiled egg with a toothpick, but it slipped from my hand. Instead, I took something with cheese. The maid handed me a red paper napkin. She smiled at me, showing a mouthful of white teeth. I pushed my way through the crowd of strangers. Someone trod on my foot, excused himself, apparently made a joke, since he himself laughed at what he had said. Salkin came up and soon Anita joined us. Salkin said, "Let's go into the bedroom. There's something I want to discuss with you."

The bedroom had a bed so wide that not one couple but two or even three could have slept in it comfortably. A painting of some red smudges hung here and a lithograph of people standing on their heads, flying through the air. There was a figure of a man with horns and the snout of a pig, and of a female with breasts in front and behind, all apparently painted by the same artist. Salkin and Anita sat down on the bed and I settled in a wicker chair. Salkin said, "We, Anita and I, have a plan to propose to you, but before you say no, hear me out first. I've already told you about our theater troupe. We leased a place in the Catskills in which to rehearse and talk over all our problems. None of us gets a penny. On the contrary, we contribute to the effort. We plan—not this year but a year from now—to put on a play that will infuse new life into the theater. What we have there is not a theater but a hotel casino. The hotel itself burned down, or the owner set it on fire. The casino was far removed from the hotel and it remained in one piece. There is a small stage there and benches and that's all we need. Anita's

parents live not far away. It was actually through her that I
learned about this casino. There is a Yiddishist summer colony
nearby, with bungalows named after Yiddish writers and Socialist leaders—Peretz, Shalom Aleichem, Mendele, Bovshover. Anarchists stay there too, that is to say, ex-anarchists who are now
businessmen, some of them even millionaires, and have bungalows with names like Rosa Luxemburg, Peter Kropotkin,
Emma Goldman. Some of these ex-revolutionaries help our
group with small donations. It would pay you to see the whole
setup. You would have something to write about. I spoke with
your brother about you and he is irked because you have isolated yourself from everything and everybody. This may be
good for an elderly writer whose career is over, D'Annunzio or
Knut Hamsum, not for a young man. I normally wouldn't take a
place in the Catskills for the summer, but since I am the founder of the group and basically responsible for everything that
happens there, we, my friend Lotte and I, rented a house in that
area and we'll be spending the rest of the summer there, at least
until Labor Day. We have a lot of rooms in this house, more
than we can use, and we would like for you to come stay with
us. First of all, you'll save the rent you're paying. Second, you'll
get some fresh air, not sit, if you'll excuse me, in a stinkhole.
Third, you can help us."

"How?"

"We've been a long time searching for a suitable play for an
experimental theater and it occurred to me that Peretz's *At
Night in the Old Marketplace* wouldn't be a bad idea. You undoubtedly know the thing. It's not for the general audience. As
often as it has been staged, it has inevitably been a flop—in
Poland and here, too. It's a play full of symbolism and mysticism. That's the very reason it would be good for us. I've translated the thing into English and I've read it to the group and
although three quarters of them aren't Jewish—American young
men and girls from Texas, Missouri, and Ohio, and what have
you—they understood the play and were enraptured by it. The
play could draw a number of the native-born Jews who are in-

terested in Yiddish art—but only if it is done in English, not in
Yiddish. The play, as you know, has a lot to do with the cabala
and Jewish mysticism, and those are unfamiliar areas for me. I
want to direct the play and you could be of great help to me.

"I want to tell you something else. I read your *Satan in Goray* and I have a high opinion of it. I told this to your brother
and he fully agrees with me. If *At Night in the Old Marketplace*
should turn out a success—I mean an artistic success not a financial one—sooner or later we would be able to dramatize
your work and I could even get you an advance of a few
hundred dollars. In brief, Anita, Lotte, and I want to drag you
out of the rut into which you've fallen or thrown yourself. And
I ask you—don't be too quick to say no. Our group has no
money, no experience, and no name, but all things start out
small. Where Times Square is now was a farm where goats
grazed a hundred years ago. Isn't that so, Anita?"

"If not a hundred years ago, then a hundred and fifty years
ago."

"What's your answer?"

"I'm not sure that I can help you."

"I'm sure that you can. Simply to discuss with you the various
attitudes would be helpful to us. You'll be able to go on writing
your articles. There is a library not far from us and a store
where you can get the magazines from which you gather your
so-called facts."

"Is there a cafeteria there?"

"What do you need with a cafeteria? Lotte is a woman with a
lot of education and she's a talented actress besides, but she's
also a splendid cook. She'll prepare your vegetarian dishes for
you. We have other girls to cook as well. We live there actually
in a kind of commune. Each person contributes whatever he or
she can. Several of the girls come from wealthy homes. Your
brother has promised to come stay with us for a few days."

"My mother and father would like to meet you, too," Anita
said. "Normally they are busy all year but they take time out for
vacations. We actually live there in that Yiddishist colony. Ours

is the David Frishman bungalow. We are sunk in Yiddishism up
to here—"

And Anita pointed to her chin.

2

From extreme isolation I was transported into extreme soci-
ability. On one side was the theater group under the leadership
of Zygmunt Salkin, and on the other the Yiddish poet Zalman
Komarov, his wife, Bessie, and the colony of Yiddishists. I
couldn't believe that such an abrupt transformation was possible. Zygmunt Salkin gave me the English translation of *At Night
in the Old Marketplace* as well as the Yiddish text. I found many
errors in the translation and Salkin promptly corrected them.

Even before, I had known that this play was too lacking in
dramatic action to interest a theater audience and I proposed
that it be played in conjunction with a dramatized short story of
Peretz's. Salkin and his group seized upon this notion and they
decided as one that I should be the one to choose the right
story and to dramatize it in collaboration with Salkin.

When Zalman Komarov and the other Yiddishists heard that I
was getting ready to dramatize something by Peretz—the spiritual leader and founder of Yiddishism—I became an overnight
target of their interest. Yiddishism in America suffered a lack of
young forces. I was comparatively young and my book had already received some notice among the Yiddishists even though
the critics complained that I failed to follow in the path of the
Yiddish classicists and gave myself over excessively to sex, as
well as demonstrating a lack of concern with social problems.

I was now surrounded by people all day and sometimes half
the night. Bessie Komarov, Anita's mother, often invited me for
lunch, for dinner, sometimes even for breakfast. Lotte cooked
my vegetarian meals. The group had many more women than
men. Everyone was young and full of amateurish enthusiasm; I

was to them an expert in Jewishness, which already at that time had begun to make inroads into American literature and theater.

Zygmunt Salkin and Anita Komarov took every opportunity to speak of my talent and to predict that I would do great things in the future. I often told myself at that time that I should be overjoyed. In the rare times when I was left alone, I posed the same question to myself: Are you happy now or at least satisfied? But the answer was always—no.

At that time I hardly ever read a newspaper, but Zygmunt Salkin received Yiddish newspapers from America, Poland, France, and even Russia, and a day didn't go by that I didn't learn of the deaths and all kinds of tragedies suffered by people who had been known or been close to me, or whom I knew through reading. And what about those whom I didn't know? What about the thousands, hundreds of thousands, actually millions of victims of Stalin's terror, Hitler's murders? What about the innocent people who had perished in Spain, in Ethiopia, in Mongolia, and who knows where else? What about the millions who suffered from cancer, consumption, or who starved to death? Even in America gangs of criminals killed and tortured their victims while phony liberals, cunning lawyers, and callous judges tolerated it all and actually helped the criminals with all sorts of pretexts and senseless theories. One would have to be totally indifferent toward man and beast to be able to be happy.

The Yiddishist colony seethed with those offering ready-made remedies for all the world's ills. Some still preached anarchism—others, socialism. Some placed all their hopes in Freud while others hinted that Stalin was hardly as bad as the capitalist lackeys painted him. Surely, no one in the colony considered the evils perpetrated daily upon God's creatures by the millions of hunters, vivisectionists, and butchers.

I had gained companionship, but my isolation from everything and everybody remained the same. All that was left were means of temporary forgetfulness. In order to get myself through the days and nights, I had to somehow muffle my senses. There were days when it seemed that Anita might provide this opportunity to me. However, something was holding us back—no moral inhibition but, one might say, a chemical one. In the course of my life I had often encountered these inhibitions. Although both sides were ready, some force that is stronger than their resolves said no. There were in the group girls who would gladly have had an affair with me, but despite my eagerness, the male within me demanded devotion and old-fashioned love.

For a while it appeared that our plan to put on *At Night in the Old Marketplace* was on its way. Zygmunt Salkin had gotten promises from alleged theater patrons that they would support the project with cash contributions. There was talk of leasing a theater in New York, if not on Broadway, then off-Broadway. But I was less deceived by these hopes than the others. Most of the boys and girls in the group had been left penniless. Zygmunt Salkin was actually the only patron of the organization and he was far from wealthy. To rent a theater required a contract and a deposit. The play needed scenery, the actors and actresses had to get enough to at least pay their rent and eat. At the rehearsals, I saw that Zygmunt Salkin lacked the skills of a director and that most of the boys and girls had little talent. Peretz's words emerged false, awkward, and often ridiculous from their mouths.

The month of August was almost over, and Labor Day—which signifies the end of many summer affairs, dreams, promises, and projects—was fast approaching. The Yiddishist colony began slowly to empty out. A number of those who in the heat of summer had preached socialism, the dictatorship of the proletariat, anarchism, atheism, even free love, went back to New York for the Days of Awe along with their elderly wives. They all offered excuses for observing the holidays. Nearly all of them had religious relatives whose feelings they didn't want to hurt.

The bungalows of Karl Marx, Rosa Luxemburg, Peter Kropotkin, and Emma Goldman closed one after the other. Zygmunt Salkin assured the members of the group that he and Lotte

would go on working for the "new theater." He had a briefcase
full of papers and a head full of ideas and hopes, but deep
inside we knew that it was all over.

I had heard some shocking news. Several of the girls in the
group had gotten pregnant and would have to get abortions. At
that time, this was no easy matter. It cost a lot (five hundred
dollars was a fortune) and it also represented a danger. The
young men appeared even guiltier than the girls.

The days had become cooler and shorter. The leaves on the
trees began to yellow and I saw birds flying in flocks—probably
on their way to warmer climates. The nights were colder and
longer. I could not sleep and I went outside for a breath of
fresh air. There was no more light coming from the bungalows
and the sky was full of stars. God, or whoever He is, was still
there, observing His Creation. A new theater? A new man? The
old idolatry was here again. The stone and clay idols had been
exchanged for a Gertrude Stein, a Picasso, a Bernard Shaw, an
Ezra Pound. Everybody worshiped culture and progress. I
myself had tried to become a priest of this idolatry, although I was aware of its falsehood. At its best, art could be
nothing more than a means of forgetting the human disaster
for a while. I walked over to the colony. It was silent as a
cemetery. Most of those whose names the bungalows bore
had departed this world, with its illusions, forever. Those who
worshiped them would follow soon. I lifted up my eyes to the
starry sky again and again as if in hope that some revelation
might descend upon me from above. I inhaled the cold air and
shivered.

One day I got into Zygmunt Salkin's car and he took me back
to New York with Lotte. They must have quarreled, because
both were silent. They did not even look at one another. After
traveling for two hours or so, we stopped at a cafeteria for a
cup of coffee and a piece of cake, and here Lotte and Salkin got
into an argument in my presence. Lotte called Salkin a "phony."
She complained, as so many worldly women do, that because
of him she had wasted her "best years."

3

I had surrendered myself to melancholy and it had taken me
prisoner. I did what it demanded—squandered my time on
empty musings; on mental probes that could bring no benefit
to me or to others; on searches for something I had never lost.
I had presented creation with an ultimatum: Tell me your secret
or let me perish. I stayed up nights and dozed by day. I knew
full well that I should have called my brother but I had lost his
phone number—an excuse for me to avoid seeing him and having to justify my lazy existence. It was quite possible that the
editorial office wanted to tell me to stop sending in the weekly
article, or maybe they had more work for me, but I hid from
them in any case. As long as they kept sending me the check, I
kept cashing it. I paid the five dollars rent and spent the rest on
meals at the cafeteria. When the checks stopped coming, I could
always commit suicide. Death had become a familiar thing for
me. In my room I stepped on vermin. One moment there was
a cockroach—winged, with eyes, a sense of hearing, a stomach,
a fear of death, an urge to procreate. All of a sudden I squashed
it with my heel and it was nothing, or perhaps turned back to
the infinite sea of life which fashions a man from a cockroach
and from a cockroach, a man.

On my long walks through New York, I passed fish stores and
butcher shops. The huge fish that yesterday was swimming in
the Atlantic now lay stretched out on ice with a bloody mouth
and blank eyes, fare for millions of microbes and for a glutton
to stuff his potbelly with. Trucks stopped before the butcher
shops and men came out carrying heads, legs, hearts, kidneys.
How frivolously the Creator squandered His powers! With what
indifference He disposed of His masterworks into the garbage!
He wasn't concerned with either my faith or my heresy, my
praises or my blasphemies. Someone had warned me not to
drink from the tap in my sink since this could give me all kinds
of sickness, but I burned with thirst in the nights and I gulped
from the rusted sink till my abdomen grew as taut as a drum. I

bought half-rotted fruit in the street and stuffed myself on it, worms and all. I stopped shaving daily and went about with a stubble, with scuffed shoes and a stained suit. Like other bums, I picked up newspapers and magazines in the garbage cans. The scientists kept on discovering new particles in the atom, which was becoming more and more of a complicated system, a cosmos in itself, full of riddles that were to be solved in the future. More evidence came out that the universe is running away from itself, a result of an explosion that took place some twenty billion years ago. Substance and energy swap roles. Causality and purpose appear more and more like two masks of the same paradox. In Soviet Russia countless traitors and enemies of the people were purged and liquidated, among them Yiddish poets who had published long odes to Comrade Stalin. According to the reviews in the book sections of the newspapers and journals I read, new and remarkable talents emerged each month, each week, each day in a deluge of genius in the United States and all over the world. Small and isolated as the Yiddishist coterie was, it raved and ranted about its achievements in literature, in the theater, and mainly in helping to bring about the redemption of the peasants and workers everywhere. There was nothing I could do but stew in my own gloom. Like the universe, I had to run away from myself. But how? And where? When I was a cheder boy I once did a thing which I always regretted. I caught a fly, put it into a little bottle with a few drops of water and a crust of sugar, stopped it with a cork, and threw it into a cellar where the janitor of our building kept broken furniture, rags, useless brooms, and similar garbage. Why I committed this ruthless act I never knew. Now I have become this fly myself, doomed to expire in darkness, a victim of a power that played games with frail creatures. All I could do was cry out to the heavenly cheder boy, "Why did you do it? How would you feel if some supercelestial cheder boy would do the same to you?" I was beginning to ponder a religion of rebellion against God's indifference and the cruelty of those whom He created in His image.

The Chassidic rabbis whose books I once studied used to

write down rules of conduct for themselves, as well as for others, on slips of paper which they called *tsetl koton* and I did the same, often in rhyme, so that they would be easy for me to remember. I fantasized about building temples of protest, study houses where people would contemplate and reminisce about the various misfortunes God has sent to humans and animals. The Book of Job would become their Torah minus God's answer to Job and the happy ending. I dreamed of a humanism and ethics the basis of which would be a refusal to justify all the evils the Almighty has sent upon us in the past and which He is preparing to bestow upon us in the future. I even played with the idea of nominating a new group of protesting prophets or saints, such as Job, Schopenhauer, Baudelaire, Edgar Allan Poe, Von Hartmann, Otto Weininger, Bashkirtsev, and some others who rejected life and considered death the only messiah. I remember calling those who flatter God and kiss the rod with which He smites them "religious masochists."

4

Outside, the autumn rain poured. Inside the office buildings on Nineteenth Street the lights were on all day long. The headlights of the passing trucks glared in the fog. I was too lazy to go out so I ate a combination of breakfast and lunch of stale bread and half-rotten bananas. On that evening I put on my shabby overcoat and went to Steward's Cafeteria on Twenty-third Street. I had paid my rent for the week and I was left with a dollar and forty-five cents. The cafeteria was half empty. At the buffet I bought a vegetable plate, a cup of coffee, and a dish of stewed prunes. Looking for a table where somebody had left a newspaper I found more than I expected: the New York *Times* and the *Daily Mirror*. I ate and fantasized. I was taking revenge for Dachau and Zbonshin. I gave back the Sudetenland to the Czechs. I founded a Jewish state in Jerusalem. Since I was the ruler of the world, I forbade forever the eating of meat and fish and made hunting illegal. I was so busy bringing order to the earth that I let my coffee get cold. I counted my change and decided to spend another nickel for a second cup of coffee. On the way back with my coffee, I discovered the Sunday *Forward* on another table. Because the typesetters always made so many mistakes in my column, "It's Worthwhile Knowing," I was not in a rush to turn to the page on which it usually appeared. Instead, I read the Jewish news. Even though the Communists in America denied it vehemently, it was clear that Stalin had liquidated not only a number of generals and such leaders as Bukharin, Zinoviev, Kamenev, and Rikov in his purges, but scores of Yiddish writers as well. A correspondent who had just returned from the Soviet Union reported that the number of victims of Stalin's purges had reached eight million. Hundreds of thousands of kulaks had died in their exile in Siberia. The "enemies of the people" were sentenced in mass trials. A lot of Communists who had come to the Soviet Union to help build Socialism were sent to work in the gold mines in the North, where the strongest man could not endure longer than a year.

I was drinking and shaking my head over the news. How could Jewish novelists, poets, and party leaders, grandchildren of our pious ancestors, defend such evil?

I was now ready to face the mistakes in my column. I found the page, but my column wasn't there. Instead, there was a long recipe for meat *kreplach*. They had stopped my column!

The cafeteria had emptied out. The lights were switched off and on to signal closing time. I paid my check to the cashier and returned to Nineteenth Street. It was still raining and in the four blocks between Twenty-third and Nineteenth streets I got drenched. I walked up the four flights to my room. It was too cold for the cockroaches to come out from their holes in the linoleum. There was no choice but to undress and go to bed. The blanket was thin and I had to put my feet into the sleeves of a sweater to warm them. I had turned out the ceiling light and was lying still. I fell asleep and dreamed. In the middle of the night someone knocked at my door. Who could it be? I had been told that Nazis lived in this building and I was afraid that someone might want to kill me. I looked around for something with which to defend myself. There was nothing except two wire clothes hangers.

"Who is it?" I asked.

"It's the night man."

The night man? What would a night man want in the middle of the night? I wondered. Aloud, I said, "What's wrong?"

"There is a cable for you."

"A cable? For me? So late?"

"The super gave it to me to give to you, but I forgot."

I rolled out of bed naked and fell to the floor. I got up, stripped the sheet off my bed and draped myself in it. Then I opened the door.

"Here."

And a black man handed me a cable.

I wanted to give him a nickel, but he didn't have the patience to wait and he slammed the door.

I tore open the cablegram and read:

STUCK IN ATHENS WITH CHILD. SEND MONEY AT ONCE.
                                                        LENA.

There was an address included that sounded Greek.

What kind of madness is this? I asked myself. Send money at once? This minute? What was she doing in Greece?

I threw off the sheet and glanced at my wristwatch. It had stopped at a quarter past five. Was it still today, or was it already tomorrow? It didn't matter either way. In Athens of all places . . . The rich uncle from America would send a check for $100,000, like in the trashy play at the Scala Theater. I felt like laughing, drinking the rusty water from the faucet and urinating. I stood for a while by the sink staring, as if seeking the means to fulfill all these three needs simultaneously. Then I went over to the window, opened it, and looked out into the wet street, its black windows, flat roofs, the glowing sky, without a moon, without stars, opaque and stagnant like some global cover. I leaned out as far as I could, deeply inhaled the fumes of the city, and proclaimed to myself and to the powers of the night:

I am lost in America, lost forever.